Endorsements for *Perseverance*

"Mark Dayton's life has been defined by compassion, integrity, and courage, and that's exactly how he led Minnesota during his long career in public service. From expanding access to health care to raising the minimum wage, Mark delivered on his promise to improve people's lives and to build 'A Better Minnesota.' Whether you're a Democrat, Republican, or independent, *Perseverance* is an essential read for anyone who wants to better understand Minnesota and the man who played such a pivotal role in shaping it for the better."
—Amy Klobuchar, U.S. Senator from Minnesota

"In *Perseverance*, Mark Dayton gives us a fascinating behind-the-scenes look at a political life defined by contradictions, challenges, and ultimately great meaning. I was delighted by his insider take on national events as well as funny and charming tales about Minnesota politics that made me laugh out loud. As Democrats grapple with what is next for our party, the story of how this Midwestern populist fearlessly challenged the status quo, delivered for the people, and won Minnesota's heart is a must read."
—Tina Smith, U.S. Senator from Minnesota

"In my interactions with Governor Dayton it was always clear to me that he was doing what he thought best for Minnesota. That same fidelity to principle and commitment to his community comes through loud and clear in this book. We can learn much about the value of public service from the governor's memoir, and these lessons are perhaps more important now than ever."
—Lorie S. Gildea, former Minnesota Supreme Court Chief Justice

"Governor Mark Dayton's story, as documented in *Perseverance*, should be required reading in our high school civics courses, mandatory for political science students, and highly recommended for anyone aspiring to serve as an elected official in Minnesota. He recognized the honor and gravity of serving as both the Governor of Minnesota and the Commander-in-Chief of the Minnesota National Guard. Every decision he made in that role reflected a deep concern for the impact on soldiers, airmen, their families, and employers. Governor Dayton's legacy is one of humility, passion, and authentic servant leadership. His story is truly an inspiration for anyone who aspires to make a positive difference in public service."

—Rick Nash, Lieutenant General (Bvt.)
USA, Ret., 30th Adjutant General

"I served in the legislature while Mark Dayton was governor, and while our political philosophies couldn't be more different, our friendship has always been a point of pride for me. In *Perseverance*, Mark brings the same humor and humility to the page that he brought to the capitol. From family stories to the grit of a political career, this is a fascinating read that reminds us there is always more to a person than their party platform."

—State Senator Karin Housley

"Mark Dayton's memoir captures the career of one of Minnesota's most remarkable public servants. I was fascinated by Mark's personal candor as well as the breadth and depth of his aspirations for Minnesota. More than anything the book reconfirmed what I know about Mark. He is a leader of great integrity—a person who acts in conformance with his beliefs even at the risk of losing friends or the support of his party. Mark's courage of conviction has always distinguished him."

—Kathleen Blatz, former Minnesota
Supreme Court Chief Justice

"In this candid, searing reflection, former senator and governor Mark Dayton shows that his rare combo of high-IQ wonk, chippy hockey goalie, and anti-war activist remains intact. He regrets 'not a cent' spending his inheritance on his candidacies for economic and social justice. Behind the scenes, he reveals, he waged a decades-long struggle for emotional and physical health. *Perseverance*, indeed. Minnesota is better for it."

— David Lillehaug, former Minnesota Supreme Court Justice

"As a Minnesota businessman who interacted with Mark on multiple topics over a number of years, *Perseverance* rang true to my experience. As reflected in the book, Mark was clear-eyed about defining problems yet willing to collaborate in discovering solutions. Mark writes, 'The path I forged was very different from today's dominant politics. I have always said that there are no saints in politics, only shades of sinners. But there are shades, and they do matter.' To borrow his words, Mark was a 'shade' of the leader that we needed."

—Greg Page, former Chairman and CEO of Cargill, Inc.

"Mark Dayton taught me that true leadership means listening to every voice and never wavering on your principles. 'Be bold, not reckless,' he once told me, words I've carried ever since. His commitment to a Better Minnesota, especially for Minnesota's children, never faltered: all-day kindergarten, expanded preschool, record graduation rates. If you want to see authentic leadership up close, read this book: It is Mark Dayton, in his own words, at his best."

—Brenda Cassellius, Commissioner, Minnesota Department of Education, 2011–2019

"I first met Mark Dayton more than twenty years ago during a Sino–U.S. interparliamentary exchange led by Senator Ted Stevens, when I was serving at China's National People's Congress and he was the U.S. Senator from Minnesota. Even then, Mark stood out as a rare diplomat: genuine, kind, and unwaveringly honest—qualities that quietly but effectively got things done. I also owe a personal debt to Mark; it was his encouragement and support that led me to pursue a J.D. in Minnesota, setting in motion a legal career for which I remain deeply grateful. Mark has a unique ability to touch lives one person at a time, creating meaningful and lasting impact while asking nothing in return. This memoir not only brings back cherished memories but also leaves a lasting imprint of a life defined by integrity, service, and humanity."

—Sally Yuanyuan Qin, Partner and Head of Asia Litigation at BakerHostetler

PERSEVERANCE

MARK DAYTON

FOREWORD BY HILLARY RODHAM CLINTON

MINNESOTA
HISTORICAL
SOCIETY PRESS

mnhspress.org @mnhspress

The Minnesota Historical Society Press is a member of the Association of University Presses.

Manufactured in the United States of America.

10 9 8 7 6 5 4 3 2 1

♾ The paper used in this publication meets the minimum requirements of the American National Standard for Information Sciences—Permanence for Printed Library Materials, ANSI Z39.48-1984.

ISBN: 978-1-68134-339-6 (hardcover)
ISBN: 978-1-68134-340-2 (e-book)

Library of Congress Control Number: 2026932558

CONTENTS

ACKNOWLEDGMENTS

I have dedicated this book to my five grandchildren: Hugo, George, Wilder, Hattie, and Margot. I have been blessed with two wonderful sons, Eric and Andrew, and two marvelous daughters-in-law, Cory and Alyssa. I also, after two unsuccessful marriages, have been fortunate to find and marry Ana, a truly extraordinary woman. All of them have brought so much richness and joy into my life. I also want to pay tribute to my brother, Brandt; my two sisters, Lucy and Anne; and my two in-laws, Tian Dayton and Mark O'Keefe, who have shared my journey with me.

I want to thank my longtime friend Lori Sturdevant, who served as my principal editor, and my brother, Brandt Dayton, and friend David Lillehaug, to whom I entrusted my early draft, and whose insights were invaluable. I also thank John Rahm, Ryan Hemmer, Shannon Pennefeather, Jim Cihlar, and the rest of the Minnesota Historical Society Press's excellent staff, who have taken my manuscript and turned it into this book.

FOREWORD

I've spent my life around people who seek public office for all sorts of reasons. Some are drawn by personal ambition alone. Others are animated by ideology. And some enter public service because they believe, deeply and stubbornly, that government can be a force for good, and that it is their responsibility to use whatever power they have to improve the lives of others. Mark Dayton belongs firmly in that last category.

Mark and I came into the Senate together in 2001. We were seated next to one another in the back of the chamber where junior senators sit and worked together on the Armed Services Committee. What always struck me about Mark is not just his integrity, though that is unmistakable, or how unafraid he was to ask tough questions and stand against political headwinds. It is his empathy. Mark listens. He pays attention. He notices who is being left out of the conversation and then he does something about it. He was especially sensitive to the needs of those who can't hire a lobbyist to walk the halls of Capitol Hill. In an era when politics often rewards volume over substance and outrage over outcomes, Mark Dayton has been guided by a quieter, sturdier compass: a belief that governing is about delivering results, not rhetoric.

Minnesota was also fortunate to have Mark Dayton as its governor, and the record of his leadership speaks for itself. When he took office, the state faced serious fiscal challenges and deep partisan divides. Mark didn't pretend those problems would solve themselves, and he didn't look for shortcuts. He made the hard, responsible choices necessary to put Minnesota on sound financial footing—choices rooted in fairness and common sense. He was willing to stand by those decisions even when doing so carried political risk.

Mark's leadership was always, at its core, about people. During his administration, Minnesota made sustained investments in opportunity—from early childhood through higher education and workforce training. He fought for all-day kindergarten so that children could begin school on equal footing and working families weren't burdened by childcare costs. He supported teachers and strengthened schools because he understands that education is the foundation of both opportunity and democracy. He expanded access to college and job training because he believes every person deserves the chance to build a life of purpose and security. Mark understands that opportunity is not self-executing. It requires personal commitment and public investment.

Mark embodied Senator Paul Wellstone's belief that "We all do better when we all do better." That's why he championed policies that raised wages, delivered new protections for equal pay, and helped ensure that a hard day's work could still support a family. He invested in infrastructure—roads, bridges, transit—because he understood that these are not abstract projects, but the connective tissue of communities and commerce. Minnesota emerged from his tenure stronger, more competitive, and better prepared for the challenges ahead.

This memoir is not simply an account of campaigns or policy debates. It is a reflection on the meaning of public service itself. It is about the discipline of showing up, the humility of listening, and the responsibility of never losing sight of the people you serve. Mark Dayton's story is a reminder that progress is possible when leaders are guided by empathy.

I've long admired Mark for the way he approached the work: with decency, seriousness of purpose, and an enduring faith in public service. At a time when confidence in our institutions can feel uncertain, his example stands as a reminder that principled leadership still matters—and that it can still make a lasting difference.

—Hillary Rodham Clinton

INTRODUCTION

"Then out spake brave Horatius,
The Captain of the gate:
'To every man upon this earth
Death cometh soon or late.
And how can man die better
Than facing fearful odds,
For the ashes of his fathers,
And the temples of his Gods.'"

— *Thomas Babington Macaulay, 1842*

I have long vowed that I would never write an autobiography. So much of my life has been lived in public view already. However, as I approached my eightieth year and faced my mortality, I reconsidered that vow. I decided that I wanted to tell my story my way, before someone else told it their way.

My life has had many twists and turns, ups and downs. Key to my surviving and thriving was one overriding lesson I learned from the great Massachusetts Senator Edward M. Kennedy.

In 1988, I spent a weekend at the Kennedy Compound in Hyannis Port, Massachusetts. After dinner on Saturday evening, Ted took me on a tour. We visited the bedroom where his brother, John F. Kennedy, slept on the night he was elected president.

Then we walked along the beach. Amidst a squall, with the waves of the Atlantic Ocean crashing around us, he told me,

"Perseverance is the prerequisite for success in politics (and anything else important in life). It doesn't guarantee success; but it is the prerequisite for success."

Coming as it did after my defeat in my first political campaign for the United States Senate, his advice had a deep and lasting effect on me. And, it turns out, he was right. Perseverance was the key to my eventual successes in winning elections as Minnesota's state auditor in 1990, United States senator in 2000, and governor in 2010 and 2014. I became one of just seven men ever to serve our state as both senator and governor, and the only one first elected to both offices by popular vote. (U.S. senators were not elected by popular vote until the 1914 election.)

My path was never easy. I faced formidable odds and strong opposition, even within my own party. My victories and my defeats cost me my inherited financial fortune.

But you know what? I don't regret a cent of it! Those opportunities to make a difference in the world, to champion the causes I believe in, and to help create "A Better Minnesota" were priceless. I wouldn't trade them for anything.

My survival in my personal life also required perseverance. Many people believe that being born into wealth puts life on an easy street.

They're wrong.

I know I'm very fortunate to have been born into a prominent Minnesota family. I'm proud of what my grandfather, father, and four uncles accomplished in starting a successful family business, Dayton's Department Store, then expanding it into the Target Corporation. (I always said that, if I could be as popular as the store, I would have won every election!)

However, my home life was hard. I had an alcoholic mother, who often directed her drunken hostility toward me. Her invectives could cut me to pieces and make me feel terrible about myself. My father was solid and steady, but he was often not around to shield me from her blows.

Then, I followed my mother into alcoholism. My battles with alcohol dominated parts of my adult life. Fortunately for me, being constantly surrounded as governor by State Patrol bodyguards removed any opportunity to sneak into a liquor store! And I have managed to preserve my sobriety after leaving office, "one day at a time."

Through my career, which I define as public service, I have always intended to make life better for future generations. I have been guided by the Zen saying: "May you leave an excellent legacy to 10,000 generations."

Born into a world shaped by the triumphs and failures of "the Greatest Generation," I always aspired that my generation would exceed it in establishing world peace and ecological sanity, eliminating global hunger and disease, and bringing social justice and full economic opportunity to all Americans. Sadly, while I can point to some areas of great progress, we have failed in too many others. And now our country's social cohesion is being ripped apart, while our very democracy is gravely threatened. Many of the Donald Trump administration's policies are disastrous, and the viciousness of their execution is abhorrent.

I saw those abuses of power before, during the Richard Nixon presidency, when I strongly opposed the Vietnam War and earned the distinction of becoming the only Minnesotan named to his infamous "Enemies List." Back then, many of us who lawfully opposed the administration's policies were labeled "Un-American" and persecuted or prosecuted for our principles.

It's said that "Power corrupts, and absolute power corrupts

absolutely." Nixon and his cronies sought that degree of power, tried to sabotage their political opposition, and brought Watergate upon themselves. Finally, enough outraged citizens spurred enough members of Congress to strip Nixon of his power and force his departure, thus preserving our democracy for the next half century.

Now we face another such test. Thus far, the results are not encouraging. But perseverance is not a characteristic only of hearty individuals. It is also a characteristic of the American people, who have faced challenge, hardship, and contradiction before. We can do it again.

— CHAPTER ONE —

MY BEGINNINGS

"For unto whomsoever much is given,
of him shall be much required."

—*Luke 12:48*

I was born on January 26, 1947, in Minneapolis, Minnesota, in the early days of what became known as the "Baby Boom" that followed the Second World War. I grew up in a Republican business family in the town of Long Lake, a small suburb in the Minneapolis metro's western region. By the time I was born, my family had already established a legacy in the state.

In 1883, my great-grandfather George Draper Dayton was sent at age twenty-one by a banking syndicate in upstate New York to run a bank in the city of Worthington in southwestern Minnesota, far from the political and financial hub of the Twin Cities. When banks everywhere were failing in the depression of 1890, he came home and told his wife that they had five dollars to their names. But he survived and eventually prospered, also becoming a farmer in the area.

In 1903, George purchased a failing dry goods store, called Goodfellows, in Minneapolis, which had previously been a tenant in the downtown retail building he had built. He changed the name to Dayton's Dry Goods and sent his two sons to Minneapolis to run it. When the older brother, Draper,

George Draper Dayton

died prematurely in 1923, my grandfather, G. Nelson Dayton, became the sole proprietor of what by 1911 was called simply, the Dayton Company. He also farmed, raising dairy cows and growing corn in western Hennepin County.

My father, Bruce Bliss Dayton, born in 1918, was the second of five sons born to G. Nelson and Grace Bliss Dayton. He and his brothers were young men, just returned home from

World War II, when they took over the single Minneapolis store, then called Dayton's, after their father died from cancer in 1950. From the original Minneapolis store, they built a diverse retail operation of department stores, bookstores, jewelry stores, and shopping malls throughout the region. And in 1961, they founded a discount chain called Target. This new retail model became the growth vehicle for the company, which was renamed Target Corporation in 2001. In 2024, it had revenues of $107 billion.

Though my father ran a high-profile business, I grew up in a relatively sheltered environment. From kindergarten through second grade, I went to a public school in Long Lake. That school is now a history museum. (You know you're old when your former school is now a history museum!) But from the time I entered third grade in 1955 to my high school graduation

Dayton's store in Minneapolis, 1937

My family: Mom, Anne, Brandt, Mark, Lucy, and Dad entering my Grandmother Dayton's Minneapolis home for a Sunday lunch, 1957

in 1965, I attended the private, all-white Blake School in Hopkins. (During my senior year, my grandmother Grace Dayton provided full scholarships to enroll Blake's first three African American students.) Some of my teachers were politically active, but they didn't talk about it. None of my fellow students were. My life consisted of playing sports, watching sports, listening to pop music, and wishing for a girlfriend!

Like so many kids in Minnesota, I wanted to be a great hockey player. Reaching that goal was initially a problem, though, because I was a lousy skater. Then, on my fifth-grade club team, I saw an opening. Our team's only goalie was unable to play in our final two games. I volunteered and went from sitting on the bench as a third-string defenseman to playing the entire game as the goalie. Miraculously, we won both games, and I was mobbed by my teammates. I was hooked on goalie!

I was not a great natural athlete, but I worked hard to develop my skills and maximize the abilities that I had. And because goalies don't need to be on the ice to hone their craft, I could practice year-round. During the summer, I would enlist my friends to shoot pucks at me against the barn at my home. That barrage paid off. In my junior year, our Blake team won the state private school championship. In my senior year, I was named a goalie on both the local CBS affiliate WCCO's "Prep Parade" all-state team and the ABC affiliate KSTP's all-state roster. I was even named one of fifty "all-state players" chosen by the Amateur Sportsman's Club, a boosters' organization. That latter honor netted me my first grainy mug shot photo in the *Minneapolis Star*, then the city's premier evening newspaper.

Becoming a good—not great, but good—hockey player did wonders for my adolescent self-confidence. It won me acceptance by classmates, and it elevated my social standing at school. In my senior year, I was elected "Head Boy," a term borrowed from the British that, roughly translated, means "president of the student council."

I also lettered for two years in varsity football and four years in varsity golf. I was not a good football player. Football is a sport in which success requires a person to be big, strong, and fast. I was none of the three! My attraction to football was like the paratrooper who when asked if he liked jumping out of airplanes replied, "Not really. But I like hanging around the guys who do."

I did like golf, and I worked hard to become good at it. I got down to a two handicap during my senior year in high school and won the season-ending private school tournament. (By college, I was working full time either at school or in summer jobs and couldn't play enough to make the shots I did before. I quit golf and didn't touch a club for twenty years.)

But other matters, far removed from the rink and links, also engaged my teenage mind. For three summers while I was in high school, I worked as an orderly at the old Abbott Hospital in Minneapolis, first in the emergency room and then in surgery. I was fifteen years old on my third day in the emergency room when two parents brought in their young son. Within just a few minutes, he died.

After his parents departed, I helped the head nurse prepare that small, naked body for transport to the morgue. It was a deeply shocking experience. But it also moved me. It made me realize in a deeply personal way that those moments in the hospital were about life and death. That realization attracted me to a career in medicine.

Another feature of those summer jobs was that starting them at 6:45 A.M. required me to be up and gone from my home before anyone else in my family awoke. So every morning, I had the same breakfast: Coca-Cola and chocolate ice cream!

I was very religious when I was growing up. In fact, long before I considered becoming a doctor, my first career aspiration was to become a minister. When I was thirteen, I was confirmed at the Wayzata Community (Congregational) Church in Wayzata, Minnesota. However, church sermons there were primarily about how to be good and go to heaven. I didn't find that message fulfilling or sufficient. I was more interested in helping others. One call to social engagement did occur during the spring of my senior year in 1965. At a church service one April Sunday, our minister called for volunteers to help contain the flooding by the Minnesota River between Chaska and Shakopee. I took a church bus down the old Highway 169 and helped fill sandbags on what a Minnesota Department of Transportation sign still marks as the day of highest-recorded river elevation.

While I considered my place in the world, my family life

My mother, Gwendolen Brandt Dayton, and my grandmother Grace Bliss Dayton, circa 1945

My mother, Gwendolen Brandt Dayton

My father, Bruce Bliss Dayton

deteriorated. My parents' marriage was disintegrating, which led to their divorcing when I was twenty-two. My mother was a brilliant woman who grew up in Columbus, Ohio. Her father had died unexpectedly from a heart attack when she was just fifteen. But despite that tragedy, she carried on. She won a full scholarship to Smith College; then worked in New York City until she met my father in the spring of 1944. They married two months later, just before my father was shipped to France during the war.

Tragically, my mother was afflicted with the terrible disease of alcoholism. Her mental state and emotional stability deteriorated with its progression. And as it did, she took her increasing resentments toward my father out on me. Her drunken dark side was very frightening; her words could cut me to the quick. "You're just like your father," she would say harshly.

Well, I *wanted* to be like my father! He was steady and reliable, and I knew he loved me. Our family dinners were nightmares. My mother dominated the conversations with her drunken rambles. I would eat as fast as possible and ask to be excused from the table.

After dinner, my mother would usually go to her bedroom, and I would often join my father in the living room, where we would share our day's events. I learned more about running an organization there than in any business school classroom.

My father always compared Dayton's performance with its top five competitors. He wanted to be the best. If not, he wanted to know it and find out why. From him, I learned that a leader must strive to be the best, but must always face reality, whether good or bad.

In the fall 1965, I entered Yale University. And in the spring of 1969, I graduated *cum laude*. But my freshman year was total misery. I had never been away from home, and even though I was leaving a very dysfunctional family environment, I was homesick. I sought some guidance from my "freshman adviser," an indifferent graduate student, who talked me into enrolling in advanced physics and calculus classes, which were over my head and plagued my academic experience for three semesters. I studied almost constantly throughout my freshman year, and although I made the Dean's List, I was miserable and exhausted.

To make matters worse, my freshman hockey experience was also horrible. Back in those days, freshman athletes played on freshman-only teams, not the upper-class varsities. I was elected our captain. However, we were lousy, losing even to high school teams. And I was lousy too. My self-esteem, the foundation of which in high school was my hockey prowess, was shattered.

One profound and positive experience during my freshman year was my association with Battell Chapel, Yale's imposing church, and its renowned minister, the Reverend William Sloane Coffin. My first Sunday at Yale, I went to the service

Playing goalie for Yale in 1967

there and found the sanctuary packed. Unbeknownst to me, the guest preacher that day was a famous Episcopal bishop, James Pike. He saw a group of us standing in the back and invited us to sit on the floor below the altar next to him. That was quite a shift from my Wayzata Community Church environment. From the pulpit, Bishop Pike railed against the social injustices of the day, which was also quite a departure from my previous church services. I initially thought, "This isn't church. It's a political science seminar!"

Over the next four years, Reverend Sloane Coffin gave many more political science seminars from the pulpit. It was there that my morally rooted political activism was born. I started reading the *New York Times* and its front pages, not just its sports pages. I began to look at the country and world around me, and I became deeply disturbed by what I saw.

My sophomore year at Yale started better, despite almost failing my final semester of advanced physics. I made the varsity hockey team but was not nearly as successful as I had been in high school. Then, in my junior year, my throat was slashed by a skate in a collision on the ice. The sharp blade tore my windpipe (trachea) and cracked my voice box (larynx).

If it had gone a half inch deeper, I would have died on the ice. Instead, coughing up blood, I was transported to the emergency room at Yale–New Haven Hospital. There, I lay in an oxygen tent with a tracheotomy kit at my side. I was forced to recognize that my dream of being the starting goalie on the U.S. Olympic Hockey Team would not be realized in this lifetime!

I was pre-med in college through my junior year. By then, however, I was becoming strongly opposed to the Vietnam War. And the 1968 presidential campaign was underway. Although two Minnesotans were running, Vice President Hubert Humphrey and Senator Eugene McCarthy, I was drawn to support New York Senator Robert F. Kennedy. He combined opposition to the Vietnam War with deep concern for the social injustices afflicting American society.

In June 1968, I returned home from college for a few days before beginning my all-time favorite summer job, as an orderly on the acute psychotic ward at Columbia–Presbyterian Hospital in New York City. (Four years before me, Dustin Hoffman had been an orderly on that ward.)

June 4, 1968, was the night of the California Democratic presidential primary, a critical test for Senator Kennedy. My parents didn't like the Kennedys, so they went to bed, leaving me to watch the primary returns on our basement television. Kennedy gave his victory speech, finishing with "And now, it's on to Chicago!" (where the Democratic National Convention would be held in August).

Robert F. Kennedy speaking to a crowd outside the Justice Department, July 1963

I leaned forward to turn off the television. Suddenly, there Kennedy was in front of my eyes, shot and lying in a pool of blood. I watched that scene repeated again and again over the following days. Something about seeing my political hero die for the causes in which he believed lit a spark of conscience in me, and I could never be comfortable being comfortable in my parents' comfortable home again.

That fall I withdrew all my applications to medical school.

As my college graduation approached in June 1969, I wanted some real-world experience. A friend who graduated the year before me had joined an organization called The Teachers, Inc. A forerunner of Teach for America, its idealistic and unrealistic goal was to transform New York City's public school system from within, by training and placing dedicated young teachers in inner-city schools.

The City of New York had initiated its own education reform experiment by establishing three "Community-Controlled Districts" within the larger school system. It gave "Community Boards" the power to hire new teachers who had not passed through the traditional school licensure bureaucracy. I was hired as one of those teachers in a district located next to the Brooklyn and Manhattan Bridges on New York's Lower East Side.

During the summer of 1969, I joined The Teachers, Inc.'s training program. To better understand the conditions in which our students lived, we trainees were housed with welfare families in the district's massive high-rise public housing projects. The summer consisted of many hours of practice teaching, as the trainers tried to prepare us for the chaos and disruption we would find in our classrooms. Still, nothing could prepare me adequately for what I would face on the day I walked into my ninth-grade general science classroom in P.S. 65, located just off Canal Street and the Bowery.

On my first day, I started to teach the way I had always been taught: with a boring, forty-minute monologue. The thirty students in each of my four classes sized me up the way a pack of hungry lions would size up a gazelle! On the second day, two girls in the second row of my homeroom class began talking. I asked them to stop, and they ignored me. I again asked them to stop, and they again ignored me. So, I fired my secret weapon, which a veteran teacher had assured me would be an effective deterrent. "All right, that's it," I said. "I'm going to write a letter home to your parents."

One of the girls sneered at me, "You write a letter home, and I'll wipe my ass with it. Then I'll give it to my mother, and she'll wipe her ass with it." Clearly, the students saw my ineptitude.

On the second week, I decided that since my monologues were not being well received, I would try to teach by experiments. I set up alcohol burners at each table and provided explicit instructions: "Mix chemical A with chemical B. Hold over the flame. Observe the chemical reaction."

I was engrossed with students at one table when I was alerted to something happening at another table behind me. Those students had decided to improvise with their own experiment. They poured the alcohol over the table, lit a match, and watched gleefully as chest-high flames erupted. (Alcohol burns at a relatively low temperature, but it still creates an impressive visual spectacle.)

Just then, the door to my classroom opened. Fortunately, it was a fellow teacher. "Bar the door," I shouted and managed to keep everyone away until the flames burned down. If that visitor had been the principal, my teaching career would have been short-lived!

However, I persevered and worked very hard on my lesson plans and improvement as a teacher. I made considerable progress. Just before the school year ended in June, the girl who had told me what she and her mother would do with my letter approached me in the hallway. She had been in the school's library and for some reason was reading through *Who's Who in America*. She came across my father's name, and I was listed as his son.

"Mr. Dayton," she said excitedly, "your father's in *Who's Who in America*. Why, you come from a very wealthy family." Embarrassed, I stumbled to find words, but nothing came out.

"That's okay," she said. "You can't help where you were born!"

When the second school year started, I had learned my lessons. On the first day, students in my most difficult class didn't bother to wait until the second day to misbehave. They just ignored me and talked among themselves.

I identified three ringleaders and right after school made unannounced visits to their homes. In that school, teachers *never* visited students' homes. I remember one boy, named Jose, squirming in his living room as he braced for what he feared would be my disclosure of his behavior that day. Instead, I assured his parents that Jose was one of the leaders in his class, and I was counting on him to help me set a good tone for everyone else.

The next day, the word spread around, "Don't mess with Mr. Dayton." I had almost no trouble with what proved to be the most disruptive class for other teachers.

However, it was very frustrating for me to work in that school, surrounded by so much poverty, misery, and violence, and to realize that I could not change it. I could not improve my students' lives in just the forty minutes I was with them five days a week. And I was very burned out trying.

While my mind and body were immersed in my teaching, my soul was caught up in our country's political turmoil. I was as involved as I could be in the anti–Vietnam War movement. On October 15, 1969, several of my students and I left school for an anti-war march up Fifth Avenue. A few hard hats attacked some of the marchers, but they only waved at my students. Then, on Saturday, November 15, I went to Washington for the Second Moratorium March, a massive protest that drew 500,000 patriotic Americans for a profoundly powerful gathering that flooded the National Mall leading up to the Lincoln Memorial. I'll never forget Pete Seeger quietly singing "Strangest Dream," a folk ballad imagining a world in which all people agreed to cease making war.

There, I got my first taste of tear gas, as the DC police dispersed us protesting in front of the Justice Department and again in front of the Washington Monument.

In May 1970, I returned to Washington for another massive protest. It was the Saturday after President Nixon invaded

Vietnam War Second Moratorium March in Washington, DC, November 15, 1969

Cambodia, and four students had been murdered at Kent State. Again, we were tear-gassed, and many protestors were beaten and arrested.

Years later, as a member of the U.S. Senate's Armed Services Committee, I was in a meeting with Republican Defense Secretary Donald Rumsfeld. I don't know what prompted his recollection, but he recounted being in a meeting with Nixon in the White House while it was surrounded by anti-war protestors. I smiled and said, "Yes. I was one of them."

But I wanted to do more. I wanted to make an impact on the events afflicting our country. At the time, the Nixon administration was persecuting the Black Panther Party in New York and had locked up Joan Bird along with other members of the Panther 21 (later narrowed to the Panther 13). "Free Joan Bird" became the rallying cry of New Yorkers opposing the White House's increasing tyranny. It was to raise money for her defense that the famous composer Leonard Bernstein had

Pin demanding the release of Joan Bird and the other "Panther 21" defendants

hosted a fundraiser in his home that Tom Wolfe lampooned in his article "Radical Chic." But Wolfe's dismissals did not change the injustice of the situation.

Bird's bail, along with that of each of her codefendants, had been set at an outrageous $100,000, which was beyond the reach of her family, friends, and supporters. So, I anonymously donated $100,000 to her defense fund. She was released on bond. New York was stunned. I felt *so, so good* about making a difference about something important. In 1971, after one of the longest trials in New York history, the Panther 13 were acquitted of all charges.

But my actions were not anonymous to the FBI, who pried out of my bank the details of my transactions. The IRS stormed into my family's office and audited my financial records. The Justice Department hauled me before a grand jury on a fishing expedition for evidence to use against other Black Panthers. (No charges were ever brought.)

Those experiences showed me the power the government could abuse to persecute and prosecute citizens who had legitimate and patriotic grievances against its actions. I believe, and I hope, that I carried those bitter lessons into my own government service.

Now I see those same persecutions and prosecutions happening today.

Esalen Institute founder and American Gestalt therapist Richard "Dick" Price in 1968

As I considered leaving my New York teaching stint, I fortunately stumbled upon a retreat and educational center in Big Sur, California, called Esalen Institute, which had been founded in 1962 with a mission to integrate spiritual and psychological insights to explore the human potential. I got a job there working first on the construction crew and then on the kitchen crew. (I became an excellent ditchdigger and dishwasher!)

I also met and worked intensively with a man who became my "Great Life Teacher," Dick Price, one of the two founders of Esalen. He was a Gestalt therapist, and with him I was able to work through some of the traumas of my upbringing as the son of an abusive alcoholic mother.

For fifteen years, my friendship with Dick grew and deepened. He became my principal confidant and best friend. Then, tragically, he was killed in a freak rockslide while hiking in Big Sur on November 25, 1985. I have never gotten over his loss. No one had a more profound impact upon my psychological well-being.

After six months living and working at Esalen, I was ready to move on with my life. I found a wonderful organization in Boston called Project Place, which, among other social services, operated a house for adolescents who had run away from homes or institutions and were living on the city's streets.

I worked as a counselor on evening and overnight shifts, from 5:00 P.M. to midnight and from midnight to 9:00 A.M. There were a couple of important differences from New York City's public school. Everyone at Project Place worked harmoniously together, and the kids wanted to be there with us. At times of crisis in their lives, there were real opportunities to change those lives for the better.

Evenings at the Runaway House were endlessly turbulent and chaotic. Strung-out and exhausted adolescents came in off the streets. Sometimes parents or police arrived unannounced to try to claim them. The local street gang prowled outside, looking for young girls. I learned to think fast and be quick on my feet.

The other transformative event in my life during those Boston years (1971–75) was the Watergate hearings in the spring of 1973. The United States Senate was investigating the previous year's break-in at the Democratic National Committee headquarters in Washington, DC's Watergate Building and President Nixon's attempted cover-up of those crimes. I was transfixed and watched every hearing on television. There I saw the president's men, who had denounced us anti-war activists as traitors and criminals, and it turned out that *they* were the criminals! I felt vindicated. Before, I had believed that my activism put me outside the political mainstream. Those hearings showed me that I was firmly entrenched inside it.

In 1971, my father and I had had a heated falling-out over his directorship of Honeywell, Inc., a Minneapolis-based firm. Although its primary products were for households, it also manufactured anti-personnel bombs for the military that cruelly killed and maimed thousands of Vietnamese civilians. In May 1970, my childhood best friend, Charlie Pillsbury, the great-grandson of the founder of another iconic Minneapolis business, the Pillsbury Company, was organizing a protest at Honeywell's annual shareholders' meeting in Minneapolis. Charlie and I each purchased one share of the company's stock so that we could attend. Within five minutes, we shut it down by speaking out against Honeywell's war practices. My father was "out of town" and did not attend.

Then we went outside, where we were joined by several hundred protestors. Someone, later believed to be an FBI agent-provocateur, threw a brick that shattered the glass in Honeywell's front door. Instantly, Minneapolis police, at the direction of right-wing mayor Charles Stenvig, unleashed a torrent of mace and attacked us on horseback. It was Minneapolis's first big anti-war protest.

By 1974, however, mainstream public opinion was turning against the war in Southeast Asia and against Richard Nixon. One night early that year, my father called me in Boston to tell me excitedly that I was the only Minnesotan named to President Nixon's infamous "Enemies List." A *Minneapolis Tribune* reporter had called him to try to find me. I have always said, "That is what I want on my tombstone!"

After those years in social service, I was yearning for a bigger impact. I had been working to help society's casualties. I wanted to tackle the forces creating those casualties. That led me to government and a job with Minnesota Senator Walter F. Mondale in Washington, DC.

— CHAPTER TWO —

FIRST POLITICAL VENTURES

"Are you a politician asking what your country can do for you or a zealous one asking what you can do for your country? If you are the first, then you are a parasite; if the second, then you are an oasis in the desert."

—*Kahlil Gibran*

Activism and social service mold a person's character and conscience. But translating those moral lessons into policy requires a thorough understanding of the institutions of power and the nuances of political craft. At the start of my life in government service, I did not yet possess that understanding. Thankfully, I had two great teachers who saw to my political education: Vice President Walter "Fritz" Mondale and Governor Rudy Perpich, both giants of Minnesota politics.

From June 1975 to December 1976, I worked as a legislative assistant to then–Senator Mondale in his Capitol Hill office. To be frank, I got the job because of my father's personal friendship with the senator. Back in 1969, my father, a Republican, approached the Democratic senator with the observation that he had no connections to Minnesota's business leaders, and if he were to be effective in Washington, he could use some. That conversation led to several Saturday morning gatherings at our house, during which Fritz talked informally with a dozen or so business executives.

I first met Senator Mondale when my father and I picked him up at the Leamington Hotel in Minneapolis to drive him to our house for one of those sessions. The next time I saw him was in his DC office six years later, to ask him for a job!

After my experience in the New York public schools, my principal political issue was education—funding it, expanding it, reforming it. Fortuitously, education was one of the senator's top legislative priorities. The Senate was reauthorizing the federal Higher Education Act, of which he was one of the principal coauthors, so he was frequently asked to speak at national education conferences. That meant I got to spend a lot of one-on-one time with him, traveling throughout Minnesota and the country.

I'll never forget flying with him to Miami in June 1976 when he spoke at the National Education Association's annual convention, just days before the Democratic National Convention. By then, Mondale had been identified as one of the finalists for soon-to-be presidential nominee Jimmy Carter's pick for vice president.

It was high drama to write the draft of his NEA speech (which he revised considerably!) and then staff him on the trip to Miami to deliver it. He deservedly received a hero's welcome at the convention and gave a flawless speech, which had to impress the Carter operatives watching him.

The Democratic National Convention in New York City July 12–15 was another unforgettable adventure. The previous December, I learned that Michael Berman, a top Mondale aide, had been asked by DNC Chairman Robert Strauss to run the convention. I asked Mike if I could take a week's vacation from my Senate duties to staff him at the convention. He agreed.

On Monday morning, the convention's first day, I arrived at Mike's office at 8:00 A.M. to find him already hard at work. His yellow pad was filled with several pages of "to dos." I spent much of the day delivering convention tickets and other documents to various party luminaries.

In the evening, after the convention formally began, I roamed the floor, looking for useful intelligence. The raging question: Whom would Carter pick as his running mate? I asked various delegates, insiders, and journalists whom they thought the choice would be. When Dan Rather replied, "I think it will be Mondale," I phoned that info to Mike, who was seated on the convention platform. I watched with satisfaction as Mike immediately picked up an outside line, presumably to pass on Rather's predication to Fritz, who was holed up somewhere. (It turned out to be a suite at the Carlyle Hotel.) The evening's other highlights included watching Senator Gary Hart and movie star Warren Beatty standing side by side, surveying the delegates!

Finally, on Thursday, the morning of the final day, the news broke: It was Mondale! Suddenly, I was thrown into the center of the convention's drama. Since Mike was consumed with convention details and the rest of Mondale's staff was still in Washington, I was suddenly the point person for all sorts of activities.

Soon it was time for Fritz to emerge from the Carlyle Hotel and travel to Madison Square Garden, where he would join with presidential nominee Carter and deliver his acceptance speech. I was sent to the Carlyle to escort him to his first moment in the national spotlight.

The hotel's entrance was surrounded by the national press corps, and a Secret Service's "diamond formation" enveloped Fritz and me. We traveled to the Garden, where I was able to use my weeklong experience to guide him through a backdoor

Jimmy Carter (left) and Walter Mondale at the Democratic National Convention, New York City, July 15, 1976

entrance to the holding room, and I met President Carter for the first time.

What a convention!

The following weekend provided another amazing adventure. That Friday, Fritz and his senior staff flew to Hilton Head, South Carolina, for high-level meetings with Carter and his top people. Naturally, I was not close to being included. Instead, University of Minnesota President Peter Magrath invited me to lunch with him at Capitol Hill's most renowned restaurant, the Monocle.

There, for the first time in my life, I was paged to come to the restaurant's telephone. (There were no cell phones in those days.) Jim Johnson, another member of the Mondale "Big Three," said urgently, "Mark, don't tell anyone this, but Fritz forgot his briefcase. Go immediately to his home, get the briefcase, and bring it to Hilton Head." I dashed out of the restaurant.

I arrived at the Hilton Head beach resort with nothing but the briefcase in my hand and my office suit on my back. I was seriously overdressed. All of Carter's campaign staff wore well-faded blue jeans. Trying to follow suit (pun intended!), Mondale's people had brand-new blue jeans, dark blue with the factory creases still intact. I hovered in the background, not invited into the meetings. But I busied myself keeping Mike Berman's car gassed and refrigerator stocked to justify staying around.

The meetings concluded on Sunday afternoon with Fritz's first southern campaign event, a "shrimp boil," South Carolina's version of a Minnesota DFL bean feed. At its end, Fritz and his wife, Joan, boarded a sedan that would drive them to the airport in Columbia, South Carolina, from which they would fly to a brief vacation.

The sedan began to move. It was to be followed by a station wagon filled with Secret Service agents and a press corps caravan. However, for reasons I never discovered, the station wagon driver's door was open, and the driver was nowhere to be found.

Skip Loescher, Mondale's press secretary, and I happened to be standing next to the driver's door. Skip appraised the situation, shoved me into the driver's seat, and said, "Mark, drive." Suddenly, I was driving the lead contingent of Secret Service agents, trying to keep up with the Mondales' sedan, which was speeding down the back roads of South Carolina.

I maintained what I considered to be a safe distance behind the sedan. The lead Secret Service agent, sitting in the passenger's seat beside me, kept saying, "Closer, closer." I thought the greatest danger to the Mondales' lives was not some terrorist attack from the weeds, but my rear-ending their car! Fortunately, neither occurred, and they flew safely to a well-deserved vacation.

That was the closest I would get to Fritz until election night in November. I was assigned to the Carter–Mondale campaign headquarters in Atlanta. The headquarters were situated in a high-rise office building about a mile from downtown Atlanta. Right next to it was an intended luxury hotel that was virtually empty, going bankrupt, and offering us rooms for ten dollars a night.

We worked around the clock, sixteen to eighteen hours, every day and night, from late July to early November. There was nothing to do but work and eat; so, I ate when I didn't work. I gained about fifteen pounds in the first two weeks, bought a much larger pair of Levi's, and went through my most grueling ordeal since final exams in college. Except these exams lasted for almost four months.

For example, the campaign plane would arrive somewhere on the West Coast about midnight. That was 3:00 A.M. in Atlanta. What would today take only a few minutes of faxing or emailing briefing materials from the policy and advance staffs at headquarters to the traveling team, back then took two to three hours of "telecopying," which, as only a few techno-archivists would remember, consisted of putting the page to be transmitted into the cylinder of the telecopier, connecting its phone line with the receiving party's machine, pressing a button, and watching that cylinder revolve for the twelve minutes it took to transmit a single page.

At that point, our friends on the West Coast would check to see if the page had been transmitted properly. If it had, we went on to the next thirty or more pages, using three machines. If not, we would repeat that process with the same page.

It was tedious, brain-numbing work after an already exhausting day, especially for the traveling crew. Afterward, we in Atlanta finally snatched a couple hours of sleep, before beginning the next day with a staff meeting at 8:00 A.M.

Finally, Election Day arrived. Our Atlanta team flew back to Minneapolis for a luncheon reunion with the traveling crew. We were all exhausted but elated. Victory was nigh!

That night, the vice-president-to-be gave me the special honor of staffing his private hotel suite, where his family, best friends, and longtime supporters gathered to watch his victory unfold. My first political campaign had become a phenomenal, nation-changing success. Little did I know then how quickly and decisively the political currents could change.

After a week's vacation, I decided it was time for me to return to Minnesota. I had been away for eleven years. If it were to be my home and the locus of my own political pursuits, I needed to get back. In December 1976, I rented an apartment in Minneapolis and began to look for a job.

I felt confirmed in my decision when I returned to Washington the next February and visited friends who were working for Vice President Mondale. Except for the vice president and his top aide, Jim Johnson, who officed in the West Wing of the White House, everyone else was housed in the adjacent Old Executive Office Building.

In our Senate office, there had been almost no privacy. Everyone's desk was crammed next to its neighbors. Thus, everyone knew not only everything that was going on in the office but also everything about everyone else's personal lives.

In contrast, in the Old Executive Office Building, most people had their own separate offices. There they sat, isolated and fearful that someone else was in on the action they were missing.

My good friend Gail Harrison, who had risen from an office secretary to become Mondale's top policy adviser through her brilliance and hard work, took me on a "Cook's tour" of the West Wing. We passed by the Oval Office, its door closed and guarded by a Marine, and went into the adjacent cabinet conference room. Suddenly, the connecting door from the Oval Office opened, and President Carter appeared. Surprised, he said softly, "Hello, Gail," and looked at me as if to say, "Who the heck are you?"

We scurried out like two children caught with our hands in the cookie jar! It was to be my last visit to the West Wing for the next twenty-four years.

Though I was glad to be home, I regretted moving out of Walter Mondale's immediate orbit. He was, without a doubt, one of the very best people I have ever encountered in politics. He was honest, principled, smart, hardworking, and politically astute. He had a nearly infallible ability to survey the scene, make his calculations, and proceed, cautiously but surely, in his chosen direction. He was always gracious to me, to all his staff and colleagues, and to his supporters and constituents. For that, he was widely liked and respected in the Senate, and he had a lock on his Senate seat in Minnesota.

Hindsight is 20/20. If Mondale had remained in the Senate, he would likely have served many years beyond his four as vice president. He would have risen to either Chairman of the all-powerful Senate Finance Committee or Senate Majority Leader. Would he, and Minnesota, have been better off? We'll never know.

He was a great public servant and a wonderful human being. Thanks for all you taught me, Fritz.

When I returned to Minnesota, Mondale's Minnesota director, Bob Hurner, put me in touch with his friend Terry Montgomery,

Rudy Perpich being sworn into office as governor in 1976

the chief of staff to the new governor of Minnesota, Rudy Perpich. I started as a staff assistant in that office the day he became governor on December 29, 1976. In the afternoon, I stood in line outside the Governor's Residence for two hours on a cold winter day to introduce myself to him.

I later learned that Rudy had serious reservations when he discovered I had been hired for his staff. He thought I was a rich prima donna who would try to work banker's hours. So, as he later told the story, one morning, after arriving in the office at 7:30, he phoned the receptionist and asked her to let him know when I showed up. He was told that I was *already* in the office and was always one of the first to arrive. He said he quickly hung up the phone!

A couple nights later, Rudy held an evening meeting at the Governor's Residence, which I attended. After its conclusion, he invited me to stay for a second meeting, followed by a third. I later learned that it was not uncommon for him to add people from an earlier meeting to stay on for the next one. He truly believed, as the sign in his office (and later in my office) said, "None of us are as smart as all of us."

It was close to midnight when the last meeting concluded. Everyone else departed, leaving used coffee cups and pastry plates on the meeting table. I saw Rudy pick up some of them and head to the kitchen; so, I picked up the rest and followed him. There I stood at the double sink in the kitchen, shoulder to shoulder with the governor of Minnesota, washing dishes! That was the beginning of our bond.

I learned so much from Rudy over the next fourteen years of our friendship. I learned the importance of a job. He had grown up on the hardscrabble Iron Range, where his father worked in one of the mines. As he put it, on mornings when his father's lunch pail was on the kitchen table, his dad was working. When it remained on the shelf, he was not. I could only imagine what that difference meant to him and his family.

So, when he campaigned on "Jobs, Jobs, Jobs," he *meant* it.

Once, when we were being driven to an event by the State Patrol, we were stopped by traffic backed up in a construction zone. I complained about the delay. He said he didn't mind because it meant people were working. And he would go anywhere, literally anywhere, throughout our country and around the globe, where there were prospects of jobs for Minnesotans.

Unlike Mondale, who was cautious and careful, Rudy was spontaneous and impulsive. He was a font of new ideas, his own and those he culled from others. I once said that working for Mondale was like waterskiing behind a cabin cruiser. With Perpich, it was like waterskiing behind a jet boat, and you were desperately holding on just trying to remain upright!

Despite our differences, or perhaps because of them, we forged a mutually respectful professional relationship and then a personal friendship. In the spring of 1978, when the commissioner of the Minnesota Department of Economic

Development resigned, Rudy appointed me the commissioner (technically acting commissioner, because the Senate never confirmed me). I was thirty-one years old.

It was my first experience leading an organization. The department had been used as a political dumping ground by the previous administration. The director of the tiny Foreign Trade Office had never even been out of the country. However, his wife was one of Muriel Humphrey's bridge partners! I called Terry Montgomery to alert him that he would hear a strong protest when I fired that director. He did, from then–Senator Humphrey's son-in-law. To Terry's credit, he backed me up.

There I learned a valuable lesson about coalition building. The state's Office of Tourism was then in the department, headed by another director who needed replacement. At the same time, the state's prestigious tourism advertising and promotion account was up for renewal. It was then held by the former governor's campaign ad agency.

I knew that people in the tourism industry were very skeptical of my appointment, believing I was just another unqualified politico. So, I formed a "Tourism Advisory Council," comprised of leading industry representatives, to review with me the candidates for both the director position and the ad agency account. We jointly made two excellent, highly regarded selections, and my standing within the industry was secured.

A particularly memorable tourism meeting occurred when I joined Governor Perpich at the U.S. Hockey Hall of Fame in Eveleth. Somehow, despite hockey's iconic status in Minnesota, the Hockey Hall of Fame had been a colossal flop, offering nothing but lifeless mannequins and obsolete graphics and perpetually losing money.

On our way to the meeting with the executive director, Rudy was primed for a major confrontation. He knew he would be asked for money, and he was determined to say no.

The meeting began with the executive director recounting

the financial plight and the critical need for $25,000 to continue operating. After about three sentences, Rudy interrupted him and began his irate response. But after only two of those sentences, the director suddenly began to bang his head on the table. "I can't stand it! I just can't stand it!" he exclaimed in a shrill voice.

Shocked into silence, the governor looked at me and whispered, "Do you have $25,000 in the tourism fund?" It was probably the only time I ever saw Rudy outjousted!

Unfortunately, my tenure in that office was short-lived. Governor Perpich lost the 1978 election to Republican Congressman Al Quie. His reelection was doomed by the circumstances under which he took office in December 1976. When Mondale had been elected vice president, he vacated his U.S. Senate seat. Then–Governor Wendell Anderson arranged to resign as governor, be replaced by then–Lieutenant Governor Perpich, and have Perpich appoint him to the Senate seat.

That self-appointment turned out to be a colossal political miscalculation. Most Minnesotans were outraged by the self-dealing stunt. Anderson's public approval rating plummeted, and Perpich was tarnished by the same brush. There was no way for either of them to recover before the election less than two years away.

I resigned the day Governor Quie took office. Elections have consequences!

The best part of my life during those years began in April 1977, when I met my first wife, Alida Rockefeller, at a conference in Monterey, California, for young progressives with inherited wealth. She was the daughter of John D. Rockefeller 3rd and the sister of West Virginia Governor Jay Rockefeller.

Alida made a presentation on the first afternoon. I was hit by a thunderbolt! The next afternoon I talked her into taking a walk along the beach with me. As the conference ended, I invited her on a date at Esalen. She later said she wasn't sure about me, but she had always wanted to see Esalen!

While I fell in love with Alida immediately, it took her a little longer to decide on me. However, we married June 24, 1978, at her parents' home in Tarrytown, New York, on a beautiful summer day.

Unfortunately, our marriage got off to a terrible start. Just two weeks after our wedding, Alida's father was killed in a tragic car accident, while being driven back to New York City. We have an iconic photograph of Alida dancing with him at our wedding reception, the last time she ever saw her father.

Although we divorced eight years later, Alida has remained a good friend and a steadfast political ally. We continue to share the same political convictions that brought us to the Monterey conference. And together we created the enduring joy of two amazing sons: Eric John Dayton and Andrew Rockefeller Dayton. (Eric's middle name was in honor of Alida's father.)

Eric was born on June 4, 1980. Andrew followed on October 19, 1983. Although Alida and I separated when they were very young, we co-parented cooperatively and devotedly and managed to raise two extraordinary boys, who are now outstanding men with their own wonderful families.

Before they were born, I read the best parenting advice I ever received, from Jacqueline Kennedy Onassis. She said that she thought if you failed to raise your children well, it didn't matter what else you achieved with the rest of your life. I took that admonition to heart and made parenting my number one priority. I coached Eric's youth hockey teams for eight years and Andrew's youth baseball teams for seven years. I loved coaching and the additional time it allowed me to spend with them. It also enabled me to impart important life lessons, such

With Eric, Andrew, Wanamingo, Mesabi, and Itasca

With my adult sons, Andrew and Eric

as working hard to become the best you can be at whatever you do.

When Eric was nine, he decided he wanted to become a goalie. I didn't want him to choose that position just to follow me, so I asked, "Why do you want to be a goalie?" He replied, "Dad, when the other team gets the puck and starts skating at you, it's SO EXCITING!" I thought, if you get that adrenaline rush and you like it, you're meant to be a goalie!

In his senior year, Eric led his Blake hockey team to its first-ever appearance in the state tournament. They won their quarterfinal game but lost a heartbreaker in the semifinals to East Grand Forks. Still, it was an exceptional capstone to his very successful high school career.

Unlike hockey, where I had extensive experience to impart as a coach, my baseball career had consisted of three strikes at my only Little League tryout. Again, however, I loved spending time with one of my sons.

Andrew was a very good second baseman. On a Saturday morning, before a playoff game, I spent an hour throwing pitches to help him sharpen his hitting. In the first inning, with two runners on base, he hit the first pitch into center field for a double. He stood on base and raised his fist toward me in jubilation. I cried with joy inside! A lesson had been learned about the benefits of hard work.

Both Alida and I tried to model my father's favorite Biblical axiom, "For unto whomsoever much is given, of him shall be much required" (Luke 12:48). As my father had with me, I wanted my sons to understand that I didn't care what they did, as long as they worked hard and were socially responsible. They have embraced my challenge.

Together, they started a restaurant, the Bachelor Farmer, and an adjoining bar, Marvel. For a decade they were among Minnesota's most popular and successful night spots, until they were wiped out by the pandemic in 2020. Since then, Eric

My son Eric and daughter-in-law Cory

My son Andrew and daughter-in-law Alyssa

has been a leader in combatting climate change. Andrew has founded a nonprofit, the Constellation Fund, which has raised millions of dollars to contribute to successful poverty-fighting organizations.

I am tremendously proud of them both. They have so much to offer a world that badly needs strong leaders with good hearts.

They have also blessed me with five amazing grandchildren: Hugo, George, Wilder, Hattie, and Margot.

After I left state government in January 1979, Alida and I co-founded a nonprofit organization, the Minnesota Project. Tom Triplett, Rudy Perpich's top policy person and his director of the State Planning Agency, headed the policy unit; I headed the community development section. This post provided me with continuing opportunities to travel the state, helping with different economic development projects, as I had been doing while commissioner.

One of my most memorable trips was to Babbitt in northeastern Minnesota, just south of the Boundary Waters Canoe Area Wilderness. I went there to help local leaders convert an empty elementary school into a business center. At the entrance to the city was a sign that, as best I can remember, said: "This town exists despite the efforts of the Sierra Club, the Nature Conservancy, Friends of the Boundary Waters, and the Audubon Society."

When I arrived, about thirty people were already seated in the room at City Hall. I walked around, introducing myself to each person: "Hi! I'm Mark Dayton." When I spoke my name, many people gave me shocked looks, followed by hostile glares.

I knew something was wrong, so I spoke to Doug Johnson, the area's state senator and a staunch Perpich ally, who knew and liked me from our previous two years working together.

He smiled and said, "They think you're Chuck Dayton." Chuck was a Minneapolis lawyer who had just negotiated the very unpopular BWCAW federal legislation on behalf of the environmental groups. "Don't worry," Doug said. "I'll take care of it."

He spoke first and introduced me. "This is Mark Dayton. He's NO RELATION to Chuck Dayton. He worked for Rudy Perpich. A good guy. He's NO RELATION TO CHUCK DAYTON."

He repeated this assurance several times. Every time, people's responses to my name improved, and their faces softened. As a result, I survived the evening!

The Minnesota Project was my base of operations until my next adventure, a two-year campaign for the United States Senate.

— CHAPTER THREE —

THE 1982 CAMPAIGN

Winning does not tempt that man.
This is how he grows.
By being defeated decisively.
By ever greater foes.

—*Rainer Maria Rilke*

By 1980, as I was approaching my mid-thirties, I began to realize that I was ready to run for political office myself, and I started quietly looking for an opening. But while my mind was turning over my options, I decided to get involved in the Democratic Party's controversial presidential primary contest that year. Despite my history with the administration, I had become disappointed and disillusioned by Jimmy Carter's lackluster presidency; so, I decided to support Massachusetts Senator Ted Kennedy's primary challenge and became the co-chair of the Minnesota Kennedy for President campaign. This move gained me the enmity of Vice President Mondale and all his aides, my former friends. I told Fritz I would proudly support him for president, but I couldn't support Carter. That distinction did nothing to appease Mondale, who let me know he was extremely unhappy with my decision.

A highlight of the campaign in Minnesota occurred at the state DFL convention in June. The national campaign sent

Kennedy's twenty-six-year-old nephew, Robert Kennedy Jr., as its surrogate to speak to the convention, whose delegates were almost 100 percent supporting the Carter–Mondale ticket.

I met Bob at the airport, and we parked outside the convention at the Minneapolis Auditorium. "Do we have time for a beer?" he asked. We did, so we first went to the Curtis Hotel across the street. In twenty minutes, he downed three beers; then we headed into the auditorium, where he was greeted by polite but muted applause.

Kennedy proceeded to deliver one of the most impassioned and frenetic speeches I have ever heard. His voice shouting, his arms and hands waving, he brought the reluctant crowd to its feet cheering again and again! Then we returned to the airport, where he departed for his next campaign stop.

In 2025, Kennedy became the secretary of Health and Human Services in the Trump administration, having deserted his family and the Democratic Party to endorse Donald Trump during the 2024 presidential campaign.

By the fall of 1980, I had set my sights on the U.S. Senate seat held since 1979 by Republican David Durenberger. He was extremely popular statewide, even among some DFLers, as he had defeated a maverick conservative Democrat, businessman Bob Short, in the previous election.

Durenberger's popularity deterred more established Democrats from challenging him. However, "Fools rush in where wise men fear to tread!" Actually, I was more carefully thoughtful than that. First, I was tremendously excited about the possibility of becoming a U.S. senator. My anti–Vietnam War activism had shown me how impactful the Senate could be in shaping world events, and my experience fundraising for Project Place had shown me how important federal policies and funds were to domestic programs.

Secondly, I recalled how important then-Senator Mondale's increasing seniority had been to his effectiveness. I would be thirty-five years old on Election Day 1982. If I could get elected and do a great job for Minnesota, I reasoned, I could over time become a senior senator and really make a difference.

I started my campaign preparation by going to Israel in October 1980. I traveled with a Minnesota friend, Paul Thatcher, and his close friend, Mark Siegel. Mark had recently resigned from his position as a senior adviser to President Carter over the administration's sale of F-15 fighter planes to Egypt and Jordan. As a result, he was a hero in Israel. We received royal treatment while touring the country, and we met with Menachem Begin, Shimon Peres, and Ariel Sharon, three then- and future prime ministers.

The most powerful experience was our trip to Masada, where Jewish nationalists held out against Roman legions for three years after the fall of Jerusalem in A.D. 70. Finally, on the night before they knew they would be overrun and either

Meeting in Israel with Paul Thatcher and Menachem Begin

murdered or enslaved, they killed almost everyone in their community.

For today's Israelis, Masada means "Never again." Never again will they be overrun and destroyed.

On that trip, we also visited Egypt and, most memorably, Luxor, which had been built by the Pharaoh Ramses II more than 2,500 years before. I'll never forget looking up at an ancient obelisk and having our Egyptian guide say to me in broken English, "See, George Washington monument. See, nothing new under the sun!"

Back home, I began the exploratory phase of my campaign right after the November 1980 election. Despite my well-known surname, I was largely unknown. I started virtually from scratch by driving all over the state, meeting with local DFL Party leaders and activists everywhere.

I was really green! My first campaign speech was to the Bloomington DFL Club in December 1980, where I stumbled through an anguished presentation. A year later, with many speeches under my belt, I spoke there again. Afterward, Jan Selness, the local party chair, came up to me and said excitedly, "Boy! Have you ever improved as a speaker."

I replied, "What you mean is, I was really awful a year ago."

"Yeah," she replied sheepishly. "You were pretty bad!"

Slowly I gained traction, especially since no other Democrat entered the race. I made the campaign official with an announcement on May 5, 1981. Not long afterward, I bought media attacking Durenberger on key issues like Social Security, which aroused state and even national attention. "Save Our Social Security" was one of my first campaign slogans.

Durenberger had been quoted in the *Ely Echo* newspaper as saying, "Social Security is like welfare." I took out a full-page ad in the *Minneapolis Tribune*: "No Senator Durenberger.

Social Security is not Welfare!" Durenberger denied making the statement, although the reporter stood by his story. It was widely reported, delighted Democrats, and propelled me into the forefront of the political landscape.

A key turning point in the campaign was my endorsement in September 1981 by the United Steelworkers of America Local #1938 in Virginia, Minnesota, then the largest local union in the entire Minnesota AFL-CIO. I had practically lived in the Eighth Congressional District during that summer. I had to overcome the stigma of being from Minneapolis's Fifth District in the aftermath of the 1978 DFL debacle, in which the party's endorsed candidate, Congressman Don Fraser from Minneapolis, had aroused the ire of Eighth District voters with his opposition to allowing motorboats in the Boundary Waters Canoe Area.

I assiduously courted the local Steelworkers Union presidents. One of them, Joe Samargia, president of USWA Local #1938 in Virginia, Minnesota, befriended me. That emboldened me to seek their endorsement at their September monthly meeting. I gave my most impassioned stump speech and was then dispatched outside the union hall while they debated.

I could hear the voices inside rising when one steelworker left the hall to visit the men's room. As he returned, I instinctively extended my hand to shake his.

A few minutes after he went back inside, the hall was filled with uproarious laughter. Shortly thereafter, the members came out and congratulated me on my endorsement. After they departed, Joe told me what had happened.

In the midst of the heated debate, the steelworker whose hand I shook stood up and said, "All I know is, anyone who wants the endorsement badly enough that he would shake a steelworker's hand after he just took a piss, I say, 'Hell, let's give it to him!'" That carried the hall.

Standing outside campaign headquarters with staffer Matt Entenza

In June 1982, I was endorsed at the DFL state convention with 78 percent first-ballot support. Only the strong pro-life caucus opposed me. That September, I defeated former U.S. Senator Gene McCarthy by a 2:1 margin in the DFL primary. Gene had represented Minnesota in the Senate from 1959 to 1971 and had run an iconic campaign for president in 1968 but had left Minnesota to live in Washington thereafter.

A particularly memorable moment occurred during our one debate, when Gene told me derisively, "Mark, I was on the Iron Range before you were born."

"Yes, Gene," I replied. "And you haven't been back there since." That ended this line of attack!

My general election campaign against Senator Durenberger unfolded during what had become a major national recession that was harshly affecting Minnesota. It had become a bona fide depression on the Iron Range, where seven of the eight taconite plants were shut down. A sense of crisis was heightened by recurring state budget deficits, which were caused by lagging tax receipts. Six special sessions of the legislature were needed in 1981–82 to keep state government solvent. With Republicans in charge in both the governor's office and the

Walter Mondale campaigning with me during my 1982 U.S. Senate run

White House, the flagging economy became a major drag on incumbent Republican candidates. Without those conditions, I probably would not have pulled as close as I did against a popular and well-respected incumbent. I was also aided by a strong campaign organization, led by a terrific campaign manager, Connie Lewis.

One of the campaign's many highlights was actor Paul Newman's appearance at a "nuclear freeze" press event on my behalf. He came to Minnesota to highlight my strong support for the movement then sweeping the country to stop the testing, production, and deployment of nuclear weapons anywhere in the world.

In June, Alida and I met Newman at the Brainerd Speedway, where he was preparing for weekend races. He was easy to find; his "office" was an enormous trailer painted like a Budweiser beer can. When he opened the door, I looked into the palest blue eyes I had ever seen.

He offered Alida a can of Budweiser, which she sipped and then brought back to the campaign office as a souvenir. The next day, someone swiped it from her desk. It was the only theft we experienced during the entire campaign.

In September, Newman flew unaccompanied on a regular commercial airline into the Minneapolis–St. Paul International

Paul Newman came to Minnesota to campaign for me

Airport, and I met him at the gate. As we walked through the concourse, it was fun to see the heads of passersby snap around and then watch their faces gaping in wonderment!

Our press conference was by far the best attended of the campaign. Members of the Minnesota press corps who weren't even assigned to the event appeared in droves. Newman was impassioned and eloquent, and I will be eternally grateful to him.

Another special moment occurred with a large event, which we organized for senior citizens, headlined by Florida Congressman Claude Pepper. He wasn't in Newman's league as a celebrity, but the effort he made for my campaign put him in a league of his own from my perspective. "The Senator," as he preferred to be called (I said, "If he shows up, I'll call him whatever he wants!"), was "Mr. Social Security" and national chairman of the "Save Our Social Security" campaign, which I had championed in Minnesota.

Unfortunately, the day before five thousand seniors were expected to arrive to see and hear Claude Pepper, the U.S. House of Representatives was holding votes, which threatened to run late into the evening and even into the next day. We faced the choice of either canceling the event and trying to notify all five thousand attendees or proceeding with it and having "the Senator" not show up.

I actually flipped a coin. "Heads, we hold the event. Tails, we cancel it." It was heads.

Congressman Pepper taught me an unforgettable lesson about keeping your commitments. This eighty-two-year-old man finished voting in the House at 1:30 in the morning, went to bed at 2:00, got up at 5:00, and caught a commercial flight to Minnesota for my event. He delivered a blockbuster, hour-long speech, which sent five thousand enthralled Minnesotans into raptures. Then he got on a plane, and I never saw him again.

What a man!

Another unforgettable evening was spent at a DFL picnic in Hallock, in the northwestern corner of Minnesota. In the middle of the event, the pilot of our small, chartered airplane called to inform us that a huge thunderstorm was rapidly approaching, and we had to leave immediately.

We raced to the airport, but we were too late to beat the storm. We were spending the night in Hallock. Our only option was the dilapidated Valley View Motel. I was fortunate in my room assignment: It was clean and dry. My Seventh District coordinator wasn't as lucky. She had a hole in her room's screen, which, she said, meant she was dive-bombed all night by mosquitoes the size of bats. My press secretary fared even worse. She discovered a dead mouse in her bedsheets.

Life on the campaign trail in Greater Minnesota!

Despite many unforgettable and encouraging moments, on election night I lost by 47–53 percent. It was close enough to be respectable but not so close that I had to agonize over one or another mistake costing me the election.

I spent $7 million of my own money on the campaign, which at the time was a record expenditure in a Minnesota election and opened me to the charge that I was trying to buy the election. The upside, however, was that I didn't have to fundraise, which I detested, and I had the resources to make myself competitive throughout.

The two years of campaigning all over Minnesota were profoundly impactful. I learned so much about myself, about Minnesota, and about the trials and tribulations of political combat. I was left bruised, chastened, and considerably poorer, but undeterred from a future opportunity.

Dave Durenberger and I became friends over the years following the election. We often commented that ours was the last of a campaign era in which political opponents could engage in strong disagreements, but not character assassination. I was honored to be invited by his family to his funeral in 2024. Rest in peace, Dave.

The campaign also launched my twenty-year political alliance and personal friendship with Paul Wellstone, which I will detail later in the chapter I have devoted to him. Rest in peace, Paul.

And the campaign deepened my bond with the reelected Governor Rudy Perpich. During the previous three years, I had been calling Rudy about once a month while he was living in Vienna, Austria, working for Minnesota-based Control Data Corp. He discouraged me from running for the Senate and said he would pick me as his lieutenant governor running mate when he returned to Minnesota to run again for governor.

When I decided to make my own run for the Senate, we remained in close contact, although we were running on two very different tracks. I was the DFL Party's endorsed Senate candidate. Rudy was running in the gubernatorial primary against the endorsed DFL candidate, Warren Spannaus.

Despite Warren's endorsement advantages, Rudy's upset victory confirmed my view that the Eighth Congressional District, especially Duluth and the Iron Range, was (then) crucially important in a DFL primary. (In 2010, that lesson persuaded me to choose Duluth State Senator Yvonne Prettner Solon as my lieutenant governor running mate, which was critical to my winning the DFL primary.)

When Rudy narrowly defeated Warren, there were fears that his victory would divide DFL Party leaders and activists against him, as had happened when Bob Short defeated endorsed candidate Don Fraser in the 1978 Senate primary. Short's victory contributed to a political tsunami that cost the DFL both Senate seats and the governor's office. It is still remembered as "the Minnesota Massacre."

The day after the DFL primary, I met publicly with Rudy, endorsed him, and put my organization to work persuading DFL leaders on the party's Central Committee to endorse him the following weekend. They did, and he cruised to a decisive general election victory. Rudy's victory meant that I would soon have a new public service opportunity to consider.

— CHAPTER FOUR —

THE COMMISSIONER

> "Each time a man stands up for an ideal, or acts to improve the lot of others, or strikes out against injustice, he sends forth a tiny ripple of hope, and crossing each other from a million different centers of energy and daring, those ripples build a current that can sweep down the mightiest walls of oppression and resistance."
>
> —*Robert F. Kennedy*

After the election, Rudy offered me a position in his administration, as commissioner of the then-expanded Department of Energy, Planning, and Development. Before I gave him a response, I considered running in 1984 for the U.S. Senate seat held by Republican Rudy Boschwitz.

After a few months of exploration, I realized that another Senate race just then would be the wrong path for me. I had two young sons, and I had been away from them and my marriage during most of the previous two years. Also, I discovered that after saying yes to every political event for so long, I was worn out from them.

I announced on May 26, 1983, that I would forgo a Senate run. Instead, I accepted Governor Perpich's offer to fill the

With my sons, Eric and Andrew Dayton

My father, Bruce Dayton, with my sons, Eric and Andrew, circa 1987

still-vacant commissioner of the newly reorganized Department of Energy and Economic Development. (State Planning had been split off into its own separate agency.)

I started as commissioner in June and served until the end of Perpich's second term in January 1987. Other than being governor myself, it was the best job I ever had. The state was rebounding rapidly from the recession of 1981–82, bringing more revenue to state coffers and a renewed desire to use those funds to shore up the state's economy for the long term. At Perpich's urging, the department had been granted new resources to assist with development projects throughout the state. For example, the 1983 legislature authorized the department's establishment of "Enterprise Zone" tax credits to encourage new businesses and existing businesses' expansions in economically distressed cities. I awarded the first credits to a startup in Thief River Falls called Arctco. It took off, became Arctic Cat, expanded, and in 2017 was sold to Textron, Inc. for $217 million.

As commissioner of the Department of Energy and Economic Development, 1985

That was the great satisfaction of the job. I could be involved with entrepreneurs, private lenders, and local officials to finance projects. A year later, I'd drive by the site and see the cars of Minnesotans who had jobs there. That's as good as it gets!

I believe this type of public–private financial and political partnership is an important contributor to a vital state economy. Later, during my terms as governor, I saw how government participation made the crucial difference in business location decisions, both large and small. I was criticized by some for committing $500 million of state and local dollars to build a new $1.1 billion stadium in Minneapolis for the Minnesota Vikings. However, our commitment kept that iconic sports franchise in Minnesota and triggered some $3 billion in additional private sector investments in east Minneapolis. Similarly, another $500 million commitment of public funds has supported Mayo Clinic's multibillion-dollar creation of a Destination Medical Center in Rochester, which secures its long-term preeminence in medical care nationally and globally.

During the Perpich years, we helped scores of Minnesota cities enhance their own local economic development effectiveness through our department's Star City Program. It had been started by my predecessor in the Quie administration, but we greatly expanded it into a rigorous, yearlong training program for local governments, chambers of commerce, and other community leaders. At its conclusion, the cities in the program proudly held ceremonial dinners, at which they were awarded "Star City" highway markers, which for years decorated much of Minnesota's highway landscape.

A couple other highlights included traveling to Edmonton, Alberta, in Canada with Governor Perpich to woo the Ghermezian brothers, real estate developers who had built the world's largest shopping mall in Edmonton. Some people and press scorned Rudy for his job-seeking ventures, but he was a true visionary and undaunted by long odds. The Ghermezians *did* come to Minnesota and created what is now the world-renowned "Mall of America," which after more than thirty successful years has expanded to 4.8 million square feet and is still growing.

Rudy's pursuit of the Ghermezians followed our unsuccessful attempt to win the competition General Motors had established for its first Saturn plant in the United States. We were told we made an excellent presentation, although we were unable to match the incentives offered by Tennessee.

One amusing moment occurred the day before we were scheduled to fly to Detroit to make our presentation. Both Minnesota senators, Republicans Dave Durenberger and Rudy Boschwitz, agreed to fly in the night before to set up our pitch, as did the chief executive officer of Rochester's IBM plant. Only Rudy's good friend Carl Pohlad, one of Minnesota's most successful businessmen and, as of 1984, the owner of the Minnesota Twins, insisted on flying into Detroit on the morning of the presentation. It was scheduled for 10:00 A.M.

Then we learned that General Motors had to move the

meeting up to 8:30, which meant Carl would not make it in time to participate. I called his secretary to ask if he would *please* fly in the night before. "Oh," she said. "I don't think that would be possible. He bought a 'Super-Saver' ticket a couple weeks ago."

I assured her that, if necessary, I would buy this billionaire another plane ticket. I heard shortly thereafter that he would change his plans, "but he was not happy about it."

My one extracurricular political activity in October 1986 was cohosting a big DFL fundraiser with my good friend Tom Borman, a leading Minneapolis attorney and nationally renowned political activist. Our headliner was Senator Ted Kennedy, who said he had accepted an invitation to Minnesota based on his friendships with Tom and me. Just two weeks before the election, we had arranged a three-tiered event: first a reception, then a dinner, followed by a several-thousand-person rally.

Like Claude Pepper four years before, Ted taught me an important lesson about keeping one's commitments. The Senate was scheduled to be in recess that week but was kept in session by Majority Leader Bob Dole for action on a major voting rights bill. As a result, Kennedy had to cancel fundraisers in other states on both Monday and Tuesday nights. His staff told us he would try his best to make our Wednesday night events but might have to stay in Washington for nationally important votes.

To further complicate the situation, that Wednesday night turned out to be the seventh game of baseball's American League Championship series in Boston. The senator from Massachusetts had the perfect opportunity to tell us he had to stay in Washington, then sneak up to Boston for the game.

Instead, he got Bob Dole to agree to hold off any Senate

votes until after midnight, then flew to Minnesota for three very successful events. I will forever be grateful to him.

My day job was very satisfying, and I loved working for and with Rudy Perpich. But by the end of 1986, I was in bad shape. My marriage had broken apart in the spring of 1985, and our divorce was finalized in the summer of 1986. I went from living in a home with a family to a townhouse, able to spend just part of each week with my young sons. My emotional pain and despair were unbearable, and I began to drink alcohol. By the end of that summer, I was drinking whenever I wasn't working.

In September, I called the Betty Ford Center in California and asked if I could reserve a room for the first week in January. The rather incredulous receptionist asked why I was not coming in the next day. I insisted on January, after I had resigned at the end of the governor's term. I expected that I could then leave quietly for treatment. I was told to call again at the end of December. I doubt the receptionist believed I would make it until then, and there were times when neither did I. But I survived, finished Perpich's term, and on January 6, 1987, arrived at the Betty Ford Center. I turned forty there. I said it was an awful place to spend a birthday, but a great place to be reborn.

I spent the next three years working on myself, coaching Eric's youth hockey and Andrew's youth baseball teams, and running my own Vermilion Investment Company, which amassed a darn good nest egg for my future political forays.

— CHAPTER FIVE —

A DIFFERENT KIND OF OFFICE

"If men were angels, no government would be necessary. If angels were to govern men, neither external nor internal controls on government would be necessary."

—*James Madison*

In January 1990, I announced that I would run for the open seat of the Constitutional Office of State Auditor. In my first try for elective office, I had aimed for the top: the U.S. Senate. Eight years later, I assessed that if I wanted to develop a career in elective office, I needed to lower my sights, seek an office I could win, and prove my ability to serve there successfully.

The state auditor was one of five elective offices established in the Minnesota Constitution. It had the responsibility to audit Minnesota's eighty-seven counties and three largest cities: Minneapolis, St. Paul, and Duluth. It could also undertake audits of other local governments and entities when situations called for them. The seat was open in 1990 because its incumbent, Republican Arne Carlson, was running for governor.

This campaign was markedly different from my Senate run. I kept within the state spending limit of $120,000 and raised all that money from other people.

As a result, my campaign staff consisted of one person,

Sharon Ruhland (née Hinde), who had just graduated from St. Cloud State University. Fortunately, she was a gem, capable of doing everything, which was pretty much what she was asked to do. Scheduling, driving, managing media, and maintaining intraparty political relationships were just part of the list.

I'll never forget our visit to the Jackson County Fair. We arrived on a Thursday afternoon, and I was surprised to find the crowd quite sparse. After obligatory blueberry pie and coffee at the Farmers Union booth, I went for my big media opportunity, a live interview on the local radio station. I gushed about the exhibits, the rides, and the pie. Then I offered that the attendees had been very welcoming. The radio interviewer, arguably a staunch Republican, looked at me scornfully and said, "Yes. And there will be even more people here when the fair opens tomorrow."

On to the next county!

During this campaign, I also met the woman who would become my second wife, Janice Haarstick, at the Seventh District DFL convention. Another highlight for me that year was the opportunity to participate in one of Rudy Perpich's many remarkable achievements, bringing Soviet Premier Mikhail Gorbachev to Minnesota. Gorbachev's liberalizing economic and political reforms in the Soviet Union had eased the Cold War, making him a respected figure in the United States. He announced that he would be coming to the United States in June 1990. His itinerary was initially set for Washington, New York, and San Francisco. Rudy invited him to add a visit to Minnesota and see our country's heartland.

The Minnesota press and Rudy's Republican critics scorned his invitation as a cheap election-year ploy. Then Gorbachev accepted! The public's excitement on an unusually cold June day was torrid. Nothing rivaling this iconic foreign leader's visit had ever happened in Minnesota. Gorbachev's efforts to

Meeting Soviet Premier Mikhail Gorbachev, June 1990

modernize and open the Soviet Union to the rest of the world was bringing him more popularity in the United States than any previous Soviet leader could claim. I was very honored to be one of fifteen Minnesotans who joined the two leaders for lunch at the Governor's Residence. It was a banner day for Minnesota, and for Rudy Perpich.

Unfortunately, this remarkable feat was not enough to salvage Rudy's attempt to win a third consecutive term. In the most bizarre political upheaval in my lifetime, the Republican gubernatorial nominee, Jon Grunseth, had to withdraw just eleven days before the election due to a sex scandal. That made then–State Auditor Arne Carlson, the second-place finisher of the Independent-Republican primary, Grunseth's replacement on the general election gubernatorial ballot. The change adhered to a little-known feature of state law that was upheld days before the election by the Minnesota Supreme Court. Carlson, an old-school moderate Republican who supported abortion rights, then narrowly won the election, which may have been decided by a massive outpouring of pro-choice voters. That same outpouring helped elect Paul Wellstone to the U.S. Senate over incumbent Rudy Boschwitz.

The Star Tribune *reported on Paul Wellstone's victory above the fold, while the state auditor's race also merited a headline.*

Iraq promises to release another 108 foreign hostages/4A

MINNEAPOLIS EDITION

Star Tribune

NEWSPAPER OF THE TWIN CITIES

It looks like a Wellstone upset; Perpich, Carlson in tight race

U.S. Senate

Underdog projected as winner

Governor

Big turnout may help IR challenger

ELECTION '90

Early returns favor Minneapolis school levy

Helms wins reelection; Bradley survives scare

Mark Dayton holds lead in race for state auditor

Surprising turnout across state could exceed 60 percent

U.S. Senate

Peterson leads Stangeland with 34% of vote counted

Democrats win governor's races in Florida, Texas; GOP wins in Ohio

Almanac

Those voters also helped elect me state auditor. I won the election with 57.6 percent of the vote, in spite of the humiliation of having the *Star Tribune* endorse my Republican opponent. Such public slights hurt at that still-early stage of my political career. However, they thickened my political skin.

My four years as Arne's successor were a considerable ordeal. While serving a vitally important role in protecting the integrity of Minnesota government, reviewing hundreds of pages of financial data compiled by the office's professional auditors was continuous and tedious. The office was filled with good people, who were mostly unenthusiastic about their jobs and most interested in their retirements, even when they were years or even decades away.

I did provide them with one moment of high drama in 1992. The office held an annual professional recertification session, which everyone was required to attend. I awoke that morning with severe intestinal cramps, which I tried to ignore. However, as I was concluding my welcoming remarks, the pain became so intense that I passed out. One auditor was heard to remark that it was the most interesting speech in the years of his attendance! I had my appendix removed that afternoon.

I was able to use the office to make my mark as an aggressive protector of public integrity. In just my second month on the job, I became aware of discrepancies in then–former Governor Perpich's claim for retirement benefits from the Public Employees Retirement Association (PERA), on whose board I served. I knew that if I challenged his questionable computation of Hibbing School Board service credits, it would destroy my fourteen-year friendship with him. However, I concluded that I could not have one high standard for everyone if I made exceptions for my friends.

I raised my objection at the next public PERA meeting. Unfortunately, a majority of the board deferred to the former governor and approved his claim. As I expected, he never spoke to me again.

The loss of Rudy's friendship was extremely painful for me. Over those fourteen years, I had developed a very strong professional relationship with him and had learned so much from him. I grew personally close to his entire family: to his wife, Lola, and his children, Rudy Jr. and Mary Sue. I liked him greatly and respected him enormously.

Rudy died in 1995. May he rest in peace.

I also prevented the outgoing mayor of Duluth from collecting an excessive pension and, most outrageously, a public school employee from collecting an unearned pension for one day's reemployment.

Most amusingly, the astute Jim Gelbmann, my deputy state

auditor and one of my best hires, confronted a local official with evidence that he had embezzled city funds. The official denied the charge until Jim told him we had bank photocopies of the suspect checks.

He was stunned. "You mean, the bank keeps copies of the checks?" he asked.

In early 1994, I announced that I would not be seeking reelection, and at year's end, my career as an auditor ended. It had been a challenging proving ground. In all four legislative sessions, I had to fight off attempts by certified public accounting firms to steal our local government clients. I was proud that by thwarting their attempts I had successfully defended the principle of public oversight over the proper expenditure of public funds.

This principle has been repeatedly attacked by the private CPA industry, members of which have dangled the prospect of cheaper audits before financially strapped local governments. However, their audits are inadequate, because they do not monitor those expenditures' compliance with applicable state and federal laws. And I believe strongly that the proper expenditure of taxpayers' dollars should be undertaken by an independent public office.

I spent 1995 and 1996 running my investment company and coaching Eric's youth hockey and Andrew's youth baseball teams. I also married Janice in May 1996. Meanwhile, I was helping Paul Wellstone's reelection to the U.S. Senate as his finance chairman. Paul had defeated Rudy Boschwitz in 1990. He stood out in Washington as a champion of progressive causes, which made him a rising star among Democrats and a target for defeat among Republicans. He faced a rematch with Boschwitz in 1996.

The finance position in Paul's reelection campaign presented me with interesting adventures, since both Paul and I hated fundraising. He had one high-priced dinner at the home of a Hollywood movie mogul. We arrived, wedged into Paul's friend's compact Ford, to be ambushed by a Republican camera crew that flooded the driveway with their lights. Paul attempted to hide under the front seat, which only added to the opposition's subsequent attack ad.

It was the last big-dollar fundraiser outside of Minnesota Paul would do during the campaign. However, as a national progressive hero, his direct mail fundraising was a phenomenal success.

One final blockbuster event was a campaign-ending rally in Minneapolis, headlined by the actor Robert Redford. He was reportedly not making campaign appearances that year; however, he made an exception because Paul had helped him on legislation affecting his home in Sundance, Utah.

It immediately became clear why he eschewed personal appearances. He was mobbed at both a reception and a dinner preceding the rally. Since I knew Bob from previously serving on an environmental board with him, I was assigned to squire him through the assembled crowds. He was even accosted by autograph seekers in the men's restroom, while standing in front of the urinal.

One woman, while waiting to be introduced to him, told me in dazed tones, "I used to have a picture of Robert Redford on the ceiling over my bed. I can't even begin to tell you what I did with that picture."

I didn't inquire further!

The rally was a huge success and another testament to Paul's overwhelming support, which propelled him to a decisive victory over Boschwitz.

Meanwhile, before my second marriage in 1996, I went on a three-week solo driving trip from Paris through Switzerland to Zurich. A highlight was dinner with my dear friend Pamela Harriman, who was then the U.S. ambassador to France. A native of the United Kingdom, Harriman was the widow of former New York Governor W. Averell Harriman, the former daughter-in-law of Winston Churchill, a distant relative of the British royal family, and a leading donor to Democratic candidates. She had hosted a fundraiser for me at her DC home during my 1982 campaign, and she told our shared consultant that I was her favorite candidate in that election year.

We continued our friendship thereafter, and when I told her I would be in Paris, she invited me to a reception at the U.S. Embassy and to dinner with her the following night at a Michelin three-star restaurant.

She was an amazing woman. She and my former mother-in-law Blanchette Rockefeller were the two bona fide "grande dames" I have known. And she was a very hardworking ambassador. Two nights before, she had flown on the Concorde from Paris to New York for a diplomatic meeting, then flown overnight back to Paris. I spent a delightful evening with her, and, of course, our dinner service was impeccable!

Pamela showed me again the merit of Ted Kennedy's axiom that "perseverance is the prerequisite for success" in life. She was ridiculed by her political opponents in our country as a "courtesan" who had slept her way to the top. However, she persevered throughout and achieved a high office, in which she was greatly respected by the French government for her diplomatic skill and dedication.

Meanwhile, as the world inched closer to a new century, I was considering my political future. I could never have anticipated all that was to come.

— CHAPTER SIX —

RUNNING AGAIN

"If not now, when?"

—*Paul Wellstone*

By early 1997, I was ready to campaign again—this time for governor. I initially sought the DFL Party's endorsement, as I had done before. I thought my hard work for Paul Wellstone's reelection in 1996 would be recognized and credited by DFL Party leaders and activists.

Instead, to my surprise, I discovered that my friend Hennepin County Attorney Mike Freeman had been wooing party delegates throughout 1996 and had amassed many commitments. I felt like a runner beginning a mile race and discovering that his competitor had already completed one lap around the track. I was hopelessly behind before I even began. And I was frustrated that my exclusive commitment to helping Paul win a vitally important reelection was being punished rather than rewarded.

I decided to forgo the party's endorsement and run directly in the September primary. That action offended many of my good DFL friends, who were staunchly committed to the endorsement process. They wanted their endorsements to determine who the party's candidates in the general elections would be. I came to believe that their endorsements should only be recommendations to voters in primary elections, who deserved to make the final decisions about whom the party's general election candidates would be. Let the people decide!

Mike Freeman won the DFL endorsement in June 1998, but he was defeated decisively in the primary by another DFL favorite son, Attorney General Skip Humphrey. (Mike is the son of the state's first DFL governor, Orville Freeman; Skip is the son of the party's founder and first U.S. senator, Hubert Humphrey.) Humphrey then proceeded to lose the general election to the wrestler/radio personality and third-party candidate Jesse Ventura.

I finished a dismal fourth in the DFL primary with only 18 percent of the vote. The only consolation was that my loss spared me an even more ignominious defeat to Ventura in the general election, in which case my political career likely would have ended. That's what happened to Humphrey, whose name was never again on a state ballot after 1998. I was determined it would not be my fate.

The 1998 defeat hit hard, and then in 2000 Janice and I divorced. While fourth place in a party primary is not an auspicious launching pad for the next campaign, I knew I wasn't done seeking elective office. As I sized up the incumbent Republican U.S. Senator Rod Grams and his DFL opponents, I decided that, despite my 1998 defeat, I had a real chance to win the contest.

I announced my candidacy for senator on April 3, 2000, by "walking my announcement" through the Minnesota press corps' offices in the basement of the Capitol. I didn't rouse much press interest that week, but I was relieved and pleased that I received no ridicule or dismissal.

In June 2000 the DFL Party endorsed State Senator Jerry Janezich, a twelve-year legislator and small business owner from Chisholm, on Minnesota's Iron Range. Jerry was a wonderful guy, but he had no statewide political standing. As I did two years earlier, I opted to forgo the party's endorsement process. Instead, I jumped into the DFL primary on September 12.

I assembled a terrific campaign team. Nationally, I hired Doug Schoen, who had been my pollster during my 1982 Senate campaign. He took a poll in June that showed me with 42 percent of the DFL primary vote, which turned out to be almost exactly my total two months later.

For media, I hired Bob Shrum, whom I had known from our Kennedy associations, and Mike Donilon, who had just helped Doug Wilder win the Virginia governorship to become the nation's first African American governor since Reconstruction. (Their business partner, Tad Devine, had just left to run Vice President Al Gore's presidential campaign.)

I also hired a terrific Minnesota staff. Jim Gelbmann, a trusted adviser during my auditor's stint, became the campaign manager. Sharon Ruhland was the deputy campaign manager and press secretary. Her niece, Dana Anderson (now Dana Bailey), started as my driver, progressed to run my 2010 gubernatorial campaign, and is now one of my closest friends.

Bob looked at Doug's poll and said, "Mark, your problem is that you haven't been properly introduced" to the Minnesota electorate. Bob and Mike set out to reintroduce me to the people of Minnesota. Our first television ads showed where I had lived and taught school in New York City. (Most Minnesotans think of that city as a combat zone!) We started running those ads statewide during the week after the Fourth of July. Their impact was amazing. On the next Saturday, I walked in the "Rondo Day" parade in St. Paul. People reached out to me. "I saw you on TV!" "I didn't know you were a teacher!"

We followed those ads right away with one of my best-ever initiatives. A few months earlier, I read about a Senate candidate in Montana who was sponsoring bus trips to Canada that enabled senior citizens to buy lower-cost prescription drugs. I took his idea, and Bob coined the phrase "Rx Express." I rode on the first bus trip to Winnipeg with about thirty Minnesota seniors, who saved anywhere from $200 to $500 apiece on their next months' medications. We ran those bus trips throughout the campaign, and they were sensationally popular.

Then we launched another of my ideas; this one was original. I had seen how many good people were being arbitrarily and unfairly denied payments by their insurance companies for medical treatments that should have been covered by their policies. (It was right out of John Grisham's *The Rainmaker.*) Our campaign set up what I called the "Health Care Help-Line." People who were being denied treatments their doctors recommended or payments for those treatments by their insurance companies could call for our help. Often our intervention and the implicit threat of bad publicity prompted the insurers to reverse their denials.

One of the most gratifying moments came on the first week of the program. We had advertised the Help-Line on a television commercial and were being swamped by requests for assistance. My son Andrew, then age sixteen, and three of his high school classmates had just begun summer internships on the campaign, and we pressed them into service fielding calls.

Andrew came up to me with the name and telephone number of a ninety-year-old woman who needed us. He had been deeply moved. "Dad," he insisted, as he pressed the note into my hand, "I *promised* her you would call and help."

I took the opportunity to say, "Andrew, that is why I do this work. It's not about the parades or the speeches. It's about the real opportunities to help real people improve their lives."

Today, Andrew heads a charity, the Constellation Fund, which he founded to raise money to fight poverty in Minnesota. I am *so proud* of him for his dedication to improving other people's lives.

Another powerful moment occurred when I visited a government class at St. Paul's Central High School. As I was preparing to leave, a girl shyly raised her hand and thanked me for helping "someone" in her family get coverage for an eating disorder that her family's insurer was denying.

I thought how important our help must have been to her and her family that she would expose what was probably her own condition to her classmates to thank me. That *is* why I did this work: to help real people improve their lives.

The summer was a whirlwind of activity. Mike Donilon's terrific television ads and my previous years of service gave me a credibility I had not had before. I was no longer the "department store heir" trying to buy a Senate seat, as if it were a yacht. My deep and sincere commitment to Minnesota was finally being recognized.

One commercial was filmed while I was driving the camera crew in my SUV to visit a farm. When it ran, to our surprise, the strongest reaction was not that I was visiting a farm, but that I was driving my own car! So many people had thought I was ferried around in a limousine.

I won the primary decisively. Importantly, I was able to win without tearing the DFL Party apart. Jerry Janezich and attorney Mike Ciresi, my two principal opponents, were gracious losers and immediately supported me.

A few days before the primary election, we took a poll. We decided to include a few general election questions. To my astonishment, it showed me defeating Rod Grams by 15 percent! I told the few top campaign people who had seen the result to bury it. I knew that kind of lead could not last. But it showed the momentum I had developed over the summer, while Grams had been inexplicably quiet.

The fall campaign was spirited but didn't change the contest's trajectory. Grams's ads and initiatives were surprisingly ineffective. His first attack ad against my Rx Express was punctuated by a very unpleasant sound, like fingernails scratching a blackboard. And he made the same mistake I had made in my 1982 campaign. He didn't have enough different ads to fill his buys, and as a result he played the same ad for too long. A friend of mine in Duluth quipped that I should pay to keep playing his ad, because people there were so sick of it! By contrast, I was fanatical about having a variety of ads, from the teaching in New York City, the RX Express, and the Health Care Help-Line to visits to farms and small businesses. Mike Donilon said he produced more different ads for me than for any other campaign.

I cruised to victory on Election Night, winning by a 5.5 percent margin. That margin would have been greater were it not for bad weather in the DFL part of the Second District, which also cost us our terrific congressman, David Minge. I was on to Washington, one of ten new Democratic senators (along with two new Republicans), which shifted the Senate from 55–45 in the Republicans' favor to 50 Democrats and 50 Republicans. That put the next vice president in position to cast the tiebreaking vote, effectively determining Senate control. But who would be that vice president? For several weeks after the election, Americans did not know. The presidential race was hung up on a too-close-to-call outcome in Florida.

On December 10, 2000, the U.S. Supreme Court, in a most egregious act of judicial activism, tore the Florida presidential election away from the Florida Supreme Court and declared Republican George W. Bush the winner of that state, which made him the next president. It also meant that with Vice President Dick Cheney as the tiebreaking vote, the Senate majority stayed with the Republicans.

The next day, I called my old DKE fraternity brother George W. Bush to congratulate him. I called him at his governor's office in Texas, left a message, and ten minutes later received his return call. We chatted cordially about our college days and mutual Minnesota friends, and he asked me how I was looking forward to the Senate. I told him I was starting out one hundredth in seniority. He laughed and replied, "Well, at least you have nowhere to go but up!"

— CHAPTER SEVEN —

SENATOR DAYTON

"Do you pray for the senators, Dr. Hale?"
"No, I look at the senators and pray for the country."

— *U.S. Senate Chaplain Edward Everett Hale, 1903*

Starting one's service in the U.S. Senate involves a considerable amount of pomp, glitz, and glamour. The swearing-in ceremony was very special. Most of my family and key staff crowded into the Senate chamber at noon on January 3, 2001. They were seated right behind President Bill Clinton, who was there to see his wife, Hillary, sworn in.

An amusing incident occurred with my assistant campaign manager Sharon Ruhland, who was seated with my family, and her husband, Joe, who was in the back row of the chamber across from her. Since one of their daughters was deaf, they knew sign language and were using it to communicate with one another.

Their hand gestures aroused the suspicions of the Secret Service, who suddenly hoisted Joe out of his seat and hauled him outside the chamber. He was shocked but managed to assuage their fears by explaining his relation to the woman sitting directly behind the president.

It was a memorable ceremony for both Joe and me!

The following Saturday night was one of the Clintons' last as president and first lady. They graciously invited Democratic senators and a few House Members to have dinner with them at Camp David. We were bused to that iconic location, where we watched the president's helicopter land, preceded by the "decoy helicopter," which was intended to draw the fire of any assassins. Not an assignment I would relish!

It was a thrill to walk around Camp David before dinner and see some of the history that occurred there, including one of the original Camp David Accords documents, signed by Israeli Prime Minister Menachem Begin and Egyptian President Anwar Sadat and witnessed by U.S. President Jimmy Carter, on the table where the signing occurred.

The dinner that evening showcased once again the superb oratorical skills of President Clinton. I hardly knew him then, but I became friends with him in the years following, through my friendship with Hillary. He is unquestionably the most charismatic man I have ever known.

Much later, in 2024, my wife, Ana, and I had lunch with

Greeting President Bill Clinton and Senator Hillary Clinton

With my wife, Ana, visiting Bill and Hillary Clinton

Hillary at a restaurant near the Clintons' New York home. We finished, and she was about to leave for an interview. Suddenly and unannounced, Bill sauntered in and joined our table. For the next hour, he regaled Ana and me with stories and remembrances as we shared a bowl of french fries.

After the initial excitement of being in the Senate wore off, I discovered to my chagrin that I had very little power to make change. Ninety percent of effectiveness there is having seniority and being in the majority, and I had and was neither. We Democrats gained the majority for a year and a half when Vermont Senator Jim Jeffords switched parties in June 2001. But our majority did not survive the 2002 election. My last four years were spent again in the minority.

Some minority senators can gain a modicum of influence by socializing and schmoozing. But that's not my style. I struggled to fit into the glad-handing aspect of Washington culture. One veteran lawyer/lobbyist told me, "Mark, you have two strikes against you here: honesty and integrity."

I learned quickly that if policies I wanted to champion had been commandeered by someone more senior, I was expected to yield that ground. For example, I wanted to immediately honor the thirty-year broken promise that the federal government would pay for 40 percent of the cost of special education. In 2001, the federal government was funding only 12 percent of those costs, and the additional burden on Minnesota school districts was staggering.

I proposed we immediately spend an additional $30 billion per year to keep the federal promise. (That was the cost of just one month of the war in Iraq.) As I expected, the Republican budget chairman opposed it. To my surprise, I also met resistance from Democratic Senator Tom Harkin, who was otherwise a good friend. He angrily accused me of trying to usurp an issue he considered his province. His amendment would have increased the federal share only over six years. Naturally, my proposal went nowhere. And neither did his.

That typified the frustration I experienced early and often in the Senate. People back home assumed I had all this power when, in fact, I had almost none. Senior citizens, who were hard-pressed to afford their prescription drug prices, knew that relatives in states like Florida had cheaper medicines and even free prescription eyeglasses, because of the way Medicare reimbursements had been established more than twenty years before.

"But, Senator Dayton, it's not fair," they'd said, assuming I could go back to Washington, tell my fellow senators, and they would jump to change it. "Fairness is an inoperative word in Washington," I would tell them, knowing it did nothing to ease their or my frustrations.

I had a distant but interesting relationship with President Bush during my six years in the Senate. On the one hand, he graciously invited me to numerous ceremonies at the White House honoring different Minnesotans. Bush was an avid sports fan, and at Yale he roomed with the star of our varsity hockey team, who had also been my next-door neighbor growing up. He and other members of our fraternity used to go to the home games and harass the visiting teams' goalies during warm-ups!

While president, he invited the players and coaches of national collegiate championship teams to the White House for ceremonies honoring them, which several times involved the University of Minnesota's men's and women's hockey teams.

On the other hand, I had major political disagreements with him. First and foremost was my opposition to his Iraq War Resolution in October 2002. I was one of twenty-three senators to vote against that resolution and one of only eleven to vote against the nomination of Condoleezza Rice for secretary of state. In my speech on the Senate floor announcing my opposition, I said that she and CIA Director George Tenet had misled me and a small group of other senators about the Iraqi nuclear threat in a meeting in the White House Situation Room just before that critical vote.

The next day, President Bush was asked at a news conference what he thought about his former fraternity brother voting against the appointment. He replied brusquely, "There are ninety-nine other senators besides that person."

My speech did provide what my sons considered one of the highlights of my Senate career: I made Jon Stewart's *The Daily Show*. He showed a clip of my saying that I had been lied to by Secretary Rice and quipped, "New to Washington are we, Senator?"

Despite my lack of seniority, I landed some great committee assignments. I had criticized Senator Grams for not joining the Senate Agriculture Committee, so that was my top priority, and I was pleased to be given a spot there. I also angled successfully for an appointment to the Senate Armed Services Committee, both for its importance and for the chance to serve under one of the very best men in the Senate, Carl Levin from Michigan.

One night, in a Senate Armed Services Committee bill markup, Senator Ted Kennedy came in, accompanied by his Bernese Mountain dog, Splash. Splash immediately went seat by seat around the table, begging for leftover scraps of food. I turned to the senator sitting next to me, nineteen-year veteran Jeff Bingaman from New Mexico, and asked, "How much seniority do you need to bring your dog into an Armed Services Committee markup?" He smiled and replied, "More than I've got!"

During the early months of 2001, we had several private and public meetings with top defense officials, who warned us about the risks of different threats around the world. However, no one ever mentioned the possibility of four domestic commercial airplanes being hijacked and turned into cruise missiles to attack the United States.

Tuesday, September 11, 2001, began as a beautiful sunny day in Washington. I walked from the Hotel George, where I was living temporarily, three blocks to the Russell Senate Office Building. At about 8:50 A.M., I stopped in the basement coffee shop before heading up to my third-floor office. However, instead of the usual line queuing before the coffee counter, everyone was gathered around the television set. An airplane had just crashed into one of New York City's World Trade Towers.

I skipped the coffee and headed straight to my office. There, my chief of staff, Sarah Jennings, was watching her television. "What could have happened?" we asked each other. It was also a clear, sunny day in New York City. Could the pilot have had a heart attack?

Suddenly, right before our eyes, another plane crashed into the second World Trade Tower. We had the sickening realization that these were not accidents.

Just around the corner from my office was Senator Ted

Kennedy's. Coincidentally, First Lady Laura Bush was waiting in his office, before the two of them would go to a Senate committee hearing nearby. We learned that they were planning to proceed with the hearing, so we held our ground.

Then the news flashed that a third plane had crashed into the Pentagon, just across the Potomac River from the Capitol. From a window, we could see a dark black plume of heavy smoke erupting from that site. We learned that the Secret Service was evacuating the first lady from our building. Seconds later, the loudspeaker system told us all to evacuate.

My terrific deputy chief of staff, Katie Sieben, maneuvered me in her car back to the Hotel George as mayhem was breaking out around the Capitol. When I entered the hotel's lobby, I ran into the general manager, who asked me if I wanted to go up on the roof with her. We stood atop that ten-story building and gazed into the blue sky, clear except for the black plume of smoke still pouring out from the Pentagon. It was eerily still and quiet, as all planes and helicopters had been grounded at Reagan National Airport, just across from the Pentagon.

Suddenly, at about 10:20 A.M., two F-15 fighter jets came streaking down the National Mall and over the Capitol, about five hundred feet above our heads. We learned later that they were trying to intercept the fourth hijacked plane, which was probably headed to destroy the Capitol.

From the 9/11 Commission's extraordinary recounting, minute by minute, of that horrible morning, it was documented that those two jets would not have arrived in time to intercept the fourth hijacked plane before it reached the Capitol; nor were they authorized to shoot it down. The reason for their delay, the 9/11 Commission found, was because they had flown from Andrews Air Force Base east over the Atlantic Ocean! All their training had directed them to do so, in the face of an expected offshore attack. The Commission's report captured an air traffic controller discovering their location, 120 miles over the Atlantic Ocean. "I don't care how many windows you break. Damn it! Push them back!" he directed.

Miraculously, the fourth hijacked plane never reached the Capitol. Heroic passengers, led by Minnesota native Thomas Burnett Jr., stormed the cockpit and brought the plane crashing at full speed into a Pennsylvania field. If that plane had demolished the Capitol, there would have been even more horrific destruction and even worse loss of life. Those passengers are great American heroes.

I returned to my hotel room and turned on CNN. It was like a dream, a terrible nightmare. No one really knew what was going on. Would there be further attacks? If so, where?

Somehow, Katie Sieben learned that a group of senators was gathering at the Capitol police headquarters, a block away from the Russell Building, at 1:30 P.M. About thirty of us assembled there. The sergeant at arms, who had started on the job just days before, began to try to contact Senate and House leaders, who had been driven to a secret secure location, Camp Hood. After a half hour trying to get through the overloaded DC telephone lines, he finally reached them. But as he was trying to turn on the speakerphone, he accidentally disconnected the line. It took another twenty minutes to reestablish contact.

The leaders had been in a car driving to their location for the previous two hours, so they knew even less than we did. We had learned that President Bush was flying back to Washington from an elementary school in Florida, via Air Force bases in Louisiana and Colorado, after the Secret Service determined that Washington no longer faced imminent danger. He would address the nation that evening.

We proposed to the leaders that we gather on the steps in front of the Capitol beforehand to also show the American people their government was standing resolute. The leaders demurred at first, until our group made it clear we would be there, with or without them. They headed back to Washington.

That night, over one hundred U.S. senators and representatives stood together on the Capitol steps. I don't remember the speeches, but I'll never forget that we closed by singing "God Bless America." It was a profoundly emotional conclusion to a profoundly terrible day.

The aftermath of 9/11 was especially harrowing. No one knew whether another attack was imminent. Just days later, letters containing the deadly toxin anthrax were opened in two offices in the Hart Senate Office Building. All the senators and staff there were instructed to vacate immediately, leaving behind briefcases, purses, computers, plants, and everything else. They were not permitted to return to the building until the following January, and several hundred had to be screened for anthrax exposure.

Standing in front of the ruins of the World Trade Center, September 14, 2001

I was fortunate that, even though I was one hundredth in seniority and thus last to choose office space, I had landed in the historic Russell Senate Office Building. My friend and Minnesota colleague Paul Wellstone was not as lucky. He officed in Hart, and thus his entire Washington staff was displaced for the following months. So, they moved into my office, and we shared our space. The advantage for me was that, in return, Paul shared his Capitol hideaway, a room that had reportedly been Daniel Webster's wine cellar when he was a senator from 1845 to 1850. I did not have nearly the seniority to qualify for such a perquisite.

Fortunately, no other attacks occurred.

Nearly three years later, I learned an emphatic lesson about the advantage in a surprise attack. After former President Ronald Reagan died on June 5, 2004, many national officials flew into Washington for his funeral. The transponder broke on the state plane carrying the governor of Kentucky, which meant the plane approached (now Reagan) National Airport, right across from the Pentagon, unidentified. Despite the countless hours of preparation by all military and civilian agencies with responsibilities to respond immediately to another 9/11–type situation, they all froze, and the plane was allowed to land at the airport uninterrupted. It was a very good thing for the governor of Kentucky that he was not shot out of the sky, as the protocol envisioned.

At the time, I was meeting in my office with a young couple from Madison, Minnesota, who were visiting Washington for the first time. The wife was eight months pregnant. When the emergency warning system instructed us to evacuate, her husband and I levitated her down the stairs and outside the back of the building. They decided to head back to their hotel in Virginia. I invited them to return the next day, but I never saw them again!

With unidentified U.S. Air Force pilot on flight into Iraq, 2002

One result of 9/11 was a congressional delegation (CoDel) trip I took to Afghanistan and Pakistan with five other senators in January 2002, just three weeks after the United States military had routed the Taliban. We would fly into Uzbekistan as our home base. However, Senate Majority Leader Tom Daschle, who led our delegation, had criticized the Bush administration just before our departure. They retaliated by assigning us to the military version of a DC-9 airplane, which required us to make four refueling stops and stay overnight in Germany en route.

We arrived in Uzbekistan the day before our scheduled flight into Kabul, Afghanistan. We learned then that the State Department was warning us not to fly into Afghanistan because of security risks. The six of us conferred and agreed we had not flown all that way to just turn around. So, the next day we flew there on a C-120 Air Force transport plane.

We landed at Bagram Air Base, an hour outside of Kabul, because that city's airport had been bombed into ruins. We were told we should walk carefully along the path to the latrines some twenty yards away, because the surrounding area had not been swept for land mines. You've never seen six senators walk so obediently in single file to the john!

Then we boarded two open-air jeeps for the drive into Kabul. We maneuvered along a narrow highway, barely two lanes wide, filled with bomb craters. Twice we inched our way past broken-down vans surrounded by six to eight Afghan men. All of them were armed.

My heart was figuratively in my mouth as we slowly drove by, looking carefully at each other. I thought, "If this is an ambush, we're dead." I asked the Marine riding shotgun, "How do you tell the good guys from the bad guys?" His grim reply: "If he starts pointing his gun at you, he's probably a bad guy." A little late to be finding out, I thought to myself.

In Kabul, we met with Afghan President Hamid Karzai. He told us that the Taliban had looted the government's treasury and pleaded with us to help him rebuild his country. We took that message back to the Bush administration, which failed miserably to support Karzai and his fledgling government. If the United States had poured financial support and technical assistance into Afghanistan, we could have showcased America's goodness to the country and the world. Instead, the country staggered along, opium became its major economic asset, and the Taliban returned.

We also visited the U.S. Embassy and its eight staff. The main embassy had been closed for a decade and was surrounded by razor wire. The ambassador and his staff shared two bedrooms in the bomb shelter, the women in one and the

In Afghanistan with President Hamid Karzai, January 2002

men in the other, which also included a tiny office with one telephone and one fax machine.

I asked the barely forty-year-old ambassador why he had taken such a perilous assignment. A career foreign service officer, he replied, "How else could I get to be an ambassador?"

Flying back to Uzbekistan, we boarded another C-120, and I was invited to sit in the cockpit. The pilot and crew were twentysomething Alabama National Guardsmen. One of the plane's four engines would not start. After repeated efforts failed, the crew debated whether to try to take off and clear the looming mountains on three engines or wait a day or two for repairs. They decided to try it, and the plane safely cleared the mountain range.

When we arrived back in Uzbekistan, I told my Senate colleagues about our cockpit drama. They had been in the cargo hold, unaware. Sometimes, ignorance is bliss!

The following day, we flew into Pakistan to meet with the country's ruling army general. The CIA told us we couldn't fly in our DC-9 because it had "The United States of America" prominently displayed on its fuselage, and they feared it could be the target of a terrorist attack at the airport. So, we boarded a CIA plane, an unmarked, two engine DC-3, to fly over another mountain range, the one where Osama bin Laden was supposedly hiding.

At the door to the plane, we were greeted by the copilot, a tough CIA agent in a T-shirt and blue jeans, with a large pistol strapped to his belt. He said gruffly, "Here is the emergency door; here is the fire extinguisher," implying, "If you need anything more, don't ask me." We flew just over the mountaintops into Islamabad. During lunch, the ruling general told us that thirty miles away, on Pakistan's border with India, there were amassed one million Indian troops.

A tough neighborhood!

During my six years in the Senate, I went on five other CoDels, which were unquestionably among my most interesting experiences there. They were not vacations. They were jam-packed, intense fact-finding trips into some of the toughest places in the world.

In June 2003, I joined another group of six senators to fly into Iraq with Senate Armed Forces Committee Chairman John Warner and Vice Chairman Carl Levin. The Republican Senator Warner was treated far more favorably by the Bush administration than had been Senator Daschle. We flew in the military equivalent of a Boeing 757 into Kuwait, which served as our base of operations. Over the next three days, we flew on Air Force transport planes into Baghdad, Tikrit, and Basra.

We drove through each city in open-air jeeps, with military escorts on each side. In Baghdad, we met with provisional government officials and with the Commander of the U.S. Forces in Iraq, General Ricardo Sanchez. He told us that we had three months to win the hearts and minds of the Iraqi people, who

In Iraq with other U.S. senators, June 2003

were still reeling from the recent toppling of Saddam Hussein. (Of course, we failed to meet that timeline, and armed resistance mounted for years.)

In Basra, we toured an oil refinery whose operations were struggling after the removal of Saddam's loyalists. In an oil-rich region, there was a seven-hour wait for gasoline. When we mentioned Saddam Hussein's name, the new manager began trembling with fear. He and others were still so terrified of him, even though he was gone, that they could barely function.

My next CoDel was a trip led by then–Senate Majority Leader Bill Frist. The Republican leader also received much better treatment than had the Democratic leader on my earlier CoDel. We flew on Air Force Two, the Boeing 757 jet reserved for Vice President Cheney. One of our stops was Beijing, during a SARS epidemic. That outbreak prompted the vice president to cancel his trip to China the week before, on his doctor's recommendation. That is how we got his plane for a very comfortable trans-Pacific flight.

First, we stopped in Seoul, Republic of Korea, where we toured the demilitarized zone on the border of North and South Korea and met with the U.S. troops stationed there. We could look across the border and see heavily armed North Korean sentries eyeing us suspiciously.

Then we stopped in Taiwan. What a vibrant country it was! The night before we were scheduled to fly into Beijing, Leader Frist called us together. The city was virtually shut down because of its SARS epidemic. However, Senator Frist, a doctor, thought it was a reasonable risk, as we would be masked and kept separate from the general Chinese population. We voted unanimously to proceed.

When we flew into China, we had to detour back to Korea so that our flight manifest would not show we were coming

In China with Premier Hu Jintao

from Taiwan. Thus, our plane landed at the Seoul airport, barely touched the ground, and took off immediately for Beijing. Diplomacy!

In Beijing, we had the opportunity to meet with the Chinese premier, Hu Jintao. At the meeting was the U.S. ambassador, another of my old fraternity brothers, Sandy Randt. The premier even complimented him in front of us for his outstanding service.

My next CoDel was back to Iraq in the fall of 2004, this time with Senator Joe Lieberman. Joe had excellent contacts both in Israel and Iraq. We stopped first in Israel and had dinner with Benjamin Netanyahu, then out of power. Presently, he is the prime minister.

Then we flew into Iraq, and again we had to stop in another country, Jordan, so that our manifest would not show the Iraqis we had departed from Israel. In Amman, we were greeted by Jordan's foreign minister. I asked him if he had ever been to Minnesota. He smiled and said that he had been there for open heart surgery at Mayo Clinic in Rochester.

In Iraq with Minnesota Company commander, 2006

In Iraq, I immediately learned everything I needed to know about the security situation in that country. It had significantly deteriorated. Eighteen months before, I had been driven around Baghdad in an open-air jeep. This time, we were not allowed to leave the Green Zone, the heavily guarded perimeter around the U.S. command.

While there, we met with Joe's good friend, the commanding general of the American forces, David Petraeus. He gave us a tour of the site and showed us some Iraqi troops undergoing a training exercise. He said that trying to train them to become effective fighters was the hardest assignment he had ever had.

I remain immensely grateful to Senator Lieberman, with whom I had other disagreements, for nevertheless taking me with him on an amazing CoDel.

My final CoDel was to China, led by Alaska Senator Ted Stevens. I particularly wanted to go for two reasons: first, because I was really interested in China; and second, because

I wanted to build a relationship with Senator Stevens, then-chairman of the Senate Appropriations Committee, to get funding for the Minnesota National Guard's pioneering, first-in-the-nation Beyond the Yellow Ribbon program for soldiers returning from Iraq.

I didn't realize until we reached China what a heroic history Ted had with that country. During World War II, he was a member of the "Flying Tigers," American airmen who flew mercy missions into China, rescuing endangered citizens and delivering food and medical supplies. Their casualty rate was 50 percent!

Thus, he was revered in China, and we received beyond first-class treatment at every stop. We met again with the Chinese premier, Hu Jintao, toured the site of the upcoming 2008 Summer Olympics, visited the Great Wall, and received a Cook's tour of the National People's Congress, where each of its rooms represents one of China's thirty-three provinces and is decorated with the most indescribable murals, paintings, and tapestries. It also houses an indoor auditorium that seats ten thousand delegates to its annual conferences.

On our last night, senators and staff gathered in Senator Stevens's suite in a Beijing hotel. I stopped at a store in the lobby and bought about thirty of my favorite cigars: Davidoff Aniversario No. 2s. They were well received by everyone and created an enormous cloud of smoke in the rooms. I never learned whether the smoke alarms had been turned off or simply didn't work, but we smoked, drank, and talked undisturbed until 2:00 A.M.

A few days after we returned to Washington, I met with Ted in his office, and he agreed to approve the first federal funding for the Beyond the Yellow Ribbon program. It was a wonderful conclusion to a remarkable CoDel.

During my six years in the Senate, many other important events occurred in Washington. At the top of the list was the Senate's vote on the Iraq War Resolution.

In the spring of 2002, President Bush's top political adviser, Karl Rove, told a group of Republican donors that the success of the fall's midterm elections hinged on "the War," by which he meant the war against those responsible for the 9/11 attacks—Osama bin Laden and his al Qaeda terrorists. By late summer, however, bin Laden had disappeared, and that war had ground to a halt. The administration needed a new war.

At the end of August, Vice President Cheney spoke to the national American Legion convention and announced that Iraq's evil dictator, Saddam Hussein, was on the verge of developing nuclear weapons. Instantly, U.S. initiatives to rebuild Afghanistan faded into near-oblivion, and the specter of a nuclear-armed Saddam Hussein seized Washington.

The administration claimed it had proof positive that Iraq possessed the uranium separation tubes used for producing nuclear warheads. The president and vice president trumpeted this threat and insisted that Congress pass a resolution authorizing a war against Iraq.

A few days before the Senate's vote on that resolution, I was invited with five other senators into the "Situation Room" at the White House, an electronically sealed chamber, in which National Security Advisor Condoleezza Rice and CIA Director George Tenet passed around tubes that they said proved Saddam Hussein was on the verge of developing nuclear capabilities.

I was unconvinced. Other reports indicated those tubes were designed for peaceful nuclear energy production. Even more important, leading senators whom I greatly respected, like Robert Byrd and Carl Levin, opposed the resolution, arguing that it was premature and improper to give the president carte blanche authority to declare war whenever he decided it was right. The United States Constitution states clearly that only Congress has the power to declare war. Bob, Carl, and others argued to make the president come to Congress later for such a resolution, if he could make a conclusive case that war was necessary.

Nevertheless, the administration stampeded Congress into voting just three weeks before the midterm elections. Democratic Majority Leader Tom Daschle and Senate Foreign Relations Chairman Joe Biden evidently decided not to challenge President Bush. In what Senator Byrd said was the most important of the 17,000 votes he had cast in Congress, the Senate resolution prevailed 77–23. Paul Wellstone and I both voted against it.

I would say it was the most important vote I cast in the Senate, too, and the one of which I am most proud. Time would prove how right we were.

Ten days later, Paul, my best political friend and most important ally in the Senate, was gone, killed in a horrible plane crash. With him were his wife (Sheila), daughter (Marcia), three staff members, and two pilots, all lost when their small airplane went down near Eveleth, Minnesota, on October 25, 2002. They were on their way to the funeral of the father of State Representative Tom Rukavina.

I was in Amsterdam when it happened, on my way to tour NATO military bases during the Senate recess, when my chief of staff called me with the terrible news. It was a bizarre night. I was in complete shock, but alone in a foreign country. There was no one with whom to share my grief. I spent the entire night on my computer to get updates and to reconfirm the horrible reality of this disaster.

For me, the Senate was never the same without Paul. His seat went to Republican Norm Coleman in the November 5 election. That helped flip control of the Senate back to Republicans, 51–49. We Democrats were consigned to the minority again and would be stuck there for the next four years.

My Senate experience was not without a few successes. One occurred when the Minnesota National Guard was scheduled to receive more modern F-16 fighter planes from the Air Force. At the last minute, the Air Force tried to renege on its commitment and send the planes to New Mexico.

I checked the list of the administration's nominations then pending before the Senate. By fortuitous coincidence, the nomination to become the Air National Guard's commander, a personal friend of the president from Texas, was on the list. I immediately placed a "hold" on the nomination, which meant that it could not be considered by the full Senate for approval.

Within an hour, I had a flock of Air Force generals in my office asking what they could do to lift the hold. I called my good friend Tex Sieben, then the commander of the Minnesota Air National Guard (and Katie Sieben's uncle) and authorized him to negotiate with the generals. I told them, "When General Sieben is satisfied, I'll lift the hold."

Minnesota got its planes!

Another memorable success occurred at the end of July 2002, when a Minnesota family asked me to help them adopt an orphan child in Cambodia. Everything had been approved, but Jim Ziglar, the head of Immigration and Naturalization Services and a former Republican Senate sergeant at arms, arbitrarily canceled the approval. That left the Minnesotans and about thirty other American families literally stuck in Cambodia.

I went to see Ziglar, who arrogantly sneered at me that he wasn't going to change his mind and there was nothing I could do about it. The month-long August recess had just begun, but I placed a hold on all the administration's pending nominations.

That immediately got the attention of the White House, who, to its credit, agreed with my position and overruled Ziglar. All the adoptions went through. A couple months later, he departed the administration.

That kind of victory was the most personally gratifying aspect of being a senator. I was invited to the family's house, in my old hometown of Long Lake, to greet their new arrival.

I also had the satisfaction of helping to secure the Senate's confirmation of President Bush's nominee for the U.S. African Development Foundation, a Minnesotan and an active Republican, Ward Brehm. In July 2002, during the final week before the Senate's month-long August recess, my son Eric, who was a good friend of Ward's son, Andy, called me to ask for my help. Ward's nomination was stalled before the Senate Foreign Relations Committee, then chaired by Senator Joe Biden.

Eric described Ward's impeccable credentials for the position, which included over thirty personal trips to Africa. I said he sounded ideal for the position. Eric then paused and said, "Dad, there's one more thing you should know. Ward was Senator Rod Grams's campaign finance chairman."

I immediately said it didn't change the obvious merit of his candidacy. That afternoon, I encountered Senator Biden walking toward the Senate chamber for a vote. I started to describe Ward's qualifications. Joe smiled, threw his arm over my shoulder, and said, "Mark, if you're for him, that's good enough for me."

The next day, Ward's nomination was reported out of the Foreign Relations Committee, and the day after, just before the August recess, it was confirmed by a voice vote of the full Senate. The following week, he was sworn in at the U.S. Federal Building in Minneapolis, and I was invited. In the audience were former Senator Grams and just about every other prominent Republican in Minnesota. All of them looked at me as if to say, "What are *you* doing here?"

Unfortunately, the occasional small victories could not offset my disillusionment with the Senate and my frustration with my inability to be truly effective there.

None of my bills or amendments ever became laws. I did have two amendments passed by the Senate. The first was an amendment to the Bush administration's "Fast Track" trade legislation. I partnered with Idaho Senator Larry Craig, then number three in the Republican leadership. We exempted small businesses from the hurry-up Fast Track procedures. Despite the Bush administration's active opposition, our amendment prevailed 62–37. Even Senator Jesse Helms, then absent, announced in favor! However, the amendment was dropped by Democratic Finance Committee Chairman Max Baucus in Conference Committee and never became law.

My second amendment would have prohibited corporate executives from claiming income tax deductions for their personal use of corporate airplanes. I waited past midnight on the Senate floor for my amendment, one of many to a Finance Committee's omnibus bill, to be brought up for debate and consideration. When the moment finally arrived, the Republican committee chairman, Iowa's Chuck Grassley, who was managing the bill, called for it to be adopted by unanimous consent. That tricky maneuver meant there was no debate; no recorded vote (so no one had to vote against it); and, of course, it was dropped by the Conference Committee.

Wonder why I was disillusioned in the Senate? Hypocrisy was often rewarded, and honesty was often penalized. There's a saying that if you like a fellow senator, you call him or her "my friend." If you don't like them, you call them "my good friend." If you detest them, you call them "my very good friend!"

To compound my disillusionment, beginning in the summer of 2004, I found myself on a downhill political slide. My troubles began in front of a high school assembly in western Renville County. A student asked me, "What grade would you give yourself in the Senate?"

It was a perfectly valid question, but one I had never been asked before and for which I was completely unprepared. I said, "An F," and went on to say that I would give the entire Senate an F for passing the Iraq War Resolution.

Unfortunately for me, the only reporter in the auditorium wrote that I had given myself an F and mentioned nothing else. It was widely reported both in Minnesota and nationally. My explanation was, of course, obscured, and the Republicans piled on.

To compound my problems, I received widespread derision for closing my Washington Senate office in October 2004 to protect my staff from a possible terrorist attack on the U.S.

Speaking with steelworkers, 2004

Capitol. In September, Majority Leader Bill Frist interrupted a meeting that about thirty of us senators were having with then–National Security Advisor Condoleezza Rice to alert us to a highly classified memorandum just received from the CIA. It said a well-placed source had disclosed that a 9/11–style terrorist attack on the U.S. Capitol was very likely before the November 2004 election. The Senate sergeant at arms told us that during his thirty years working in national security, no warning had been so definitive.

I tried unsuccessfully to get both the Republican and Democratic Senate leaders to hold a closed Senate session to review and discuss this urgent prediction. I should have pressed the matter further with them and other Senate colleagues. Instead, I erred in going my own way and announcing my office's closure alone.

Never stand alone in Washington.

The mayor of the city, *Time* magazine, and other prominent authorities denounced my actions. (Most of my Senate colleagues were graciously silent.) My Minnesota approval rating quickly dropped from 56 percent to 44 percent.

No attack on the Capitol occurred.

At the end of 2004, I faced the prospect of spending the next two years doing what I most detested about politics—raising millions of dollars—to finance a tough reelection campaign. I felt that I had been ineffective in the Senate, and that Minnesota deserved better. In my view, that's what it got in my successor, Senator Amy Klobuchar, who has been an outstanding senator for Minnesota.

I announced in January 2005 that I would not run for reelection. I spent my final two years demoralized. The day after my announcement, I passed an ornery Republican senator in a hallway. "Quitter," he sneered. I responded by raising my middle finger in his face and, quoting Senator Frank Lautenberg, said, "Conrad, you're Number One with me."

In January 2007, I returned to Minnesota, sadly feeling like a failure. However, Republican Governor Tim Pawlenty had just been reelected, which meant the door was open for a Democrat to run for governor in 2010.

I decided to go through that door.

— CHAPTER EIGHT —

HILLARY AND PAUL

> "The political leaders with whom we are familiar generally aspire to be superstars rather than heroes. The distinction is crucial. Superstars strive for approbation; heroes walk alone."
>
> —*Henry Kissinger*

Washington, DC, does not reward heroism, and someone looking for heroes will probably have better luck looking elsewhere. It attracts ambitious people eager to acquire power, already powerful people seeking even more of it, and cynical people attempting to influence the powerful. But occasionally, Washington surprises you.

Robert Kennedy was my first political hero, just as I was coming into political consciousness in 1968. After his brother's assassination, he was elected to Congress as a U.S. senator from New York in 1964. In office, he promoted human rights, toured the country to understand the hidden depth of American poverty, and championed policies designed to fight poverty, provide employment, and promote community investment where it was needed most. Despite his brother's role in expanding the U.S. military presence in Southeast Asia, by 1968 Robert Kennedy was one of the loudest critics of the Vietnam War.

His convictions were what led him to seek the presidency that year. And ultimately, he gave his life pursuing them.

Robert Kennedy wasn't exactly an outsider in Washington. Despite his youth, he'd been given the kinds of opportunities that only wealth and political influence can provide. But his moral vision led him to use those opportunities to champion outsiders. I identified with him. He wasn't tall or handsome or poised, like his older brother. But he was fearless and tenacious in fighting for the underprivileged and for social justice. Watching him die for the causes he believed in lit a flame of political consciousness in me that has burned to this day.

Leaders like Robert Kennedy, though, have passed into legend. In today's Washington, it is hard even to imagine that he and others like him once walked through its halls of power. But during my years in the Senate, I found two new heroes. Both were just as fearless, willing to take strong stands and champion great causes, whether currently popular or not. And like RFK, both of their careers in Washington were far too short.

"There cannot be true democracy," Hillary Clinton said, "unless women's voices are heard. There cannot be true democracy unless women are given the opportunity to take responsibility for their own lives." Hillary Clinton is one of the most outstanding people I have ever known. I first met her when we were both elected to the U.S. Senate in 2000, and we developed a lasting friendship when we sat next to each other in the Senate chamber for the next six years. She was the smartest, hardest-working senator there, and I learned so much from her.

The week before we took office, we had a Democratic Senate Caucus meeting. The *Washington Post* that day had quoted Senator Robert Byrd, arguably the body's most powerful member, saying that Senator Clinton would get along well there if she were "a workhorse, not a show horse." At that meeting, Hillary looked him in the eye and said, "Senator Byrd, I want you to know, I'm here to be a workhorse, not a show horse."

Of course, as a former first lady and one of the Democratic Party's most prominent leaders, she couldn't avoid also being a show horse. But she was a masterful working senator, always impeccably well prepared, and she amazed her Republican colleagues, as well as skeptical Democrats, with her interpersonal and legislative skills.

She joined the Senate Prayer Breakfast to connect with more conservative, mostly Republican members, whom she would not have reached otherwise. She established a tutorial for the twelve new members of both parties with Senator Byrd, where he taught us about the culture and traditions of the Senate. (He had already sent each of us his four volumes on the history of that body!)

The first session was scheduled for 4:00 P.M. in Senator Byrd's enormous Capitol office. I had been told that he was a stickler for punctuality, so I walked in at 3:59. There I saw him on one side of the table and Hillary sitting respectfully right across from him, pen and notepad at the ready. Needless to say, she'd gained a new friend and staunch ally.

I remember one late night in the Senate, when we sat together in the chamber. On Hillary's desk was a stack of plain white paper the size of a New York City telephone directory. She was assiduously writing "Hillary R. Clinton" on each page.

"What are you doing?" I asked. She was pre-autographing cover pages for her upcoming book. "Can't you just make photocopies?" "No," she replied. "Buyers will dab the signature with water to see if it is authentic."

As she plowed through a couple hundred pages (She was to sign some 27,000 of them and give herself the beginnings of carpal tunnel syndrome), I sheepishly pulled a half dozen letters from my briefcase and began to write responses. That was the kind of workhorse I got to see firsthand.

What I admire most about Hillary is her phenomenal resilience and incredible resolve under the most extreme pressures. I have never seen anyone subjected to as much political abuse and assault. She took it all and soldiered on.

She was always superbly well prepared, even amidst the enormous demands on her time and energies. And I admire her rapier-sharp intellect and wit. With her intelligence, experience, and skill, I always thought she should be president.

As I was leaving the Senate at the end of 2006, I told Hillary that I would support her presidential run in 2008. During 2007, I represented her in about twenty Iowa Democratic events, leading up to the state's first-in-the-nation caucuses on January 3, 2008. I joked that "Wherever three or more Iowans were gathered, her campaign sent Hillary or Bill. If fewer than three, they said, 'I wonder what Mark Dayton is doing tomorrow night?'"

But 2008 was Barack Obama's year. Despite Hillary's understandably disappointing run for the presidency that year, she joined the president-elect's team as secretary of state. She did an incredible job in that high office. In four years, she visited 112 countries and traveled almost one million (956,733) miles. She not only championed our country's best interests but also served as a beacon for women's hopes and aspirations throughout the world.

Then, 2016 looked to be Hillary's year. I proudly helped host her in Minnesota for several events in 2015 and 2016. On one May 2015 morning, she flew into St. Paul's Holman airport to begin a caravan into Iowa. That day turned out to be the coldest temperature on record for Minnesota and Iowa. I brought two winter vests and a large thermos of hot coffee to fortify her for the ordeal. Her top aide, Huma Abedin, later told me that both were essential to her survival that day!

Thus, I was thrilled and greatly honored to be asked to give an endorsing speech for her during the Democratic National Convention's final evening. I was given a prime slot in the evening program leading up to her acceptance speech. It was the culmination of sixteen years of friendship and shared political commitments.

Once again, she was brutally savaged by opposing political forces, including even the director of the FBI. Election night 2016 was one of the worst of my life. It was an unspeakable horror to watch Donald Trump squeak by to victory, despite losing the national popular vote. Although Minnesota went for Hillary, that was no consolation.

The best political leader of my lifetime had been denied the presidency, despite her overwhelmingly superior qualifications, because of a confluence of forces, all of which are damning of the American electorate. Someone smarter than I will someday have to explain how Donald Trump could draw so many voters to his side. What have we become?

Hillary's defeat in 2016 signaled the end of her career in elective office. And despite her numerous achievements on behalf of the American people during her three decades in Washington, I can't help but imagine the good she would have accomplished if she'd been able to stay longer.

Hillary is my hero of modern Washington, but I also had another, Paul Wellstone. Paul liked to say that he represented "the Democratic wing of the Democratic Party." He was truly one in a million—as a person, a politician, and a leader. His victory over Rudy Boschwitz in the 1990 race for U.S. Senate

With Senator Paul Wellstone and Vice President Walter Mondale, 2001

in Minnesota was the greatest political upset in my lifetime. And his death in 2002 during his campaign for reelection was the greatest political tragedy in my lifetime. "Politics," he said, "isn't about big money or power games. It's about the improvement of people's lives." He believed that and practiced it.

I first met Paul at the DFL state convention in June 1982, where I was endorsed for the U.S. Senate election that November. Throughout the spring, I had encountered at party events a very earnest young man, Frank Altman, who was seeking the endorsement for state auditor. He was unopposed until the first day of the convention, when a Carleton College professor named Paul Wellstone, who had had little prior involvement with the DFL Party, arrived and announced his candidacy for that office.

The auditor's endorsement was held on Sunday morning, the convention's last day. Most of the 1,200 or so delegates were dead tired, hungover, or both. Frank Altman was the first to address the unruly crowd with a very serious description of the auditor's responsibilities. Then Paul Wellstone spoke in what was to become known as his special style: shouting, gesticulating, over-the-top exuberant. "NUCLEAR FREEZE! ECONOMIC JUSTICE! ENVIRONMENTAL PROTECTION!" None of which had anything to do with the auditor's job, which mattered naught to the delegates, who were aroused by Paul's frenzy. Someone called for a voice vote, and Paul was endorsed overwhelmingly.

He and I both lost our elections that November, but in our campaign travels together we began a friendship which deepened over the next twenty years. After our defeats, I was appointed commissioner of the Minnesota Department of Energy and Economic Development by Governor Rudy Perpich. Then he tapped Paul to organize Community Energy Councils throughout the state. I gave Paul my conference room for his office, and we spent the next years working closely together. At the end of long days, we would put our feet up on a table and solve the problems of the world!

In the fall of 1989, I decided that I wanted to run for state auditor the following year. Unsure of Paul's continuing designs on the office, I visited him for lunch in Northfield, where he had returned to teach at Carleton. I began the conversation tentatively, saying that I was interested in running for state auditor but would defer to him, if he ran again.

A big smile spread across his face. It turned out that he wanted to run for the U.S. Senate and was worried it would conflict with my ambitions. So, we switched our campaigns from 1982, and both achieved different results.

Paul's race was a true "David vs. Goliath" matchup against a very well-financed Republican incumbent, Senator Rudy Boschwitz. Paul had almost no money, but he overcame that deficiency with uncanny political instincts and superb television advertising. "Fast-paced Paul" was his introductory ad, where he established himself as the underdog prairie populist. "Looking for Rudy" was another brilliant play on a then-renowned "Looking for Roger (of General Motors)" spoof by Michael Moore.

Trailing Boschwitz by over forty points in the polls on Labor Day, Paul steadily closed the gap. Still, on the last weekend before the election, he was seven points behind and out of money to contest the final Republican media blitz. Our faces were grim as we boarded the DFL Party bus for our traditional last swing throughout the state.

Suddenly, the news broke of a letter Boschwitz had written to prominent Jewish citizens, denouncing Paul, who was also Jewish, for raising his children as Christians, as was his wife, Sheila. In a state that was about one percent Jewish and 99 percent Christian, it was not a good political play. At each campaign stop (there were no cell phones) Paul would be updated by his campaign manager, Jeff Blodgett, and a glimmer of hope appeared.

On Monday, the day before the election, former Vice President Mondale publicly chastised Senator Boschwitz for his comments. It received massive statewide coverage. Paul's final statewide media blitz had occurred at no cost to his campaign. He won the next day's election by a narrow, but clear, margin. The college professor from Northfield, Minnesota, was now a United States senator.

Paul's first decade in the Senate was a challenge. From the beginning, he caused a stir in Washington by haranguing

1990 Election Night with Paul Wellstone, who won the U.S. Senate election

then–President George H. W. Bush at a White House reception. His brash, outspoken style was viewed askance by some senior senators. Paul himself told the story of being confronted on the floor by Democratic Senator Fritz Hollings. "Young man, you remind me of Hubert Humphrey. You talk too much."

But Paul had unyielding determination and the utmost courage of his convictions. Over time, he gained the respect of more and more of his colleagues. As one Republican senator later said to me, "He might be a little pink, but he really believes it."

In 1996, Paul was challenged for his first reelection by former Senator Rudy Boschwitz. As I said before, I was asked to serve as Paul's finance chair, which meant I had to do what I disliked most in politics: ask people for money. I did learn, however, that it was easier to ask for someone other than myself, especially someone in whom I deeply believed. Nineteen ninety-six was the first election after the Republican right wing had seized control of the U.S. House of Representatives with its "Contract for America." If the Senate's leading progressive could be defeated, it would have a chilling effect on all the causes Paul and I believed in.

I received my first indications that Paul was going to do better than some pundits predicted when I asked my father

Speaking with Senator Paul Wellstone, 2002

and one of my uncles who they were going to vote for. To my surprise, both said Paul. They didn't agree with him on many issues, but they admired his independence and his passionate convictions. Sure enough, Paul won his reelection decisively. And in 2000, it was my great honor and thrill to join him as Minnesota's two United States senators.

As 2002 unfolded, Paul was receiving intense attacks from Republicans in Washington and Minnesota, who were trying to upend his reelection that November. By October, President Bush and Vice President Cheney had manufactured the threat that Iraq President Saddam Hussein possessed nuclear weapons. Just twenty-five days before the election, the Senate held a vote to authorize President Bush to declare war on Iraq.

It was a momentous vote—for our country, the world, and the senators soon facing their voters. In Minnesota, polls showed that over 80 percent of voters supported President Bush's call for Senate support of the war resolution, as they believed, wrongly it turned out, that he was telling them the truth.

The pressure on Paul was enormous. He was neck and neck in polls with his Republican opponent, Norm Coleman, who supported the resolution. Yet Paul believed, as I did, that it was wrong.

On October 11, he and I were two of twenty-three senators who voted against that Iraq War Resolution. Paul was the only senator facing reelection to vote against it. His unsurpassed political courage and integrity shone through once again.

Ten days later, the Senate adjourned until after the upcoming election. I saw Paul for the very last time as we gathered on the Senate floor. He was ebullient! He had just received an internal poll showing him six percent ahead of his opponent. Even Minnesotans who disagreed with his war vote respected him for those qualities of courage and integrity that made him so exceptional.

We said goodbye, and he headed back to Minnesota to finish his campaign. I flew to Brussels for a tour of NATO bases. We planned to rejoin each other for that traditional DFL bus ride on the campaign's final weekend.

I will never forget the incredible horror of the phone call from my Washington chief of staff informing me that Paul, his wife, Sheila, his daughter, Marcia, DFL Vice Chair Mary McAfee, two campaign aides, and two pilots had been killed in a terrible plane crash on the Iron Range.

What an impossible, indescribable, horrible catastrophe. To make matters even worse, eleven days later former Vice

President Mondale, the party's last-minute replacement, lost a close election to Coleman.

Minnesota and America had lost a one in a million leader. His sons had lost a father, mother, and sister. I had lost my best political friend.

For me, nothing was ever the same in Washington. Nothing could ever be the same. When I pass, if I get thirty seconds up above before being sent down to serve my penance, I'm going to ask the Good Lord, "Why did Strom Thurmond get to live to over one hundred, while Paul Wellstone couldn't make it to sixty?"

— CHAPTER NINE —

BACK ON THE TRAIL

"The credit belongs to the man who is actually in the arena, whose face is marred by dust and sweat and blood, who knows the great enthusiasms, the great devotions, and spends himself in a worthy cause; who at best, if he wins, knows the thrills of high achievement, and, if he fails, at least fails daring greatly, so that his place shall never be with those cold and timid souls who know neither victory nor defeat."

—*President John F. Kennedy, paraphrasing President Theodore Roosevelt, 1961*

My campaign for governor of Minnesota began quietly in November 2008, less than two years after I left the Senate. In January 2009, when the Minnesota Newspaper Association invited all the announced and possible candidates for governor to its annual banquet, there were fifty-two of us. By the following January—seven months after incumbent Governor Tim Pawlenty announced that he would not seek a third term—there were twenty-two. The following January, after the election, there was one: me.

I'd faced formidable odds. My DFL opponents included the

speaker of the Minnesota House of Representatives, Margaret Anderson Kelliher; the mayor of Minneapolis, RT Rybak; and a popular Iron Range legislator, Tom Rukavina. When I announced that I would not seek the DFL Party's endorsement in June 2010, but rather run in the August primary, most party activists turned from personal friends to political opponents. In fact, DFL Party leaders locked me out of their state convention in Duluth. (The two ringleaders, RT's and Margaret's campaign managers, Tina Smith and Jaime Tincher, later became my lieutenant governor/U.S. Senate appointee and chief of staff. As Hubert Humphrey once said, "In politics, as in religion, forgiveness should be immediate and absolute!")

As the 2010 election year unfolded, I faced the challenge of reintroducing myself to the people of Minnesota. I started with a political dinner on the Iron Range. I had learned long ago to always start my campaigns on the Range! It was a longtime DFL stronghold—and, back then, anyone who predicted it would become otherwise would have been laughed out of politics.

After blanketing the Range, I turned my attention to the rest of the state. Party events that spring were futile, as I was not seeking the endorsement. Instead, I launched one of my best-ever ideas: a tour throughout Minnesota. I called it "87 counties in 87 days!" My campaign pooled every list I had ever collected, and we invited everyone to meetings in each county. Turnouts ranged from more than fifty people in several counties to just one in Lac qui Parle. I also met with newspaper editors, key local officials, and longtime friends.

Those meetings were invaluable. They reeducated me about the key issues on people's minds throughout the state. They reminded me how much I loved traveling everywhere and meeting everyone in Minnesota. And they provided me with new credibility when I spoke about key problems and offered my solutions during the following months.

Supporting a nurses' strike, 2010

One of our most memorable evenings occurred in Pipestone. We checked into the local hotel, whose lobby and rooms looked like something out of *The Twilight Zone*, and went to our evening meeting. There, a newspaper reporter asked if I was staying in Room 407, which was rumored to be haunted. Undaunted, I returned to the hotel and switched my room to 407. One of my drivers, Katie Tinucci, was so distraught that she borrowed my cell phone and went to sleep connected to our campaign manager in St. Paul, Dana Bailey.

Surviving unscathed to the next morning, I told Katie that I had been tempted to knock on her door at 2:00 A.M. and moan "Whooo!" She assured me that she would not be alive if I had.

Among the highlights of a summer campaign in Minnesota are an endless number of parades. I always walked them, running from side to side to shake as many hands as possible. I also wanted people to see me working hard and sweating for their votes. Popular that summer were Super Soaker squirt guns, brandished by kids perched at the edge of parade streets. I ran up to them and said, "Who wants to shoot a politician?" Several usually responded, and I received refreshing showers throughout otherwise very hot parades. The watching adults were entertained as I moved quickly down the block.

I should add that no parade, like no campaign, can be successful without the well-coordinated teamwork of campaign staff and volunteers. I am deeply indebted and forever grateful to the many devoted staff, friends, and supporters who propelled that campaign under the fantastic leadership of my dear friend Dana Bailey.

The issue that won the primary and general elections for me that year was raising the state's income tax rate by two percentage points on the wealthiest two percent of Minnesotans. In national politics at that time, any mention of a tax increase was considered suicidal. However, our state government was in a serious fiscal crisis that recurred repeatedly throughout the last years of Pawlenty's governorship. Minnesotans in 2010 knew that the state was likely facing a huge budget deficit for the next biennium. (It was projected at $6.2 billion when I took office the following January.) Many of them also knew that the state's total state and local tax burden (income, property, and sales taxes combined) was regressive, meaning that our richest citizens paid a smaller percentage of their incomes in total state and local taxes than the rest of Minnesotans.

In my speeches, events, and paid advertising, I made this injustice and my solution to it the principal focus of my campaign. Because others shied away from it, I stood out.

On primary night, I was having dinner with my two sons, Eric and Andrew, at Mancini's in St. Paul, when my campaign called to tell me that I had lost. I was trailing Margaret Anderson Kelliher by 14,000 votes. By their calculation, there weren't enough votes still uncounted to make up that gap. Needless to say, I lost my appetite!

Still, after dinner, we stopped in the intensive care unit at Regions Hospital to visit one of my interns, Chelsea Skog, who had been in a horrific car accident, struck by a drunk driver while delivering campaign brochures for me. Fortunately, she and her passenger survived.

When we arrived at my campaign headquarters around 10:00 P.M., our outlook was still bleak. To compound our misery, the air conditioning there had malfunctioned. Stuffed with workers, friends, and press, the office was stifling.

Over the next hour, the air conditioning and my prospects came back to life. The Eighth District was coming through! My selection of popular Duluth State Senator Yvonne Prettner Solon as my running mate and my standing on the Iron Range propelled us into a narrow lead, which held up for the rest of the night.

As a result, I won the three-way primary contest, topping second-place finisher Anderson Kelliher by a narrow seven-thousand vote plurality. "This is like Lazarus coming back to life," said David Schultz, a political science professor at Hamline University in St. Paul.

The general election campaign was also tough and uphill. Previously, Minnesota Democrats had won only three of twenty-eight gubernatorial elections during a Democratic presidency. This time, President Obama's first midterm election immediately followed the Great Recession and the wrongly maligned Affordable Care Act. As a result, 2010 was a terrible political year for Democrats nationally. I had two principal opponents, Republican Tom Emmer (now the majority whip in the U.S. House of Representatives) and the Independence Party's Tom

Horner, a public relations businessman and a former Republican. Our first debate occurred just days after the primary in Winona, sponsored by the Coalition of Greater Minnesota Cities. Tom Emmer did not appear, and the event's organizers placed an empty chair with his name posted on it on the stage with Tom Horner and me. That picture received statewide attention, with the result that all three of us attended every one of the thirty-plus remaining debates. No other statewide campaign in Minnesota memory featured as many in-person debates. It was hailed by editorial writers as an outstanding exercise in democracy.

A highlight of my campaign was President Obama coming to Minnesota and headlining a rally. It was planned for the mall at the University of Minnesota campus, and we expected a crowd of well over ten thousand. Unfortunately, after a week of perfect fall weather, it rained that Saturday afternoon, and we had to move the event to three different indoor venues on campus. That reduced the size of the crowd, although it did not dampen the enthusiasm.

I spent that morning in western Minnesota at Congressman Collin Peterson's Pheasant Hunting Opener. My driver, Dan Lopez, and I sped back to the Minneapolis airport to greet the president's plane. As we approached the checkpoint, we realized we had two shotguns in our car! We detoured to a nearby friend of Dan's, stashed our guns, and made it to the terminal just in time to greet Air Force One.

Another highlight of the afternoon was the blockbuster rendition of "The Star-Spangled Banner" by nine-year-old McKaia Ryberg from Bird Island, Minnesota. That spring, I had traveled to her hometown for a benefit to raise money for a foundation established in the memory of a young man who had lost his life to cancer. I walked into the auditorium just in time to see a tiny girl belt out unaccompanied the best version of our national anthem I had ever heard in my life. I told her then that if I were elected governor I would invite her to sing at my inauguration. When President Obama arrived in early October, I was not certain I would be having an inauguration. So, I took the opportunity of that big occasion to ask her to sing, which she again did so well, and she also had the chance to meet the president.

All in all, despite the rain, a wonderful day!

Polls showed me closely ahead right up to the election. That night started out very well. Unlike the primary, I was ahead early and by about 10:00 P.M. had a lead of almost 120,000 votes.

Then a bomb exploded. Hennepin County announced it had incorrectly tallied about 55,000 votes to me that should have gone to the Republican candidate. The switch of some 110,000 votes put the election on the knife's edge, where it remained until the next day. The preliminary final tally had me winning by 9,800 votes, less than half of one percent, which under Minnesota law required a recount.

The next five weeks were unrelenting uncertainty. Would there be somewhere in one of the other eighty-six counties an error like Hennepin County's that would hand the victory to Tom Emmer?

Fortunately, Ken Martin, who would go on to become the best DFL Party chair in my political lifetime and is, as of 2026, the chairman of the Democratic National Committee, organized a phenomenal cadre of volunteers to attend every recount hearing throughout the state. Finally, on December 10, Emmer graciously called me to concede the election. (By contrast, Al Franken's victory in the U.S. Senate election two years earlier had been contested by the Republicans and kept unresolved for almost six months.)

Nationwide, it was a bad year for Democratic governors. Republican candidates won twenty-three of the contests; Democrats only thirteen. At year's end, our country had twenty-nine Republican governors, only twenty Democrats, and one Independent.

But I was one of them!

How did I win that year when so many other Democratic candidates, both in Minnesota and across the country, fared so badly? One of my axioms is that in Minnesota, "Populist campaigns win!" Rudy Perpich and Paul Wellstone had proved that point. By focusing my campaign on raising taxes on the wealthiest Minnesotans and opposing the drastic cuts my Republican predecessor had made to education and human services, I established myself as the populist candidate in both the primary and general elections. And it became clear to people that I was taking those stands not for political expediency but because I strongly believed they were right for Minnesota.

And I was right!

— CHAPTER TEN —

EXPECTATION AND REALITY

"I do the very best I know how—the very best I can; and mean to keep doing so until the end. If the end brings me out all right, what is said against me won't amount to anything. If the end brings me out wrong, ten angels swearing I was right would make no difference."

—*President Abraham Lincoln, 1863*

I left campaign mode to face the most overwhelming challenge of my lifetime. The recount's uncertainty meant that I had less time to prepare to take the gubernatorial oath of office on January 3, 2011. I had to finish hiring an office staff, choose thirty-three agency heads, and prepare a budget to resolve a projected $6.2 billion deficit for the next biennium.

Fortunately, I had a nucleus of terrific staff to help me. Dana Bailey, my fantastic campaign manager, stayed with me and began to manage a staff. A longtime close friend, Lee Sheehy, took over the recruiting and screening of potential agency commissioners. And I was incredibly fortunate to have recently met an amazing woman, Tina Smith, who took over as my chief of staff.

Tina had been Minneapolis Mayor RT Rybak's chief of staff

With Tina Smith, who served at different times as my chief of staff, lieutenant governor, and U.S. Senate appointee

and had managed his gubernatorial campaign. After I won the primary, one of my advisers urged me to meet with Tina, whom I did not know. In late August we sat for lunch in the patio of a south Minneapolis restaurant. Three hours later, we were still there!

Tina is one of the most amazing people I have ever known. She is extremely smart and possesses excellent political judgment and impeccable integrity. Most importantly, she genuinely likes people, and they almost immediately like her. She was the mother lode of an office of very talented people who worked incredibly well together through the most difficult circumstances. She is now a United States senator.

My first important action on the morning after taking office was signing an executive order that qualified 95,000 low-income Minnesotans for Medicaid, a public health program funded by federal and state governments. (In Minnesota, that program is also known as Medical Assistance.) President Obama and Democratic congressional majorities had opened the door for states to expand their programs. But in Minnesota, expansion had been staunchly opposed by the state's previous Republican administration. It epitomized a fundamental difference between that Republican governor and the Republican majorities in the legislature and me. I believe that government exists to help people in need.

It was a tumultuous first full day in office. That morning at 6:00 A.M., Dakota, one of my two wonderful German shepherds, died after a three-month battle with cancer. Then I had a 7:30 meeting with the Iron Range legislative delegation, who wanted new highway funding in the upcoming legislative session. Immediately afterward, I went into the ornate Governor's Reception Room to sign the Medicaid executive order.

The room was packed with both proponents and opponents of the order. The opponents carried posters and threatened to disrupt the ceremony. Spontaneously, I invited their representative to come to the podium and offer their rebuttal.

I hadn't thought twice about it. But I later learned that it was very unusual, if not unprecedented, for a governor to invite his opposition to share the podium in his own reception room. Even the hard-bitten Capitol press corps was impressed.

My first day in office combined success with disaster. It was the first of many similar days to come.

Throughout my following eight years as governor, I heard

With Wanamingo and Itasca

countless stories from people whose lives had been saved or whose quality of life had been transformed by their new Medicaid coverage. There is nothing better in my line of work than to learn that something you have done has made a positive difference in someone else's life. Or, in many of these cases, saved someone's life.

Less than two weeks after I took office, state law required me to submit a complete two-year budget to the newly assembled Minnesota legislature, in which both the House and Senate were controlled by Republican majorities. Fortunately, Lee Sheehy had found me an outstanding commissioner of human services, Lucinda Jesson. Cindy, an accomplished attorney whose career had included a stint in the state attorney general's office, had already played an important role in the transition, doing a superb job organizing the portfolios of commissioner applicants.

I offered her the job on the Friday before I took office. She said she wanted the weekend to think about it. As she recounted, that Sunday she went to church, and the title of the sermon was "Here I am, Lord!" She took that as a message and accepted the job.

Thank God that she did. Our first budget meeting lasted four hours as we looked for cuts of over a billion dollars from the state's human services budget. At its conclusion, I looked at Cindy. "Here we are, Lord?" I asked.

My balanced budget was dead on arrival with the extremist right wing of the legislature. My campaign proposal to increase income taxes on the wealthiest Minnesotans was denounced and immediately rejected. Republicans would not consider any tax increase to reduce the deficit, and they also would not specify where they wanted to reduce spending.

I found their rigid position unconscionable. We faced having to make drastic cuts in services many of our citizens depended upon in order to meet our constitutional requirement of a balanced budget for the next two years. The services on the chopping block included personal attendants for the severely disabled, mental health care for adolescents, and emergency social services for abused spouses and children—all badly needed. Yet Republican legislators, reinforced by some business lobbyists, would not consider raising one dollar of additional revenue from the wealthiest Minnesotans.

I had won my election by championing that principle of greater tax fairness, compounded now by budget necessity. But my victory made no difference to conservative ideologues, who would not budge an inch. Still, those hypocrites would not accept even a smidgen of responsibility to specify which human services they wanted to cut even more. That, they insisted, was my agencies' responsibility.

Further, they constantly ranted about the "waste and fraud" in government to justify their unspecified funding reductions. They were fundamentally anti-government, especially when a Democrat was in charge of it. I thought to myself, "If you don't believe in government, why do you insist upon running it? If you think the private sector has all the answers, go work in the private sector." I prudently kept those views to myself!

Yes, there are excesses in some government programs, and unwise or wasteful spending accompany them. Those flaws should be attacked and eliminated. But they shouldn't obscure all the wise spending and effective services that improve so many people's lives.

President Ronald Reagan coined the phrase, "Government is not the solution to the problem; government is the problem."

That political tagline has become the conservative mantra. "Cutting taxes" (or not raising them) has become their Holy Grail, any additional need be damned.

If we had fair and equitable tax systems, that resistance would be more defensible. But we don't. Our federal, state, and local tax structures are all regressive, meaning the wealthy pay smaller percentages of their incomes in taxes than middle-income taxpayers. So, when the middle class believes they're getting screwed, they're right.

My proposal would have raised the state income tax rate by two percent on the wealthiest two percent of Minnesotans. Ninety-eight percent of our citizens would have received no tax increase under my proposal. It would not have eliminated the projected deficit, but it would have made a big dent in it. And it would have made the tax burden fairer for our citizens.

But the Republicans of 2011 would have none of it.

As the session neared its May constitutionally mandated conclusion, we were $3 billion apart. I proposed that we compromise and meet halfway. My offer was scorned and rejected. Many Republicans in the legislature were ideological zealots who considered compromise a weakness and intransigence a virtue.

In my ten previous years dealing with legislators as state auditor, Department of Energy and Economic Development commissioner, and a governor's staff member, I had prided myself on being able to "get along with everyone who could get along with me." In January, I invited groups of all the legislators and their spouses/partners/guests to receptions at the Governor's Residence. I hosted weekly breakfasts with the leaders of both parties. I tried to build personal relationships with legislators, particularly Republicans, which could overcome our serious policy differences. I invited them to agree with me "to" something we did not necessarily agree "with." That's what shared governance requires.

To my dismay, I learned that when the chips were down in the final days of that legislative session, my personal relationships failed to budge their intransigence. In meetings with top Republican leaders House Speaker Kurt Zellers and Senate Majority Leader Amy Koch to try to find compromises, they said to me, "If we agreed with you, we would be deposed this afternoon." I said publicly, "I offered to meet them at the fifty-yard line, but they refused to leave their end zone."

As a result, we remained $3 billion apart at the session's conclusion and still $3 billion apart on June 30, the day before the next biennium would begin. Without an agreed-upon budget, state government could no longer operate. The next day a government shutdown began.

That night I issued a statement that said in part, "I cannot accept a Minnesota where people with disabilities lose part of the time they are cared for by personal care attendants so that millionaires don't have to pay $1 more in taxes."

A few days later, I expanded on my case in an opinion essay that was published in the *Rochester Post-Bulletin* and other newspapers around the state. "I believe that the future of Minnesota is at stake," I wrote, citing the importance of state investments in higher education, public safety, and services for the elderly that allowed them to remain in their homes. "Our way of life, what makes Minnesota special and successful, hangs in the balance" in the state budget negotiations, I wrote.

It fell to a court-assigned special master, former Minnesota Supreme Court Chief Justice Kathleen Blatz, to decide which state services were essential to the public safety (such as prisons) and which would have to be suspended during a shutdown. The shutdown's impact was felt more widely than most Minnesotans likely would have predicted. Among the enterprises affected were road construction, housing projects, timber harvesting on state lands, an environmental study of a potential new mine on the Iron Range, and—most painfully for some—the licensing of liquor distributors, which interrupted the flow of beer in Minnesota. There seemed to be no way to break the impasse.

After almost three weeks, I was approached by two distraught state employees at an event in St. Cloud. They were panic-stricken that their unemployment benefits were about to run out and they and their families would be destitute. I realized the shutdown had to end, and there was only one way. I agreed to the Republican proposal to raise their missing $1.4 billion through an additional school aid shift of $700 million and another $700 million in bonds from the Tobacco Trust Fund. With both of those steps, the state was, in effect, borrowing from its own future. In return, the Republicans agreed to no further budget cuts and the elimination of all their policy changes in the budget bills, such as a 15 percent reduction of state employees, restrictions on abortion, and a requirement for voters to show a government-issued photo ID to be issued a ballot. They also agreed to pass a bonding bill in that session of not less than $500 million to put people back to work throughout Minnesota.

Some of my allies were unhappy with my compromise, but I believed I had made the necessary decision to return state government to the people of Minnesota after twenty-two days. I felt further confirmed when a subsequent poll showed approval for the Republican legislature at 17 percent. (A year later, it had dropped even more, to 11 percent!)

It was an enormous relief to have the budget impasse resolved and the legislature dispatched until the next January. I was so thankful for five-month legislative sessions!

The session had the unintended but welcome effect of boosting and solidifying my standing among Minnesota's Democrats, many of whom had viewed me suspiciously after the 2010 DFL primary. I vetoed fifty-eight bills passed by the Republican majority. Those bills would have made draconian changes to the social fabric of Minnesota. Meanwhile, across the river, Wisconsin's Republican governor and his legislature were passing much of the same legislation that I was vetoing. It was very clear to everyone what a difference having a Democratic or a Republican governor made.

A highlight of those first months in office was my first National Governors Association meeting in Washington. On the last morning, President Obama addressed the governors in the East Room of the White House. He stood underneath a famous portrait of President Abraham Lincoln. Chills raced down my spine as I realized that here was our country's first African American president standing in the light of the president who had signed the Emancipation Proclamation and sacrificed his life for doing so. It was one of the most profoundly powerful moments in my life.

In an Oval Office meeting with President Barack Obama

One enormously important project began in the 2011 legislative session: the massive renovation of our State Capitol. That magnificent structure, designed by famed architect Cass Gilbert and completed in 1905, had been in decline for years, and previous administrations had ignored its growing problems. Finally, enough pieces of marble were falling near people's heads to persuade all of us working there that there could be no further avoidance.

The 2011 legislature established the Minnesota State Capitol Preservation Commission, which I chaired. Its twenty-two members consisted of legislative leaders from both parties, the chief justice of the Minnesota Supreme Court, and four public members. The commission met regularly throughout my two terms, worked remarkably well together, and oversaw an extraordinary $301 million renovation of the Capitol.

Unfortunately, the renovation was extremely disruptive to all of us there. I led by example by vacating my office for two and a half years. I moved into cramped quarters in the Veterans Service Building at the other end of the Capitol Mall and traded my scenic view of the mall for one of a parking lot. Being removed even a few blocks from the action during legislative sessions proved challenging, but we survived.

The reward was that in January 2017 we moved back into a magnificently renovated building. Our commission oversaw the multiyear, multimillion-dollar project with no partisan rancor, and it was completed on budget and on time. A few months later, over 60,000 Minnesotans came to the opening weekend to see *their* Capitol. It was one of the most rewarding—and lasting—undertakings of my state stewardship. It is why, when I had my official portrait painted, I stood in front of the renovated Capitol building.

Another project which I began that year and continued throughout my two terms in office was the transformation of the Minnesota judiciary, which until then had been almost entirely male and white. At first, we received little response to our outreach to women and minority attorneys. So, I enlisted my great friend Lee Sheehy to spearhead our initiative. Lee did a superb job building relationships, especially among minority legal organizations, and recruiting well-qualified candidates.

The results speak for themselves. After eight years, I had increased the racial diversity of Minnesota's judges by 98.5 percent. I had appointed 82 percent of all Hispanic judges in Minnesota (nine of eleven judges). I had increased the proportion of women judges in Minnesota by 37 percent and the proportion of female judges in Greater Minnesota by 78 percent.

I appointed Minnesota's first African American female Supreme Court justice, Native American Supreme Court justice,

With the WNBA Champions Minnesota Lynx, 2011

LGBTQ Supreme Court justice, and Hispanic appellate court judge.

This reform is one of my proudest and most lasting achievements. Great credit belongs to Lee Sheehy, without whose herculean efforts it would not have succeeded.

The 2012 legislative session started out more promising than the previous year's. No budget changes were necessary. (In fact, the state's improving economy had boosted revenues and lowered future deficit projections.) There was nothing I had to have from the legislature and, thus, nothing I had to give in return.

In February came the enormous announcement by Mayo Clinic, Minnesota's largest employer and a world-renowned medical center, that it wanted to build a Destination Medical Center in its hometown of Rochester over the next twenty years. That multibillion-dollar investment was essential to making Mayo and Rochester competitive with other premier medical facilities. Theirs was a proposal that would anchor in Minnesota the nation's number one rated medical center, one of the state's best assets for building both prosperity and well-being. What a sensational gift to Minnesota!

To my surprise, some legislators reacted negatively to the proposal, criticizing its cost and the public expenditures necessary. I immediately sprang to the defense of Mayo, saying there were forty-nine other states and several other countries who would jump at the chance being offered to us. That silenced the dissent, and the project proceeded down the legislative gauntlet.

I assigned my chief of staff, Tina Smith, to spearhead the legislation from our office. She was, of course, so superb that, at the session's conclusion, Mayo officials asked me to appoint her to the newly established Destination Medical Center Board, where she was immediately elected its chair. The project is underway today, and Mayo recently announced another commitment of $5 billion to finance its next phase. What a phenomenal boon to Minnesota!

Another huge project appeared during that legislative session. In December 2010, the roof of the Metrodome, home of the Minnesota Vikings and Twins, collapsed under the weight of a heavy, wet snowstorm. Fortunately, it happened on a Sunday morning at 2:00 A.M., so no one was injured. I went to the thirty-year-old stadium in downtown Minneapolis that morning to see the collapsed dome roof, under melted snow and on top of the field.

The Vikings had already said they would not renew their lease, which expired in 2012, and, without a new stadium, would move elsewhere, probably to Los Angeles. That threat had a particular sting for Minnesota sports fans. In 1960, the then–Minneapolis Lakers professional basketball team had moved to Los Angeles to become the Los Angeles Lakers.

The Wilf family, owners of the Vikings, proposed a billion-dollar stadium, about half of which would be financed by the City of Minneapolis and the State of Minnesota. This largest-ever publicly financed project in Minnesota's history attracted intense opinions on both sides. Liberal Democrats denounced a large public subsidy to multimillionaires, while conservative Republicans opposed any such public expenditure.

On the other side were the many thousands of stalwart Vikings fans throughout the state. To them, the loss of the team would have been catastrophic. After fifty years, the Vikings had achieved iconic status in Minnesota. It was far and away the state's most popular sports team.

I strongly supported the project, not only to keep the Vikings in Minnesota, but also to anchor economic revitalization in east Minneapolis. It was a part of the city that had been decimated by the decline and exodus of the flour milling industry, which had begun a half century earlier. Despite that long decline, little had been done to revitalize what had been for nearly a century the economic epicenter of the entire region. I believed this was a chance for revival that Minnesota could ill afford to pass up. It was another example of where government's financial partnership with a private business venture would make the critical difference between success or failure.

The legislation authorizing state funding for a new stadium traveled a rocky path through the session. Fortunately, it had two terrific authors, Senator Julie Rosen of Fairmont and Representative Morrie Lanning of Moorhead. Both were Republicans, since that party was still in the majority. Significantly, both were also from Greater Minnesota, helping to sell this project as an asset for the entire state.

As the final showdowns loomed at the session's end, a fabulous political drama erupted. The Vikings pulled out all the stops and brought their star running back, Adrian Peterson, to the Capitol. He was followed around like the Pied Piper by a gaggle of infatuated legislators. Another star, defensive end Jared Allen, appeared before five hundred raucous fans at a pro-stadium rally in the Mall of America on a Saturday morning, an hour before the mall officially opened. Finally, the day before the House and Senate votes, several hundred more Vikings fans, all dressed in or painted purple, descended on the State Capitol for a thunderous rally. They then set out in a colorful mass to lobby wavering legislators.

As I had predicted, the Vikings' overwhelming popularity created a political tsunami. We even had legislators who had publicly opposed the legislation call us at the last minute and ask for reasons to justify changing their votes! On May 10, the

With Minnesota Vikings players at the Capitol to get U.S. Bank Stadium bill passed, 2012

bill passed 36–30 in the Senate and 71–60 in the House. The *Star Tribune* editorially credited me with "savvy and indefatigable leadership" in removing a threat that had hung over Minnesota sports fans for far too long.

Today, U.S. Bank Stadium is considered one of the finest stadiums in the country, home to the Vikings, to college and high school teams, and to music concerts, monster truck shows, and

Cutting the ribbon to open U.S. Bank Stadium, the new home of the Minnesota Vikings

weekly rollerblading. The stadium has triggered some $3 billion of private sector investment in the area around it. Those private and public investments have totally revitalized east Minneapolis.

One grim event, which occurred on August 17, 2012, was the commemoration of the 150th anniversary of the beginning of the 1862 US–Dakota War. On September 9, 1862, then–Governor Alexander Ramsey proclaimed, according to a Minnesota Public Radio report, "Our course then is plain. The Sioux Indians of Minnesota must be exterminated or driven forever beyond the borders of the State. . . . If any shall escape extinction, the wretched remnant must be driven beyond our borders and our frontier garrisoned with a force sufficient to forever prevent their return."

On the day before the anniversary, I replied,

> I am appalled by Governor Ramsey's words and by his encouragement of vigilante violence against innocent people; and I repudiate them. I know that almost all Minnesotans, living today, would be just as revolted. The viciousness and violence, which were commonplace 150 years ago in Minnesota, are not accepted or allowed now.
>
> I call for tomorrow, the 150th anniversary of August 17, 1862, to be "a Day of Remembrance and Reconciliation in Minnesota." I ask everyone to remember that dark past; to recognize its continuing harm in the present; and to resolve that we will not let it poison the future.
>
> To honor the American soldiers, Dakota people, and settlers who lost their lives in that war, I order that all state flags shall be flown at half-staff from sunrise to sunset on August 17, 2012.

Greeting President Barack Obama as he arrived in Minnesota on Air Force One, 2012

> And I urge everyone participating in the events commemorating this 150th Anniversary to practice not only remembrance, but also reconciliation.

Another enormous event in 2012 was the November election. The reelection of both President Obama and Senator Amy Klobuchar looked secure in Minnesota. However, a couple of the state's eight congressional elections were going to be close. And the Republican majorities in the Minnesota House and Senate were in jeopardy. They had suffered in the court of public opinion for their role in the 2011 state government shutdown and had failed to recover.

Two other ballot measures were hugely important. The Republican-controlled legislature placed two constitutional amendments on the November ballot. Unfortunately, even though I strongly opposed both amendments, Minnesota's Constitution does not permit the governor to veto those legislative actions.

The first proposed, "Shall the Minnesota Constitution be amended to provide that only a union of one man and one woman shall be valid or recognized as a marriage in Minnesota?" As debate over the proposal deepened among voters and elected officials, the *Star Tribune* reported that Roman Catholic bishops from Minnesota's dioceses were told during an audience with Pope Benedict XVI that they ought to support the preservation of traditional (i.e., heterosexual) marriage. Minneapolis–St. Paul Archbishop John Nienstedt became a central figure in organizing religious support for the amendment. He committed $650,000 to the cause and joined other religious leaders and supporters of the amendment for a demonstration at the State Capitol in September.

That was a formidable lineup in favor of the amendment. A similar amendment had been approved every time it was voted upon in thirty other states. The initial prospects in Minnesota did not favor its defeat.

Throughout 2012, an unprecedented grassroots movement developed to defeat the amendment. The lead organization, Minnesotans United, had 27,000 volunteers knock on over 400,000 doors and make over 900,000 phone calls in the final eight days of the campaign alone.

Polls showed shifting public opinions throughout the year. In July, a SurveyUSA poll had 52 percent of Minnesotans supporting the amendment, while 37 percent opposed it. On October 26–28, another SurveyUSA poll showed 48 percent in favor of the amendment and 47 percent opposed.

It took the enormous efforts of thousands of grassroots volunteers to make the difference. On election day, more than 51 percent of Minnesota voters opposed the amendment, while 47 percent supported it. One and a half million of my fellow citizens spoke out in favor of marriage equality. It was one of the moments I was most proud to be a Minnesotan.

The other Republican constitutional amendment was also awful. It was part of their party's long-running nationwide efforts to twist America's democracy in their favor. Making bogus claims of voter fraud, which were unfounded and untrue, they proposed that a form of government-issued photographic identification would be required before anyone could vote in Minnesota's municipal, state, and federal elections. It asked, "Shall the Minnesota Constitution be amended to require all voters to present valid photo identification to vote and to require the state to provide free identification to eligible voters, effective July 1, 2013?"

The amendment sounded innocuous to many voters, but it was not. Government-issued photo ID cards bearing an up-to-date address are standard pocketbook items for most middle-class Minnesotans. But for the youngest and the oldest voters, such cards can be hard to find or come by. Seniors in care facilities whose driver's licenses have lapsed; homeless and

With civil rights leader Julian Bond, circa 2012

impoverished people who don't drive; and students seeking to vote on campus rather than at their parents' home precincts all would have found voting more difficult had the amendment been approved.

At first, the amendment appeared headed for easy passage. In July, a SurveyUSA poll had 65 percent of Minnesota voters supporting the amendment, while only 28 percent opposed it. On October 26–28, SurveyUSA found that 55 percent favored the amendment. Only 40 percent opposed it.

However, by November 1–3, support and opposition were tied at 48 percent. And on election day, November 6, the amendment was defeated by almost 54 percent opposed to 46 percent in favor.

What happened? A major media campaign educated Minnesotans about the true motives of the amendment's proponents and the pitfalls caused by its passage. Former Republican Governor Arne Carlson and I teamed up for a television commercial, expressing our bipartisan opposition to the measure. Although we proved ourselves not quite ready for prime time, I was told that the ad was a very effective persuader. Once again, the collective wisdom of most Minnesota voters prevailed.

The election produced very decisive victories for DFL candidates and progressive causes. The most far-reaching development of the night was the switch in control of the Minnesota legislature from Republican to DFL majorities. As a result, the 2013 session would mark the first time in twenty-two years that Democrats controlled the governor's office and both branches of the legislature—a political lineup that has come to be called a trifecta.

Thus, 2012 proved to be a very good year. Despite opposition majorities in both the House and Senate, very important legislation, financing both Mayo Clinic's Destination Medical Center and U.S. Bank Stadium, was approved. Two awful proposed constitutional amendments were defeated. And majority

Touring the Terracotta Army at the Qin Shi Huang Mausoleum during a trade mission to China, 2012

control of both the Minnesota Senate and House was flipped from Republican to Democrat.

I had an important role in all those outcomes. I had effectively branded Republican legislators as unreasonable for their unwillingness to agree to a budget compromise in 2011 and forcing the state government shutdown. Their resulting disapproval ratings of 17 percent in the fall of 2011, down to 11 percent in the fall of 2012, precipitated their defeats that November.

For me personally, the major downer in 2012 was that my legs were experiencing unusual weakness and often shooting pains when I walked. I was diagnosed as suffering from stenosis, or constriction in my lower spine. Thus, I underwent the first of what would turn out to be six spinal surgeries during the next eleven years.

Thanks to the skill of my superb Mayo surgeon, Dr. Jeremy Fogelson, and Mayo's fabulous nursing and support staffs, my surgery was successful. The shooting pains in my legs permanently disappeared, and the weakness in my legs improved. Thus strengthened, both physically and politically, I was ready to face the challenges and exploit the opportunities that 2013 presented.

— CHAPTER ELEVEN —

MAKING UP GROUND

> "Better the occasional faults of a government that acts in a spirit of charity, than the consistent omissions of a government frozen in the ice of its own indifference."
>
> —*Franklin D. Roosevelt, 1936*

The year 2013 started out as a promising one. State government still faced a projected $1.1 billion deficit, according to the Department of Management and Budget, but that was far less than two years before. It gave me an opening to advance my signature proposal from the 2010 campaign: to raise the state's personal income tax rate on the richest Minnesotans. A two-percentage-point tax rate increase on the wealthiest two percent of Minnesota taxpayers would raise $2.1 billion, eliminating the projected deficit.

The Minnesota Department of Revenue's biennial "Tax Incidence Study" had documented for years that Minnesotans with the highest incomes paid a smaller percentage of those incomes in total state and local taxes (personal income, property, and sales) than almost everyone else in Minnesota. Another study, by the Institute on Taxation and Economic Policy, confirmed the Department of Revenue's analysis. It found that middle-class Minnesotans paid 26 percent more state and local taxes per dollar of income than did the top one percent of our state's income earners.

In other words, our state's tax system was seriously regressive. Raising the personal income rate by two percentage points on couples making over $250,000 per year and individuals earning more than $150,000 did not eliminate that regressivity, but it did significantly reduce it. And it should be noted that those higher tax rates applied not to entire incomes, but only to the share of one's income that exceeded those levels.

In my State of the State address that February, I said,

> What do I believe offers the best hope for a better future to most Minnesotans? I want Minnesota to provide the best jobs for our citizens, the best lives for their families, and the best environment for our businesses to provide those jobs.
>
> Those who measure "business climate" only by tax rankings will question my strategy, although many surveys rate Minnesota lower in overall taxes than most are led to believe. We're 15th among the states in taxes, according to the Minnesota Center for Fiscal Excellence. And we rank 11th highest in per capita income.
>
> However, Minnesota has not been considered a "low tax" state during my almost four decades of public service. And the facts show that states offering businesses and their top executives the lowest taxes usually provide the rest of their citizens with the lowest incomes, the fewest public services, and the highest crime rates. Furthermore, their job growth typically lags "high value and high performance" states like Minnesota.
>
> So, yes, I absolutely meant what I said. I want

> Minnesota to provide the best jobs for our citizens, the best lives for their families, and the best support for our businesses to provide those jobs. I want Minnesota state government to provide the best value for everyone's hard-earned tax dollars and the most efficient, effective services anywhere.
>
> I want Minnesota to offer the world's best educations for ALL of our citizens, children, and grandchildren. Educations which begin early in life and continue throughout life; so that all of us can learn the skills, and relearn the new skills, necessary to succeed in a rapidly changing and ever-more-competitive global economy.

Thus, I proposed state funding for all-day kindergarten statewide. I had seen the benefits to the educational opportunities it provided to five-year-old children. What I didn't appreciate initially was its financial benefits for the parents of five-year-olds, who would be relieved of a year of very expensive childcare. Several of my young office staffers opened my eyes to this phenomenon!

There were many other progressive measures that DFL legislators and I cosponsored in the legislative session to increase funding for all elementary, secondary, and higher education, which had been savaged by the previous Republican governors' and legislators' unwillingness to raise revenues in the face of budget shortfalls.

My critics criticized my "spending increases." In my State of the State, I pointed out that most were necessary to make up for previous spending reductions. I said, "Analyzing other areas of state government spending yields similar results. During the past decade, our state leaders reduced expenditures for many public services, both in real dollars and in comparison to other states. The latest survey places Minnesota 33rd among the states in total expenditures for K–12 education per $1000 of personal income; 37th for health and hospitals; 19th for police protection; and 48th for fighting fires."

We had important ground to make up.

The most dramatic triumph of the 2013 session was the passage of a state guarantee of marriage equality. At the session's beginning, just two months after voters defeated the Republican-backed constitutional amendment to prohibit same-sex marriage, I did not imagine there was a chance to legalize those unions. Nevertheless, in my State of the State address that February, I reiterated the support I had expressed for marriage equality the year before. I said, "Let me mention one other cause, which is controversial, but consistent with my faith and my principles. And, more importantly, consistent with this country's founding principles and its Constitution. I believe that every Minnesotan should have the freedom to marry legally the person she or he loves, whether of the same or other sex.

"Last year, Minnesotans began a conversation about why marriage matters, and we found our common belief that it is about love, commitment, and responsibility. I want Minnesota to be a state that affirms that freedom for one means freedom for everyone, and where no one is told it is illegal to marry the person you love."

To my surprise, the same overwhelming grassroots support that prevailed in November 2012, combined with effective lobbying, brought the legislation to the floors in both chambers.

There, its passage reminded me of President John F. Kennedy's book *Profiles in Courage*. Several legislators who knew they were risking their careers voted in favor of it, even when their votes were not needed for its passage. They just knew that it was the right thing to do—and so enormously important.

Addressing a crowd before signing the Marriage Equality Act, May 2013

On a brilliantly sunny May 13, 2013, I had the privilege and the thrill to sign that bill into law on the lawn in front of the Capitol before several thousand cheering supporters. It was a profoundly emotional moment for me and even more so for all whose lives were changed by it. One elderly woman approached me with tears streaming down her face. "I thought I would never live to see this day," she told me.

In June, at the Minneapolis Gay Pride parade, I received the most overwhelming appreciation from any crowd throughout my entire career. It still sends shivers down my spine! It's the reason I did this work: to make a difference in other people's lives.

How did Minnesota fare under these new policies? And, further, how did Minnesota's experience differ from that of its neighbor, friend, and friendly rival, Wisconsin?

The two states share much in common: similar populations, histories, and political traditions. But they chose quite different paths beginning with the 2010 midterm elections. While Minnesotans were experimenting with entrusting their state government to Democrats, Wisconsin was running the opposite scenario. There, voters had elected conservative Republican Scott Walker governor in 2010 and had given Republicans a governing majority in the state legislature. University of Minnesota political science professor Lawrence Jacobs called it "a natural experiment" in which the results of modern conservatism and modern progressivism could be directly compared at the state level. (Of course, I didn't have a Democratic legislative majority until after the 2012 election.)

In a November 23, 2013, *New York Times* article, Professor Jacobs asked a simple question: "Which side of the experiment—the new right or modern progressivism—has been most effective in creating jobs and improving business opportunities, not to mention living conditions?" He crunched the numbers and presented the experiment's early results.

The argument then in vogue during the Tea Party era was that tax cuts and deregulation not only would keep state budgets balanced but would also lead to the kind of robust economic growth that was still needed several years into the recovery from the financial crisis of 2008. In Minnesota, we'd rejected that argument. Instead, we raised state revenues through a tax increase on the wealthiest residents. But instead of money and business fleeing the state, Minnesota had the fifth fastest growing economy in the country in 2013 and *Forbes* ranked it the eighth best state for business. However, Jacobs reported, "Three years into Mr. Walker's term, Wisconsin lags behind Minnesota in job creation and economic growth." Tax cuts and deregulation did not deliver their promised results. Wisconsin was thirty-fourth in the country in job growth and in the bottom half of states in *Forbes*' ranking of best states for business.

The taxes raised in Minnesota were not only used to pay overdue bills or to support existing state obligations; they were also invested in several major projects that hinged on forging partnerships between the state government and some of the state's largest businesses and institutions, including the Mayo

Clinic Destination Medical Center, U.S. Bank Stadium, and the Mall of America. These public–private partnerships showed that Minnesota was serious about growth and was willing to be creative to achieve it.

Policymakers and business leaders in Minnesota have long understood that a major part of the state's economic power is built on its education system. By investing in education, businesses throughout the state can hire the best and brightest and know that more homegrown talent is receiving the education needed to succeed in the future. So, while many states slashed education funding as they grappled with economic challenges, we invested most of the new revenue into schools, including statewide all-day kindergarten. At the same time, as Jacobs noted, "By contrast, Mr. Walker's strategy limited Wisconsin's ability to invest in infrastructure that would have catalyzed private-sector expansion, and he cut state funding of K–12 schools by more than 15 percent. Per student, this was the seventh sharpest decline in the country."

One of the most contentious issues during these years—not just in Minnesota, but across the whole country—was the passing and implementation of the Affordable Care Act (also called "Obamacare"), which President Obama signed into law in 2010. Under the new law, the federal government provided money for individual states to establish health insurance exchanges as well as expand their Medicaid coverage. Though the federal money was available for all states, each state had to decide whether to accept that money.

In Minnesota, Medicaid expansion under the Affordable Care Act enabled us to cover an additional 35,000 residents. And insurance premiums for Minnesotans ranked among the lowest in the nation. Wisconsin took a different approach, refusing the federal dollars to support the state exchanges and refusing to expand its Medicaid coverage.

Jacobs was blunt: "Evidence and common sense should

matter more in our overheated political debates. The lesson from the upper Midwest is that rigid anti-tax dogma fails to deliver a convincing optimistic vision that widens economic opportunity and security. The excesses of liberalism may lurk, but Minnesota is building a modern progressivism that plows a hopeful path."

While I greatly appreciated Dr. Jacobs's analysis and agreed with it, I always managed to have a cordial relationship with Governor Walker, as I also did with North Dakota's Republican Governors Doug Burgum and Jack Dalrymple (with whom I grew up in Minnesota!). I have always said that politics is like a sandbox: "You don't get to choose your playmates. You play with whoever else shows up!"

Governor Walker and I worked together to build a much-needed, four-lane bridge over the St. Croix River, just south of Stillwater. Stillwater's downtown streets had become clogged by traffic waiting to access an archaic, two-lane lift bridge that was the only nearby connection with neighboring Wisconsin communities across the river.

We both pledged half of the necessary funds from our transportation budgets, and the bridge was built from each state's shore to meet in the middle. However, when the two sides met at the midpoint, their heights differed by six inches! The correction cost a couple months and a few million dollars to complete; then we attended the grand opening together.

On October 1, 2013, as required by the federal Affordable Care Act, we launched "MNsure," a state-run online marketplace for Minnesotans lacking health insurance to shop for health plans and receive financial assistance to afford them. It was initially an operational disaster and easily the most traumatic governing event I had experienced since the state government shutdown in July 2011.

In hindsight, I saw why sophisticated companies like Target launch their new product lines and technologies in small, obscure markets, so they can work out the bugs in their systems before they go national. We launched MNsure full-scale from the beginning in the face of strident Republican opposition and under the glare of statewide publicity. It was not a pretty sight.

The day before it launched, I asked MNsure's executive director if she was sure the system would perform properly. She said she was. She was wrong. The computerized system suffered major breakdowns, and some callers were placed on hold for as long as two hours before they were connected to it. The number of staff was woefully inadequate to handle the flood of complaints.

MNsure struggled through its first year but showed consistent improvement thereafter. By 2016, out of roughly 190,000 total customers in the individual market, 60 percent bought their insurance through MNsure's exchange, a 34 percent increase in enrollment, which in 2014 included only 12 percent of the individual market.

"Altogether, Minnesotans are poised to save $372 million in tax credits," said Allison O'Toole, MNsure's new chief executive officer. "That is real money for Minnesotans."

Some residents weren't eligible for federal subsidies, but they did qualify for state aid under a one-time program passed by the Minnesota legislature. That $310 million program provided 25 percent premium discounts to people who weren't eligible for the federal tax credits. (And it was another benefit of our rectifying the state's fiscal situation, which generated the funds to provide that assistance.)

Ten years after its launch, the *Star Tribune* reported in 2023 that "Minnesota's health insurance marketplace has reason to celebrate: a record of successfully delivering benefits to Minnesota families. MNsure has matured in its operational efficiency and customer service and has achieved record enrollment while delivering nearly $2 billion in health care cost savings to Minnesotans over ten years." Despite the initial challenges, the success of the program was hard to deny. When combined with the expansion of private health insurance and Medicaid, "MNsure has played an important role in reducing the statewide uninsured rate from 8.2 percent in 2013 to a record low of 4 percent."

Vitally though, the program's effects were felt not just in high rates of insurance and lower costs of insurance, but in actual health care savings for Minnesotans. Problems as complicated as health care aren't solved without a lot of patience for complexity and willingness to adapt. But sometimes that patience is rewarded.

Despite all its successes, 2013 turned very painful for me physically when I tore the tendon from my left hip bone. I was racing down the stairs in the Governor's Residence to get to an event, reached the first-floor landing, and made a sharp right turn. I heard and felt a loud "pop" in my hip, and my next step became very painful. Every step hurt for the rest of the year.

Doctors at Mayo Clinic, who were otherwise so accurate in their diagnoses and effective in their treatments, missed the boat this time. After numerous tests, I was prescribed platelet transfusions, which twice did nothing to relieve my pain. I had to gut it out every day for months, waiting for those platelets to effect a reattachment. Finally, another doctor told me that surgery would be necessary to reattach the tendon to the hip bone and would require me to wear a body cast for the following three months.

Welcome to the new year.

I had the hip tendon reattachment surgery in January 2014 and found myself in a body cast that extended from my waist down to my left knee. Although I was thus limited in my movements, my energy and enthusiasm for my work remained unabated. When asked by the press, I replied that my brain did not reside in my hip, so my ability to function on the job was unimpaired!

That wasn't entirely true. I couldn't travel around the state, as was my wont. I couldn't even travel very comfortably to my office in the Capitol.

So, my wonderful staff brought my office to me at the Governor's Residence, three miles west of the Capitol on historic Summit Avenue. The study next to my bedroom was converted into a small conference room, and I held meetings there. The residence's elevator enabled me to get downstairs for legislative breakfast meetings, which were a long-standing tradition of my residence hospitality during legislative sessions. Since almost no one ever objected to going to the lovely English Tudor mansion that had been donated to the state in the 1960s, I heard almost no complaints about these arrangements. And since the legislature's activities dominated state government's work during those winter months, my physical location was hardly noticed.

Fortunately, I recovered in time to meet on March 1 with His Holiness the Dalai Lama on his visit to Minneapolis. We met in his hotel room so that I could welcome him to Minnesota before his public appearances. His staff evidently expected it to be a brief meeting and appeared ready to whisk him away. However, I told him that in 2007 I had traveled to Lhasa, Tibet, which he had been forced to leave at age three. For the next half hour, we engaged in a wonderful conversation in which I shared my impressions of his country and he mused about life there. He gave me a silk prayer shawl, which I treasure to this day.

With a group of children at an event for the Muslim American Society Minnesota, circa 2014

Early in the 2014 session, I also unveiled an idea I had been germinating for some time: an “Unsession.” Years before, the soft drink 7UP had billed itself the “Un-Cola!” I borrowed this brand and applied it to my proposal: a legislative session devoted to undoing the hundreds of obsolete laws, rules, and procedures that had wormed their way into state statutes.

The idea had been proposed many times in previous administrations. But it finally caught on. Briana Bierschbach reported at the session’s end that, despite past failures at this statutory decluttering, “With 1,175 unsession proposals already signed into law by Wednesday afternoon—covering everything from tax preparation to business permitting—the governor claims a successful exception to the government-reform rule. And the count could rise, since Dayton has more time to sign or veto bills.” Seeing the “Unsession” idea catch on was gratifying, but there was more for me to love about the 2014 session. It produced the first increase in the state's minimum wage since 2005. The state wage floor went from $6.15 to $8.00 in August 2014, to $9.00 in August 2015, and to $9.50 in August 2016—after which it would be indexed to inflation to keep climbing. Thanks to that legislation, the 2025 minimum wage in Minnesota is at $11.13—not as high as California's $16.50 or Washington State's $16.66, but a far cry from Wisconsin's meager $7.25.

More than 325,000 of Minnesota's lowest-wage workers received that 2014 raise. I pointed out that a worker with a family of four, working a forty-hour week, would still be earning below the federal poverty level. I said that people should be able to work their way into the middle class, and studies had shown that those increased incomes would be spent immediately and locally for family necessities.

What's more: I was able to secure $72 million in bonding authorization for a major Greater Minnesota water project called the Lewis & Clark Diversion. I pushed hard to secure that funding, knowing how desperately a new source of water was needed in the southwestern corner of Minnesota. By 2014, a water shortage in that region had reached a crisis stage. Worthington was enforcing severe water use restrictions on lawns and other outdoor areas. Limits on water usage in the region were also restricting business expansions at, for example, Worthington's large turkey-processing plant.

A potential new source of abundant fresh water was from the already-built Lewis & Clark Water Diversion Project in South Dakota. It channeled water from the Missouri River to areas of southeastern South Dakota, right on the Minnesota border. There the project stopped.

That first leg had been financed almost entirely by federal funds. They had been obtained primarily by South Dakota Senator Tom Daschle, the powerful U.S. Senate majority leader.

When Tom left office after losing to Republican John Thune in 2004, federal funding essentially stopped at the state line.

I recognized that if the pipeline were to be extended into Minnesota, state funds would have to pay for it. However, convincing DFL legislators to include funding for it in the state bonding bill, thus benefitting counties like Rock, which were rock-solid (pun intended!) Republican, was an extremely difficult task.

Some also said that I favored Worthington because it was my great-grandfather's first Minnesota home. That was untrue. I championed this project because it was the right thing to do. The economic vitality and quality of life in the region were being severely harmed by the lack of water, and this pipeline was the solution.

I insisted the necessary funding be included in the bonding bill. In 2015, the water reached the Rock County Rural Water District outside Luverne, the county seat. Then it flowed to the Lincoln–Pipestone Rural Water System, which served an area that included thirty-eight cities in ten counties. The water allowed Luverne to become the site of Minnesota's first shrimp hatchery and harbor, a commercial-scale shrimp producer. When the project was completed, more than 300,000 residents and important industries received Lewis & Clark water over an area of five thousand square miles.

DFL legislators were right about one thing: Rock County is rock-solid Republican. In my 2010 gubernatorial election, I lost Rock County by 20.62 percentage points. In 2014, after getting life-enhancing fresh water for the county, I lost it by 21.29 percent. (I also lost neighboring Nobles County, including Worthington, both years but by a slightly smaller margin in 2014.)

In politics, virtue is sometimes not "its own reward." It is the *only* reward!

Laying sandbags during flooding in Moorhead, Minnesota

Shortly after my cast was removed that spring, Minnesota experienced a rash of major flooding. I was able—as governor, not as a reelection candidate—to travel widely to view the damage, meet with local officials, and bring in emergency and natural resource officials, who could provide follow-up funding and help. I invited the area legislators from both parties to show that my visits were nonpolitical. They almost always showed up! And, of course, my appearances were widely reported in the press.

It was the perfect way to get ready for my campaign for reelection that November. And I had gained a wonderful running mate and political partner, my chief of staff, Tina Smith. My first lieutenant governor, Yvonne Prettner Solon, was ready to retire. Although Tina did not bring to our ticket Yvonne's geographical balance, she proved to be a terrific campaigner and a superb fundraiser.

At the outset, the political climate was not favorable. According to Dr. Eric Ostermeier in *Smart Politics*, Minnesotans had elected a Democratic governor with a Democrat in the White House in just four of twenty-eight cycles since statehood. Our Democratic gubernatorial candidates were 0–12 historically when their president was serving in his *second* term (or greater, with FDR). That was the situation I faced in 2014 with Barack Obama serving his sixth year in the White House.

Nevertheless, in my State of the State address on April 30, I made the case for my reelection. Like every politician in those years, my successes and failures were measured by job creation and employment numbers. I proudly reported that in 2014, there were more jobs in Minnesota than at any point in its history, and 150,000 more than when my term began. Collaboration between the public and the private sectors was delivering results across the state, including U.S. Bank Stadium, the new home for the Minnesota Vikings, the presence of which promised to revitalize a neglected portion of downtown Minneapolis.

That collaborative spirit hadn't only delivered for the Twin Cities. I called attention to developments outside the metro area as well. I argued that "Perhaps the most transformative development project anywhere will occur in Rochester, thanks to the world-renowned Mayo Clinic's decision to build its expanded Destination Medical Center there. Already Minnesota's largest private employer, Mayo expects this multi-billion-dollar expansion to double its employment over the next twenty years." That expansion would not be solely the result of private investment. The state legislature, the city of Rochester, and Olmsted County were major investors as well. The Mayo Clinic was already world renowned, but this new endeavor, I argued, "will establish Minnesota as one of the world's best locations for advanced medical research; the

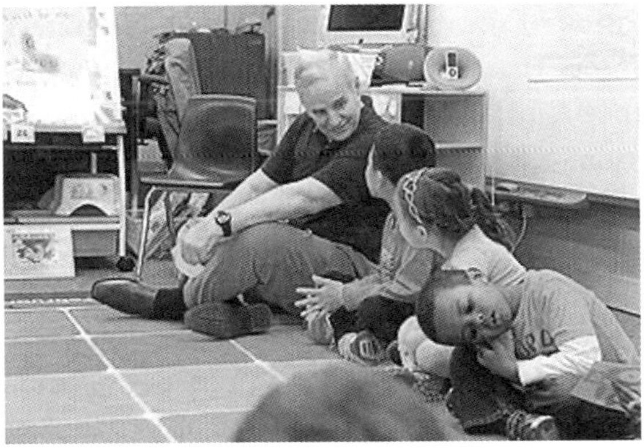

Visiting with students at Westview Elementary, May 2015

development of new medical treatments and technologies," as well as thousands of new jobs.

High-skill jobs require high-skill workers. And the state's long history of educational investment was a major reason why so many of those jobs exist in Minnesota. At the beginning of my first term that investment was in decline. But instead of cutting it further in the face of a budget deficit, we'd increased K–12 funding by $223 million, created an alternative pathway for securing a teaching license to ensure every classroom had a great teacher in it, and started a "Read Well by Third Grade" literacy initiative. The legislature had made a $485 million investment in education in 2013, increasing the per-pupil formula used to calculate school funding allotments, supporting special education, and enacting one of my biggest education priorities and proudest political achievements: all-day kindergarten.

I also wanted to remind voters that we had accomplished all of these things with fiscal discipline. "[D]uring the past two and half years," I noted, "we have repaid all of the $2.8 billion previously borrowed from our schools. Now, school districts can put their money into classrooms, not bank loans. Let us vow that no more will we balance state budgets by creating deficits in school budgets."

I had no intention of resting on these educational laurels, though. I told voters that if I were given a second term, I wanted to go farther. A major area of concern was state support for higher education, which had fallen to its lowest level since 1981. While we'd begun to reverse that trend with a $248.5 million increase in state funding that year, I insisted we still had a long way to go.

And despite all the criticisms of and court challenges to the Affordable Care Act, Minnesota had made tremendous strides in coverage and cost under its provisions. The MNsure program had a rough start. But things were looking up. And the proof was in the numbers. "Among the states, we have the fifth lowest percentage of citizens without health insurance coverage. Eight percent of our residents are uninsured, compared to the national average of 14.8 percent. And our state's entire health care network deserves credit for enabling MNsure to offer the lowest insurance rates of any health exchange. These low rates have helped MNsure enroll over 206,000 Minnesotans in affordable health coverage—many for the first time. MNsure didn't start well, but it's gotten better, and it will keep

Getting ice-cold water poured on my head for a charity fundraiser at the Minnesota State Fair, 2014

on improving." In fact, later in 2014, I was able to announce more good news about MNsure. After its rocky start, MNsure in 2014 was performing as intended. "For the second year in a row, Minnesota will have the lowest insurance exchange rates in the country," I said in October.

I'd made my case to the voters of Minnesota. Now it was up to them to decide if I'd done enough.

To my good fortune, the 2014 election in Minnesota broke with the expected midterm election pattern. Unlike four years previously, my reelection contest was never close, even though the year proved to be another bad one for Democrats nationally. The Republican Party endorsed a little-known Hennepin County commissioner and former suburban legislator, Jeff Johnson. He had spent the previous years assiduously courting the right-wing activists who controlled their party's election apparatus.

I learned later that Johnson's operatives believed they would best me in the five televised debates, but they were proven wrong. To begin, every time we were introduced as "Governor Dayton" and "Commissioner Johnson" it worked to my advantage. And Johnson proved to be a doctrinaire but uninspiring spokesperson for his very conservative ideology.

Nor was he all that well informed. One of my favorite moments came at a Sunday morning KSTP-televised debate, during which we were asked what our definition of "middle class" was. I immediately answered, "Between $50,000 and $60,000 (annual income)." Johnson basically didn't know.

Another great moment occurred during our last televised debate on Twin Cities Public Television's widely watched *Almanac* public affairs program the Friday night before the election. Commissioner Johnson's campaign had been running a commercial showing him with a pair of hand-held clippers

President Bill Clinton came to Minnesota to campaign for me in 2014

trimming some protruding tufts of grass. When he used his opening debate remarks to criticize one of my supposed failures, I replied, "Jeff, you're just like your commercial. You're clipping at one small clump of grass, while ignoring that the rest of the lawn is in great shape."

He appeared completely flustered and taken aback by my rejoinder, and all the steam seemed to go out of his subsequent jabs. I left confident that I was ending the campaign unscathed and heading for victory.

On election night, we had a small dinner gathering for Tina's and my immediate families and key staff. It ran long, so I excused myself and went alone to my hotel room to watch the first returns at 8:00 P.M. Just as I turned on the national network news, ABC announced at 8:01 that Tina and I had been elected in Minnesota! After the late election night in 2010 that had turned into a month-long marathon, it was a great relief and thrill to win so quickly and decisively.

The final count had us winning by 109,856 votes. For the first time in twenty years—a period in which Minnesotans dabbled extensively in third-party politics—the winning gubernatorial candidate in Minnesota received more than 50 percent of the vote.

Unfortunately, our decisive victory did not transfer to the legislative elections. Republicans preyed upon the increasingly stark divide between metro and rural Minnesota. While Tina and I won overwhelmingly in the seven-county Minneapolis–St. Paul metro area, Duluth, and the Iron Range, we lost in fifty-three of the eighty-seven counties. DFLers maintained a narrow majority in the state Senate, but the House flipped to a Republican majority. I knew that change and the way it was wrought was likely to impede the work I wanted state government to accomplish.

Nationally, it was a bad midterm election for the Democrats. Republicans won twenty-four governor's seats; Democrats, only eleven. Only eighteen of our fifty states would be led by Democratic governors. It was even worse in the congressional elections. With a final total of 247 seats in the House and 54 seats in the Senate, the Republicans gained their largest majority in the U.S. Congress since 1929. It would be a tough last two years for President Obama. And a tough next four years for me.

— CHAPTER TWELVE —

DAYTON UNBOUND

"Democracy is the worst of all forms of government . . . except for all the rest."

— *Winston Churchill (paraphrased)*

I began my second term as governor on January 5, 2015. It was something Minnesota hadn't seen in twenty-eight years: the second-consecutive-term inauguration of a DFL governor.

I stated my priorities in the 2016–17 biennial budget proposal I submitted to the legislature in late January. My plan used most of a $1 billion projected budget surplus to extend preschool to more four-year-olds, offer childcare tax credits to families, and provide free breakfast for all students up to third grade. The proposal also eliminated a series of corporate tax loopholes.

I also proposed major new legislation that would require buffers of vegetation beginning fifty feet from lakes, rivers, streams, and water-bearing ditches on all the state's lands, public and private. The fouling of Minnesota's waters by agricultural and other runoff had reached critical proportions in too many areas of our state. The Minnesota Pollution Control Agency reported in early 2015 that of ninety streams inspected in southwestern Minnesota, only three could fully support aquatic life, and only one was deemed safe for swimming. Though this problem had been building for a long time, no one previously had proposed doing anything significant about it.

This was the kind of initiative I believed had to wait until my second and—as I had already announced—my final term. As I expected, it aroused the fervent opposition of some farm organizations, whose support I had needed politically for my reelection. Now I was free to do the right thing. I said at the beginning of the year that I would be "Dayton Unbound."

In my State of the State address on April 9, I defended my budget and buffer proposals. I noted that growth in employment, incomes, and profits—not tax increases—had caused our state's biennial budget forecast to go from a $6.2 billion deficit in 2011 to a $1.9 billion surplus for the 2016–17 biennium. Minnesota's economy was flourishing again. And people were noticing. That year, *Politico* magazine ranked Minnesota as "The Best American State," while Forbes ranked the state second for "Quality of Life" and third for "Best Place to Make a Living." With a robust economy and budget surplus, I believed it was time for state government to reinvest in the government service Minnesotans valued most: education. In my first term, the major education policy achievement was all-day kindergarten. Some questioned the interest, others the need, and still more worried about the cost. But only a year after the bill was signed into law, the rate of five-year-olds enrolled in all-day kindergarten went from just 54 percent to 99.6 percent. State funding made all the difference.

I wanted to go further. So, I asked for an additional $694.6 million. The significance of that figure was not lost on me. We had achieved a major reinvestment in public education and had done so under both Republican and DFL legislative control. The per-pupil formula had increased. A new literacy initiative

Signing a bill into law with a special witness

was in place. Special education funding was up. We'd even increased funding for school breakfasts and lunches. Given all these changes, some people were asking, "Well, haven't we done enough?"

But, in my address, I wanted to put all this in perspective. I noted that the most recent Census Bureau report on public education finances ranked Minnesota twenty-fourth among the states in per-pupil expenditures for K–12 education. I felt that an *average* commitment to educating our children was not nearly good enough. They deserved more. Years of cutting education to pay for other priorities had added up. We were way behind. And only consistent public investment, year after year, was going to get things back to where they needed to be.

My budget proposal for that year also included initiatives for funding pre-kindergarten programs for all the state's four-year-olds, growing the childcare scholarship funds, eliminating the waitlist for Head Start, and expanding tax credits to help parents cover the cost of childcare. My proposals added up to

372 million additional dollars flowing to programs supporting children four and under.

Parents and students were feeling the fiscal pressure at the other end of the education spectrum too. We hadn't only disinvested in pre-K and K–12 education; we'd also neglected higher education. The University of Minnesota and Minnesota State systems were tremendous assets to the state, but they needed the state's support too. Nearly $250 million was cut from higher education in 2011. In 2013, the legislature restored what was cut. But that was not enough.

Families in both systems were facing higher tuition bills, and students were graduating with far too much educational debt—the fifth highest in the country. We had enacted tuition freezes the previous year. But it was time to do more. In my address, I explained, "I am proposing those tuition freezes be continued into the next two years. I also ask the legislature to support needed increases in the state's financial aid programs for Minnesota students."

The speech also afforded me a chance to let legislators and Minnesotans know that despite the opposition my buffer strip proposal had attracted, I had no intention of backing down. Clean water is Minnesota's signature natural resource. I would not sit by and do nothing while it was spoiled. I explained that some lakes, rivers, and streams had become dangerously polluted. I recalled speaking with a Minnesotan who lived in a town that provided free bottled water to its residents when its water treatment plant malfunctioned and noted that "That's just the way it is, living here." I couldn't accept unhealthy water as "just the way it is," and I felt that most Minnesotans could get on board with this buffer initiative.

So, I challenged the legislators to pass the bill, despite its opposition: "You, our state's 201 legislators, *are* the bill's future. Passing it is your responsibility."

I expected that 2015 would be a very good legislative session. Despite losing a DFL majority in the House, I thought Tina's and my reelection mandate from Minnesota's voters would give us strong momentum.

I was severely disappointed. Republican legislative leaders, following the lead of their congressional counterparts, showed no interest in collaborating with Democrats on a shared agenda. Then I was skewered by most Republicans and many Democrats for proposing significant salary increases for my cabinet officers, whose salaries had been frozen for more than a decade. Back in my early days in politics, I had learned an important lesson from then-Governor Rudy Perpich about supporting my top people, financially and otherwise. If I wanted them to stand up for me, I needed to stand up for them. A new Salary Commission had greatly increased the top salaries permitted, and I took full advantage of it.

However, immediate commissioner salary increases of $30,000 and $40,000 were too much for legislators, for whom those amounts were more like annual salaries, and who had not received a raise since 1999. I was advised to propose phasing in increases over several years, but that would have meant denying my own commissioners a raise so that my successors and their commissioners would receive the benefits. I stuck it out, endured the attacks, and finally prevailed at the cost of considerable political capital.

Since the 2015 legislative session set agency and program budgets for the following biennium, we had to resolve our considerable fiscal differences in the final days. My proposal for protecting the state's water from agricultural pollution was also a major sticking point at the session's end. It took a veto and a second try in a special session to enact something I disliked but could "agree to."

The final compromise required 50-foot buffers adjacent to public rivers, creeks, and wetlands, but just 16.5-foot buffers along publicly owned ditches. In both cases, implementation of the requirement was delayed longer than I had originally proposed. Privately owned bodies of water were not covered by the new state requirement but would need to answer to orders made by the state's ninety county soil and water conservation districts. Counties were authorized to issue up to $500 fines to property owners who did not comply.

This buffer law was called by the Nature Conservancy the "most significant advancement in Minnesota water policy" since the 1991 Wetland Conservation Act. Others were less charitable. I was greatly disappointed by the final outcome, but it was achieved over the strident opposition of some legislators, beginning with the Republican House author of my bill, Paul Torkelson. (Since Republicans held the House majority, bills' authors had to come from that party.)

I asked Torkelson why he had insisted on authoring the bill, since he opposed it. "So I can control it," he replied. That convinced me nothing meaningful would have passed unless I held firm, up to and including a veto of the legislature's first attempt at minimal compromise.

The year brought other disappointments. I failed to get the funding I wanted for increased highway improvements and for universal pre-K education. I had proposed increasing revenue from the state's gasoline tax by adding a wholesale tax before it reached the pump. Any increase in any tax was a complete nonstarter for Republican legislators, regardless of how badly the revenues were needed or how well they would be used. Taxes were their kryptonite. And, of course, they were unwilling to offer any alternative, except to take money from the remaining surplus in the general fund. So, increased highway improvements were punted into the next legislative session (and beyond).

Republicans also opposed full funding to provide pre-kindergarten education to our state's 40,000 four-year-olds. The reason, as expressed by House Speaker Kurt Daudt to a couple Republican fundraising groups, was that more pre-K classes in the public schools meant more public school teachers. Most teachers joined the teachers' union. And most union members voted for Democrats.

That meant 40,000 four-year-old children were denied better starts in their lives due to Speaker Daudt's petty political calculations.

These and other major differences remained unresolved heading into the session's final week. The legislative leaders and I met for several hours each day at the Governor's Residence to thrash through our budget differences. Speaker Daudt picked every possible nit. Every expenditure was debated ad nauseum. Meanwhile, the clock was ticking toward the constitutionally required ending.

Finally, after more frustrating hours of debates, the Speaker and DFL Senate Majority Leader Tom Bakk retreated into my study and returned with a budget agreement they had concocted without me. It failed to increase pre-kindergarten funding—one of my top priorities—and was too stingy with higher education, MinnesotaCare subsidies, and clean water protection. They promptly went outside the residence to inform the waiting Capitol press corps of their "achievement."

I was furious. I expected to be blindsided by the Republican Speaker but not by the DFL Senate leader. I considered it an unforgivable and unacceptable betrayal.

I insisted on a meeting with the entire Senate DFL caucus. When I walked into the caucus meeting room on June 11, the eve of the special session, I was still livid. In an attempt to dampen my remarks, Senator Bakk invited the entire Senate staff to attend the meeting. Their presence didn't soften my tirade. I reminded the caucus members that I had been reelected by over 100,000 votes, and my proven leadership deserved, if not their agreement, at least their support.

The budget was finally resolved with a one-day special session on June 12. While the education bill still did not contain funding for the universal pre-kindergarten program I sought, it doubled a preschool scholarship program for four-year-olds from low-income families. At a middle-of-the-night meeting after the special session adjourned, the DFL Senate caucus also opted to retain Tom Bakk as their leader. Evidently, no one else wanted the job!

As 2016 began, political insiders wondered about my relationship with Senator Bakk. After our blowup at the end of the last legislative session, would we be able to work together? To his credit, Tom was respectful and constructive throughout the session. (Of course, it helped that he and the entire legislature were up for reelection that November.)

One of the many things I like about Iron Rangers like Tom is that they can throw a punch, but they can also take a punch. It's one of the ways they communicate!

Lacking any constructive ideas, Republicans started a rumor in January that I would leave office before the end of my second term, then three years hence. I found most Republican legislators to be like mosquitoes, buzzing around me looking to draw blood. I often wondered why, if they didn't believe in government, they didn't devote themselves to working full-time in the private sector instead of opposing almost everything I was trying to accomplish for our citizens through government.

Just before that year's legislative session began, House Minority Leader Paul Thissen (whom I later appointed to the Minnesota Supreme Court), Tom Bakk, and I made a joint statement in the *Star Tribune*. We noted that "Overall Minnesota is doing better—much better—than in recent years. We have a $900 million budget surplus, unemployment is at a 15-year low, and businesses are creating jobs." But those numbers didn't tell the whole story. "Still, too may Minnesotans are feeling left behind in an economy that too often favors the wealthy few." We knew, of course, what Republicans would propose: tax cuts, especially for corporations and the wealthy. "But that choice," we argued, "threatens to put our state back into deficit and will not address the economic challenges facing Minnesota families. Instead, we must build an economy that works for all Minnesotans—not just the wealthy few."

We outlined our ideas around five major imperatives: build a better transportation system; invest in education; clean up our water; expand economic opportunity for all; and cut taxes for the middle class. And we concluded, "That is our vision for an even better Minnesota; it's what we as Minnesotans can accomplish together if we choose reasonable leadership, make rational decisions and believe—as we do—that Minnesota's best days are ahead of us."

Of course, the Republican majority in the House immediately rejected almost all of our proposals, and therefore, very little of our agenda was passed in the session. In fact, many of the priorities we outlined in 2016 did not advance into law until voters granted DFLers a "trifecta" in 2023.

One example of the Republican resistance we encountered was the fate of my proposed $1.4 billion bonding bill. Legislative sessions in even-numbered years were typically vehicles for major bonding bills. Since such bills require 60 percent majorities for passage, a minority caucus generally had a major say in them. And, again that year, Republicans held the majority in the House.

My bill proposed wide-ranging statewide projects, including building renovations on the University of Minnesota and state university campuses, improvements at state parks, tunnel and bridge modernizations for railroad safety, and subsidized housing preservation. A major piece, $220 million, was for projects to improve water quality by replacing aging sewer systems, upgrading water treatment plants, and overhauling wastewater facilities across the state.

Republicans, predictably, said my bill was too large. I responded that I had received over $4 billion in requests, most of which deserved support. Meritorious and urgently needed water quality projects alone could have comprised the entire bill.

However, for the Republican caucuses, a number was more important than merits or needs. They failed to understand that bonds were investments in our future. Building projects also provided jobs for working Minnesotans. Republicans insisted that the bill's total cost could be only $800 million. As a result, many worthwhile projects were eliminated, although some were accommodated by an addition to the bill of nearly $300 million in immediate cash spending

Even with that sweetener, the bill was not approved when the session ended in May. It died in the session's final minutes when the House and Senate could not agree on a provision that would have allowed Hennepin County more borrowing authority for the Southwest Light Rail project. Republicans apparently could not abide a bill including any assistance for light rail transit, while many DFLers refused to vote for a bill without it.

Also remaining undone after adjournment was a $291 million tax relief bill, which would have lowered some taxes for farmers, students, and veterans. I did not sign it because it contained a $101 million error. I immediately started negotiations with legislative leaders for a special session that would remedy both omissions. Unfortunately, despite repeated meetings to try to resolve our differences, no agreement could be reached. Like most governors before me, I would not call a special session without an ironclad prior agreement from legislators of both parties. Otherwise, once they were back in session, they could stay as long as, and do whatever, they wanted.

My commitment to improving the quality, and thus the safety, of Minnesota's water extended beyond my bonding bill. I called for 2016 to be the "Year of Water Action." I proposed further strengthening of the buffer requirements that had been pared down by their opponents in the previous session. I also convened a statewide water quality conference on February 27 in hopes of building momentum for the issue.

At the August State Fair, I held a water quality event at which I asked fairgoers to take a clean water pledge. It stated:

"I know that water is critical to my life. Because water is so critical, I vow to be a good steward of our water. Today I take the Minnesota Water Stewardship Pledge, affirming my commitment to:

- Rethink how water affects my life and the lives of future generations.
- Use water efficiently and wisely in my everyday activities.
- Learn more about what people can do to preserve and protect water.
- Factor water use efficiency and protection into the choices as a consumer.
- Talk to others about clean water protection and preservation."

Another very meaningful event at the State Fair was to recognize the Minnesota National Guard's Beyond the Yellow Ribbon program. As I described before, when I was a United States senator, I obtained the first federal funding for Minnesota's pioneering program to provide continuing help for returning Iraq war veterans and their families. At the fair, Major General Rick Nash, Minnesota's terrific adjutant general, noted that over 290 cities, counties, businesses, and nonprofit organizations had become involved in the program. It remains one of my proudest Senate initiatives.

But, earlier that summer, a major crisis had occurred. On July 6, a car driven by an African American public school employee, Philando Castile, was stopped in Falcon Heights for a suspected defective taillight. The police officer making the stop shot and killed Castile. The incident prompted over a thousand people to gather the next morning outside my residence. My security discouraged me from going outside and into the crowd. However, I followed one of my axioms: "Always go to trouble."

While amidst the angry demonstrators, I said, "Would this have happened if those passengers, the driver and the passengers, were white? I don't think it would have. So I'm forced to confront, and I think all of us in Minnesota are forced to confront [that] this kind of racism exists."

My statement sparked considerable controversy in Minnesota and received national attention. However, it accurately represented my views. It also calmed the angry crowd and prevented, I believe, an outpouring of violence on the site then and during the days following, when several hundred people remained camped on the street.

Thereafter, I met with Mr. Castile's family to express my deepest condolences. Later, I appointed his uncle to the state's Board of Peace Officer Standards and Training.

The Saturday night after the shooting, the protest outside my residence threatened to escalate. A large group broke away to stop traffic on nearby Interstate 94. My security feared protestors would storm the residence (which they did not). So, for the first and only time during my two gubernatorial terms, I was evacuated to a nearby hotel.

With protests ongoing, I greatly appreciated then–U.S. Representative (now Attorney General) Keith Ellison coming to my defense. In a *Star Tribune* op-ed, he wrote, in part, "I don't know about you, but I'd never heard a sitting governor say race may explain why a black person was killed in an officer-involved shooting. . . . And I couldn't have been prouder of him. I knew he would be attacked for saying it. . . . I got a little worried for him. Honesty makes you vulnerable. I know why our society systematically churns out different racial outcomes: race. I was born knowing it, and everything I have seen, heard, and experienced in my fifty-two years has confirmed it. But rarely do powerful white men admit it. When myths prevail, stating the obvious is a radical act. And it takes guts. Thank you, Gov. Dayton."

One of the year's highlights for me was being asked to give a presidential nominating speech for my friend Hillary Clinton on the final night of the Democratic National Convention.

I said, in part, "When I was elected to the United States Senate sixteen years ago, I was seated next to the new senator from New York, Hillary Clinton. For the next six years I saw, up close and in person, precisely the kind of leader this country needs right now.

"She listened to people explain their problems, not just from New York but throughout our entire country. She championed their causes, because she shared the belief of Minnesota's great Senator Paul Wellstone that 'We all do better when we all do better.'"

Despite the high hopes at that convention to elect our

nation's first woman president and defeat a clearly unqualified Republican opponent, November 8 brought the despairing result of Hillary Clinton's defeat and Donald Trump's election as president of the United States. To compound that blow, Republicans won majorities in both chambers of the Minnesota legislature. That meant I would serve my final two years as governor under a Republican president and with a Republican legislature.

A grim prospect.

— CHAPTER THIRTEEN —

ENDINGS AND BEGINNINGS

> "In questions of power, then, let no more be heard of confidence in man, but bind him down from mischief by the chains of the Constitution."
>
> — *Thomas Jefferson*

My last two years in office ended the same way my first two years began, with both the Minnesota Senate and House controlled by Republican majorities. Their electoral successes emboldened them and increased their already excessive obstinance.

In my January State of the State address, I set forth my priorities. I said, "When I took office in 2011, I promised to increase Minnesota's investments in K–12 education every year I was governor—with no excuses, no exceptions. With your support we have kept that promise, and I'm not going to abandon it now." I knew, of course, that support would now be more difficult to find.

In my subsequent biennial budget proposal, I increased per-pupil spending in public schools by two percent in both of those years, costing $311 million, and added $75 million for voluntary pre-kindergarten programs. Republican legislative leaders had previously opposed pre-K funding because, as House Speaker Kurt Daudt had said, more public school funding would mean more teachers, who would be likely to vote Democratic.

I said, "We cannot expect our schools to be successful or our economy to flourish, if we fail our kids before they even enter their classrooms. The best way to close the achievement gap is to stop it before it begins."

I also proposed a $318 million increase for the University of Minnesota and Minnesota state universities and $68 million for college scholarships.

My other top priority was transportation. Estimates at the time indicated that Minnesota would need $18 billion in additional funding over the next twenty years to bring its roads and bridges up to standards. I proposed a ten cents per gallon increase in the gasoline tax, which I said would cost the average Minnesotan only $75 per year. However, the tax-averse Republicans immediately rejected it, citing the projected $1.65 billion budget surplus (conveniently ignoring that it was my two percent income tax increase on the wealthiest two percent of Minnesotans, which they had opposed, that had generated much of it).

I also proposed a variety of tax cuts, including the expansion of the childcare tax credit to 95,000 families. Even so, the gas tax was a nonstarter in the legislature.

By 2017, I was showing the wear and tear of years of 24/7 governing. The aging process had taken its toll on me. Forty-five minutes into my planned fifty-minute State of the State address, I suddenly felt a lack of oxygen and fainted. I quickly regained consciousness and was helped from the House chamber. I returned to my residence and passed the night without incident.

The next morning, I disclosed to the press that I had just been diagnosed with prostate cancer. On March 8, I underwent surgery for its removal at Mayo Clinic. Subsequent tests did not indicate any spread of cancer cells to other parts of my body. However, almost five years later, in December 2021, a cancerous node was detected in my right lung and removed surgically. Six months later, two cancerous nodes were detected in my pelvis and right thigh.

Fortunately, the Mayo Clinic had pioneered the development of a machine that could target a radioactive laser to within one millimeter of a site within the body. This miraculous procedure meant that, instead of general and debilitating radiation, I could be "zapped" at those two locations with minimal discomfort and achieve complete eradication.

I am *very pleased* to report that there has been no reappearance of any detectable cancer since!

Shortly before the session's end, I was very encouraged by the *Star Tribune*'s Minnesota Poll that showed me with my highest approval rating ever. Sixty-two percent of those polled approved of my performance as governor, while only 29 percent

With Senator John Hoffman and Melissa Hortman, who became House minority leader in 2017 and the 61st speaker of the Minnesota House of Representatives in 2019

disapproved. I hoped that display of public support would persuade Republican legislators to moderate their opposition to my proposals. I was wrong.

As a result, the 2017 legislative session was difficult and unproductive. We argued incessantly over every tax and spending measure. Nevertheless, this session looked poised to finish its work by the constitutionally mandated date in May. My public school funding increase remained intact, and $50 million of the pre-K funding survived.

After another very late last-night session, the legislature's omnibus appropriations bill was forwarded to me. Without my knowledge, the Republican legislative leaders, with the connivance again of DFL Senate leader Tom Bakk, had slipped in a provision intended to force me into signing their tax bill, which contained several measures I opposed. It said that if I didn't approve the tax bill, funding for the essential Minnesota Revenue Department would be eliminated.

I could have vetoed the tax bill and challenged this idiotic legislative action in court. However, that would likely have shut down the Revenue Department into the next fiscal year, which was only a month away. Instead, I decided upon a different course of action. I signed their bill, which did contain numerous provisions I liked, and took advantage of the following provision in the Minnesota Constitution:

> Article IV, Sec. 23: If a bill presented to the governor contains several items of appropriation of money, he may veto one or more of the items while approving the bill.

That provision empowered me to line-item veto the funding of the legislature's operations for the next two years. However, I knew legislators had an undisclosed amount of money stashed away in their private accounts.

This action was unprecedented, completely surprised legislators, and aroused the fury that I expected. However, I felt certain that I was right, both legally and ethically. So, I punched back hard. And I also defended the structural integrity of our state's executive branch from outrageous threats like the one leveled at the Revenue Department.

The legislature filed suit, and the case went all the way to the Minnesota Supreme Court. There, on November 16, Chief Justice Lorie Gildea (a Republican appointee to the court) courageously signed a 5–1 decision that upheld my action. (Republican-appointed Associate Justice Barry Anderson cast the one dissenting vote; another Republican appointee, Associate Justice David Stras, recused himself.) That episode thoroughly antagonized Republican leaders toward me, justifiably, and the chief justice, unjustifiably, for the following year (and toward her even thereafter). Legislative pettiness should never be underestimated.

As I suspected, the legislature's hidden accounts held sufficient funds to enable them to continue their operations until the 2018 legislative session, at which time their regular appropriation could be restored.

One of the most consequential events of 2017 was the resignation of U.S. Senator Al Franken. Al had been, in my judgment, an outstanding senator for Minnesota. I got to know him and his wonderful wife, Franni, when they were campaigning for the Senate seat in 2008. Although he was running for office in Minnesota for the first time that year, he was well known. Franken grew up in St. Louis Park, went to college at Harvard University, then became an acclaimed comedy writer and performer during the formative years of NBC's long-running sketch comedy show *Saturday Night Live*. Later, he became a national political commentator and bestselling author, known for witty, biting criticism of the right-wing populism that had come to dominate talk radio and cable television. Franni's sensational apple pies and Al's good humor gained DFL converts all over the state, and he won a cliff-hanger election that was contested and remained undecided for six months into 2009.

After I was elected governor, Al and I developed a strong working partnership on behalf of our state, and we campaigned successfully together in 2014, when we both decisively won our reelections.

However, Al was caught in the tsunami of the "#MeToo" movement that swept the nation in late 2017. The movement called out and condemned sexual assault, particularly by men in positions of power. One picture of Al with a fellow USO (United Service Organizations) show female performer was especially damning. Several of his Democratic Senate colleagues called for him to resign, and pressures built both within and outside of the Senate for him to step down. On December 7, 2017, he announced his intention to resign from the Senate, which he did on January 2, 2018.

It fell to me to appoint his successor. There were several extremely well-qualified candidates, but one stood above the rest: Lieutenant Governor Tina Smith. As I said before, I had not met Tina until August 2010, during my campaign for governor and after her candidate, Minneapolis Mayor RT Rybak, had withdrawn from the contest. Right away, she was clearly the best I have ever encountered in the political arena. She had been outstanding as my chief of staff from 2011 to 2014 and as lieutenant governor starting in 2015. She was extremely smart, politically astute, and good-natured. She genuinely liked people, and people naturally liked her. The choice was clear.

Initially, Tina was reluctant to accept the appointment. Some were recommending that I appoint a "placeholder," who would not run in the special election that would be required in November 2018 (followed by the end-of-term election in 2020).

Senate Majority Leader Chuck Schumer had other ideas. He strongly believed the appointee should run in both elections. Based upon Senator Amy Klobuchar's and my recommendations, he invited Tina to his Brooklyn home to discuss her appointment. As Tina and I both know, Chuck can be *very* persuasive! She returned from Brooklyn, discussed the decision with her family, and informed me on Sunday morning that she would accept the appointment.

After a day of rapid preparation, I announced her ascension. The choice was very well received. Tina undertook the enormous tasks of learning the Senate job, organizing a campaign for that fall's special election, and continuing to both serve in office and campaign for reelection two years later. Fortunately, her superb talents were more than equal to both the tasks. She has been an outstanding senator, a great credit to Minnesota, and an important national leader during these critical times. In early 2025, she announced that she would not seek reelection in 2026.

Another important event in the fall of 2017 was the development and approval of plans for the diversion of the flood-prone Red River around Moorhead and Fargo. The Red River twists and turns, running slowly from south to north along the Minnesota–North Dakota border and into Canada. It often floods during springtime snowmelts.

In 1997, it swamped the Fargo–Moorhead area and, even more severely, the Grand Forks–East Grand Forks region. Downtown Grand Forks was flooded and then burned, destroying several buildings, including the *Grand Forks Herald* newspaper headquarters, which I had visited just the week before.

I drove to East Grand Forks right after that year's flood to help with the cleanup. It was awful. People's homes had been flooded up to the second stories, and their ruined belongings—rugs, sofas, chairs, and clothes—were piled onto the sidewalk for disposal. Entire blocks were lined with debris in piles so high they looked like snowbanks. Cars and even garages were swept downriver.

The river flooded again in the spring of 2009. Schools closed so that students could help fill seven million sandbags, and hundreds of National Guard members were mobilized. It flooded again in 2010 and 2011.

Minnesota did much more than North Dakota to alleviate our cities' flood exposure with several years of bonding to fortify banks and raise levees along the river. Then, Fargo, which remained at great risk for serious flooding, proposed an ambitious multibillion-dollar project to divert the river around the two cities.

At first, the proposed route would have caused major flood damage to primarily agricultural areas in Minnesota south (upstream) of the diversion. As a result, in December 2016, the Minnesota Department of Natural Resources denied the necessary permit for the project to proceed, citing the adverse environmental effects on our state.

Things were at a standstill. Some Minnesotans in the area wanted me to continue to block the project, saying it would provide greater benefit to Fargo than to the Moorhead area.

However, I thought that position was too provincial and shortsighted. More than a quarter of North Dakota's economy is based in the Fargo–Moorhead area, which is home to three major universities, many successful businesses, and much critical infrastructure in the at-risk area, which would be protected by the diversion. Moorhead, Clay County, and that entire region of Minnesota had vital stakes in Fargo's prosperity.

Nevertheless, opponents were right. The proposed project was too costly to Minnesota and too environmentally damaging for the benefits it provided. That is why our DNR rejected it.

North Dakota Governor Doug Burgum then approached me about collaborating to develop a revised plan. Over three months, from October to December, I made five trips to Fargo–Moorhead for meetings of the sixteen-member, bistate task force we assembled. At the conclusion of those sessions and after hundreds of hours of meetings by our staff and technical experts, we developed a project which would travel primarily through North Dakota and be financed mostly by that state and the federal government. Its permit was approved by the Minnesota DNR on December 27, 2018.

Since I left office, the project has become an enormous $3.2 billion undertaking, which appears to be managed well by the responsible authorities. When completed in 2027, it will shield 44,000 acres and more than 235,000 people—along with their homes and businesses—from flooding.

Other controversies emerging in 2017 were two copper-nickel mining projects, one at the former LTV plant site east of Aurora/Hoyt Lakes and another next to Ely and the Boundary Waters Canoe Area Wilderness. Environmental activists were implacably opposed to any copper-nickel mining because of the large amounts of toxic residue generated by the extraction that could leach into rivers, lakes, and groundwaters. Proponents of the project insisted that modern mining is safe for the environment—and that the good-paying jobs the project would bring were worth the risk.

After careful and extensive environmental review of the proposed PolyMet project, I believed it posed an acceptable risk. The site was in the remote location of the former, abandoned LTV taconite plant, in a different watershed from the BWCAW's.

Those reviews and proposed protections were unacceptable to environmentalists, who filed lawsuits, administrative objections, and any other means to defeat the project. They managed to delay a final decision past my departure from the governorship in 2019.

(In the November 2024 election, a Republican, pro-mining candidate won decisively in a Minnesota House District encompassing that region. The DFL had lost its political grip on the Iron Range—a change that would have shocked several previous generations of Minnesotans.)

On the other hand, I opposed the proposed copper-nickel mining project adjacent to the Boundary Waters because I believed the risk of pollution to that priceless national treasure was unacceptable. I also believed that a construction project of that magnitude, bringing up to a thousand workers right next to downtown Ely, would destroy the popular town's unique character and visitor appeal.

Once again, this project split job-seeking mining advocates and environmental protectors. The pro-mining Trump administration will likely intensify that split and fight.

A humorous footnote to this year occurred one spring morning when my chief of staff called me at 6:30 A.M. to inform me that I would soon receive a call from the president of the United States, Donald Trump. My phone rang, and his assistant asked me to hold. When he came on the line, I said, "This is Governor Mark Dayton."

There was a pause. The president said, "I was trying to reach Matt Damon." (!)

We had a brief but cordial conversation, in which I thanked

him for recently signing a bilateral trade agreement with Canada that would benefit Minnesota farmers. Then we went our very separate ways!

My final legislative session as governor in 2018 was almost certain to be unproductive, given Republican majorities in both bodies and their resentments after their defeat the previous year in challenging my veto of their budget. Their first action was to restore their own funding, which I did not oppose.

In my final State of the State address on March 14, I said, "Restoring fiscal stability to our state budget is one of the most important legacies I can leave Minnesota. During my final year in office, I will not support any budget, tax, or policy proposals that would threaten that stability. I urge legislators to do the same."

Since it was a traditional bonding bill session, I also proposed $1.5 billion of bonding with significant investments in colleges, universities, and water treatment facilities. I said, "It's almost impossible to provide world-class educations in antiquated buildings with leaky ceilings, dilapidated bathrooms, worn-out exteriors, and in classrooms without advanced technologies and other learning aids."

The session concluded, as I had predicted, with little effort by the Republicans to find suitable compromises. As a result, I vetoed fifteen of their bills, including two major tax and spending measures.

I vetoed the tax bill because the benefits went primarily to people with the highest incomes. In my veto letter I wrote,

> **Individual Rate Cuts.** The bill provides little in tax reductions to low- and middle-income families and instead prioritizes rate cuts that benefit

wealthy Minnesotans the most. One in five Minnesota households do not have enough taxable income to benefit from the bill's rate reductions.

Under this bill, when comparing the tax impact of the rate cut for a married joint filer with two children:

- Earning $30,000 or less would see no tax reduction
- Earning $65,000 (state median income) would see a $92 tax reduction
- Earning $150,000 would see a $262 tax reduction
- Earning $250,000 would see a $263 tax reduction

Under my tax bill, when comparing the tax impact of the new personal and dependent credit, a married joint filer with two children:

- Earning $30,000 or less would see $240 tax reduction
- Earning $65,000 (state median income) would see a $240 tax reduction
- Earning $150,000 would see a $240 tax reduction
- Earning $250,000 would see a $72 tax reduction

Fiscal Responsibility. This tax bill also seriously jeopardizes Minnesota's future fiscal stability. The rate cuts in the bill are phased-in to hide their full costs. The personal income rate cuts cost $136 million in FY 18–19, but the full cost will be $395 million a biennium. The corporate rate cut costs $23 million in FY 18–19, but the full cost will be $170 million. These future revenue losses are in addition to the average $200 million per biennium that will be lost from freezing business property

> taxes last year. I will not sacrifice our state's hard-earned fiscal stability, as this bill does.
>
> I have been very clear about my commitment to fiscal sustainability for the State of Minnesota. . . . The long-term fiscal stability of the state is my highest priority. I have worked over the past seven years to restore the state's fiscal stability, and I will not support any bill that threatens that stability.

I felt vindicated when in August our state's Standard & Poor's bond rating was upgraded to AAA, the highest possible level. That new rating matched the top rating we regained from the Fitch agency in 2016 and received again for the third straight year.

I also vetoed the Republicans' omnibus supplemental budget bill for reasons that epitomized the impossibility of working constructively with them. I wrote:

> Repeatedly over the past several months, I implored the legislature to send separate bills on Minnesotans' most urgent priorities. We agreed that we must reform elder care, address the opioid epidemic, and ensure safe schools for our children. Yet, instead of coming together to find shared solutions to these critical issues, you have deposited them into a 989-page budget bill, with 51 policy provisions, which I oppose. This legislative gamesmanship was terrible, and I will not sign the result.
>
> Despite efforts over the past several months to strengthen existing elder abuse laws, this bill fails to meet the expectations of a large number

of lawmakers and of the coalition of nearly every consumer advocacy organization in the state working to stop elder abuse. This legislation does not ensure that there will ever be licensure or protections for assisted living or dementia care. It provides no private rights of enforcement for elderly and vulnerable adults who suffer preventable harm or even death at a long-term care facility. It fails to provide even the basic public right of action protections for elderly people being evicted from their care setting and residence. In fact, advocacy groups believe changes made in this bill would actually make current law less protective. This failure is unacceptable.

The bill also does far too little to combat the opioid epidemic plaguing our State. Several months ago, I proposed investing over $12 million annually in high impact strategies to treat and prevent opioid abuse, funded through an Opioid Stewardship Fee that would hold partially accountable the pharmaceutical companies, who created this deadly epidemic. Instead, this bill spends only $7 million in FY 2019 and about $10 million in FY20/21, entirely from the general fund. Not one penny is ascribed to the drug companies, through either a "penny-a-pill" or a licensing fee. Evidently, the industry's thirty-two lobbyists and whatever promises they made outweighed the interests of the people of Minnesota.

The bill does not support a comprehensive approach and instead provides one-time grants and a small rate increase to providers. There is no funding targeted to communities of color or tribal

> communities that have been devastated by this crisis. The disparities between tribal communities and communities of color and white residents are the highest in the United States. You could have and should have done more.
>
> Included in this enormous bill are workable responses to problems that I sincerely hoped would become law: school safety and HAVA funds. I was sincere in my oft-stated desire to work with you and make these provisions become law. However, you knowingly prevented their enactment by inserting them into a bill, containing policies and agency budget cuts that I had said I would not sign.
>
> I made my objections to this bill very clear throughout the session. My administration sent you over 100 detailed letters throughout the session, carefully explaining my concerns with each of the proposals.
>
> This terrible bill and the resulting veto are your creations. Never have I seen a legislative session so badly mismanaged, less transparent, and more beholden to monied special interests.
>
> For the above reasons, I have vetoed this bill.

One good result did come out of the session: a major public pension fund stabilization. Our state was facing a future debt of $16.2 billion for its public pension obligations. However, during the previous two legislative sessions, political gamesmanship resulted in bills that I had to veto. Finally, legislators from both parties came together to do what had to be done. Great credit goes to Republican Senator Julie Rosen and Republican Representative Tim O'Driscoll, who shepherded the bill through both bodies to unanimous passage. Senator Rosen was one of my favorite legislators and one of the very best.

At the bill's signing ceremony, I said it would be the last legislation I would sign as governor. "I can't tell you how many retirees and active employees have spoken with me in the last few days and told me how vitally important this is for their peace of mind, for their financial security, for their sense of being able to rely on pensions, on the promise that they've earned."

Fortunately, it was a moment when partisanship was set aside for the well-being of Minnesotans who must depend upon their government. It was, unfortunately, too infrequent an occurrence during my eight years at the helm.

I had intended to spend the last couple months of my final term traveling around our state, highlighting the policies and projects we had successfully established. However, as John Lennon sang, "Life is what happens to you while you're busy making other plans." (And no one learned that lesson more emphatically than he did.) Despite two previous surgeries to address the stenosis in my spine, I was still having problems with weakness and tiredness in my legs while walking. October seemed like a good time to address it, with the upcoming elections diverting press and public attention away from me. My terrific Mayo orthopedic surgeon, Jeremy Fogelson, wanted to stabilize my lower spine from both front and back, which would involve two surgeries. The first entailed repairing my spine from my backside. Two days afterward, he approached the spine through my abdomen.

Two more days later, my son Andrew was visiting me when I started to pass out. I was wheeled into the Intensive Care Unit with my kidneys failing, my lungs filling up with fluid, and a staph infection.

That was the onset of what proved to be a forty-day ordeal at Mayo, as I slowly recovered from the surgeries. Some in the press later accused me of hiding my hospital stay. I pointed to a newspaper report about my surgeries on October 16. I continued to work from Rochester, and we continued to issue releases from there. The press was, understandably, too focused on the governor's race and other election contests to care about where I was.

I was still very weak when I left Mayo and, while mentally fit, in no physical condition to travel the state. One of my favorite groups, Jefferson Airplane/Starship, advised to "Sing it now while you still have a song." I will always regret that I had to end my governorship with my final song unsung.

However, I did receive some much-appreciated acknowledgments of progress I had helped achieve. One of my top priorities had been increased funding for early childhood education. I wanted to follow up my successful push to fund all-day kindergarten statewide, which was achieved with the support of a DFL legislature in 2013, with pre-kindergarten funding for all four-year-olds.

With persistent efforts every year, I was able to significantly increase funding that gave more four-year-olds better starts in their lives. Those efforts were recognized in a *Star Tribune* article near the last month of my time in office. The article recognized that the push for educational funding was not some lame-duck hobby but a consistent priority that I had been pursuing aggressively from my first days in office. But while it's easy to talk about education dollars abstractly as a line item in a state budget, it is quite another thing to notice what those dollars mean in the concrete. There were now, as the *Star Tribune* put it, "visible results of Gov. Mark Dayton's long quest to bolster the state's public education system . . . sitting in the tiniest desks and chairs." The heated debates were over and a new educational status quo was in place across the state and, the *Star Tribune* noted, "both the governor's supporters and those who have sparred with him over education issues say the governor will leave office early next year having changed the way Minnesotans talk and think about the state's youngest students." In politics, changing the terms of policy debate is essential to long-term policy achievement. And finally, at least in early education policy, those terms had changed. The additional funds for and expanded scope of public education in Minnesota was proof of that. As I told the paper, "I feel proudest of providing the resources that were lacking before."

Other important acknowledgments were published in my final year as governor. While issues like education and transportation were major, ongoing priorities of my administration and matters of vigorous debate, other issues I championed were no less important. I had started the Governor's Pheasant Opener in 2011 and continued the tradition each year of my two terms. Going into the pheasant season during 2018, I was delighted to read an October article in the *Star Tribune* that took the time to outline what our administration had done for conservation and environmental protection during the past eight years:

- 43,500: Acreage added to state Wildlife Management Areas since 2011.
- 385,351: Minnesota cropland acres enrolled by 615 farmers in the state's voluntary Agricultural Water Quality Certification Program, which began in 2013.
- 38: Trout-stream easement miles acquired by the state since 2011.

Governor's Pheasant Hunting Opener (which I originated), October 2015

- 26: Percentage increase in annual overnight campers in Minnesota state parks between 2011 and 2017—from 286,000 to 360,000. Additionally, annual state park permit sales have increased 37 percent during the period.
- 58.3 million: Twin Cities regional park visits in 2017, up about 25 percent since 2011 and fueled in part by 2,244 acres added to these parks since 2011.
- 21,700: Number of Minnesotans who attended Department of Natural Resources "I Can Fish" programs designed to show people new to outdoor activities how to participate. Another 15,000 residents signed up for similar introductory programs on rock climbing, mountain biking, and paddling.
- 13: Shallow-water lakes since 2011 designated as Migratory Waterfowl Feeding and Resting Areas, totaling 3,435 acres. Also, water control structures

have been added to 21 existing Feeding and Resting Areas covering 14,000 acres.

- 26,700: Acreage added to Minnesota's Walk-In Access program, granting permitted hunters and others permission to enter private land.

Of course, the controversies over my opposition to Twin Metals Minnesota's proposed sulfide mine and advocacy of waterway buffers were part of that record too. I wanted to show that recreation, agriculture, and public health all had a vested interest in protecting Minnesota's natural environment. I told the *Star Tribune* interviewer, "The natural resources we inherit from our fathers and mothers are our sacred responsibility to protect and enhance for future generations." My view was that most Minnesotans agreed with me. "It's a silent majority," I said. "But it's an overwhelming majority."

In February 2018, another article opined on what we'd done over two terms to advance racial and economic equity. It was blunt: "No Minnesota political leader in modern times has had more impact advancing the cause of racial and economic equity and improving our natural environment. Dayton's credo of 'A Better Minnesota' has meant reducing overall economic inequality and otherwise improving the lives and potential of people of color, women, the variously disabled and middle- and lower-income folks."

Some of the policies we pursued were aimed at racial inequalities. As the article noted, "The percentage of workers of color employed in state government has risen from 8 percent in 2011 to 12 percent. In 2017 alone, 16 percent of new hires were people of color. This is real progress toward an eventual Dayton goal of 20 percent, matching the state's overall of-color percentage." We'd also pushed for more considerations on minority hiring on projects that were utilizing public funds, made it a priority to name people of color to administrative posts and judicial appointments, and worked to close education and employment gaps.

But, as the article pointed out, "most low- and middle-income households in Minnesota are white." And while steps were taken to address racial disparities in the state, our economic agenda aimed to put Minnesotans of all races on firmer financial footing. That's what drove tax policy, health care policy, education policy, environmental policy, and social policy.

The article concluded, "We can admire the efforts and achievements of a governor born to wealth and privilege, who has been driven since his youth by an idealistic zeal to improve the lot of those without such advantages. Mark Dayton has shown us that justice need not impede economic growth, a kind of Minnesota exceptionalism that gives us a competitive advantage."

Of all the retrospectives published about my time in office, though, few meant as much to me as a letter to the editor from one of my former senate staffers, Seng Vang, that the *Star Tribune* published during my final days in office. Vang wrote:

> As Gov. Mark Dayton's time in office winds down, I feel compelled to share my personal observations about his leadership and why this wealthy and powerful politician will always be remembered as a "man of the people."
>
> I was fresh out of college when I landed a job as a staffer working for then–U.S. Sen. Mark Dayton. I couldn't believe it. A girl born in a Thai refugee

camp to parents who were never formally educated and spoke little English was walking the halls of the U.S. Capitol. After needing help most of my life from publicly funded programs, I was now in a position to help others. By day, I staffed Sen. Dayton's health care help line, helping families in crisis navigate the health care system. By night, I came home to our three-bedroom house in East Side St. Paul that was shared by my parents, four younger sisters, and my brother's young family. After my parents were sworn in as new U.S. citizens, Dayton threw a party for them. My parents were grateful for the party, but were genuinely touched when he listened intently to my mother's tearful story about our journey to the U.S. Eventually, I left the senator's office for graduate school. As Minnesota's greatest cheerleader, he lobbied me to stay and attend the Humphrey School of Public Affairs. I did so and then settled into a quiet life.

Seven years after I left Dayton's office, my father passed away. His funeral was set for Jan. 8, 2011. On a whim, I informed the office. The office initially told us that was the same day as Gov. Dayton's inaugural ball, and we understood that he was busy. Then they informed us that the governor wanted to stop by the funeral before heading to the ball. He didn't do it for the TV cameras. He didn't do it to impress others. Our family has never publicly shared this story, but this act illustrated the kindness and decency that have defined Mark Dayton's tenure in public service. My father died thinking he was a "nobody" in this country. I wish he would have known that the highest-ranking elected leader of this state thought he was a somebody. To be clear, it wasn't just my

> father. Gov. Dayton, through his policies and leadership, has worked tirelessly for all Minnesotans, like my father. Beyond balancing the state budget, it was critical for him to increase health care coverage and expand early childhood opportunities so that Minnesotans now and into the future will have better opportunities and lives. While his background and upbringing are far from common, his legacy will be that he fought for the common man. Gov. Dayton, thank you for your service. You will be missed.

I left office on January 7, 2019. I had the satisfaction of watching the inauguration of my outstanding successor, Governor Tim Walz. It was the first time since 1976 that a Democrat had succeeded another Democrat as governor in Minnesota.

Me (second from left) with, left to right, my sister Lucy Dayton, brother-in-law Mark O'Keefe, sister Anne Dayton, sister-in-law Tian Dayton, and brother Brandt Dayton

Going back to being a civilian was a hard adjustment. For forty-four years, I had been consumed by government and politics. Now, suddenly, it was gone. Overnight, I lost my career, my home, my staff, and, most importantly, my life's purpose.

Rudy Perpich joked that before losing his election in 1978, he had read that in some third-world countries they took the losers of elections out and executed them. It wasn't until he lost that he realized it was an act of mercy!

I so much liked a joke my 2010 opponent, Tom Emmer, used against me that I used it on myself thereafter: A man drives up to the Governor's Residence and says into the intercom, "I want to see Governor Mark Dayton." "Mark Dayton is not the governor," the trooper replies.

The next day, the same man returns. "I want to see Mark Dayton." "Mark Dayton's not the governor," is the same reply.

On the third day, the man drives up again. "I want to see Mark Dayton." The trooper, exasperated, exclaims, "I keep telling you, Mark Dayton is *not* the governor. Why do you keep coming back?"

The man replies, "I just like to hear you say it!"

Leaving an office isn't the same as losing an office, but it's close enough. The phone stops ringing. I always said, "It's amazing what winning an election does for your social life. But I know it's not because people have suddenly discovered I'm a wonderful human being!"

At the other end, those invitations dwindled. The press and the public no longer cared what I thought about every event of the day. At least I had a successor who kept the continuity with what I had accomplished, unlike Presidents Obama and Biden, who had to watch their successor, Donald Trump, ravage much of what they had done. Nevertheless, it was all being done without me. I suddenly felt very old—and alone.

During my eight years as governor, I had never looked for a new love relationship. I knew that I needed, and wanted, to devote all my time and energy to being the very best governor I could be. I felt so incredibly fortunate to have that opportunity. And I knew it was time limited.

Now, relieved of all those responsibilities, I wondered if such a relationship were still possible for me. In December 2018, I ran into a former intern, Ana Orke, in an elevator while going to a friend's fundraiser. We had dinner shortly thereafter, but she was moving to Atlanta.

In the fall of 2019, she emailed me and said she had moved to San Francisco. On January 30, 2020, I was in the city and invited her to dinner. There I told her that I would like to pursue a serious relationship with her.

It was in the midst of the pandemic; so, my initial courtship was limited to telephone calls and FaceTime. That June, Ana was able to move back to Minnesota. In July, in front of my kitchen counter, I asked her to marry me. Fortunately, she said "yes" anyway! In September, I gave her an engagement ring at a more romantic setting in Sedona, Arizona. We were married on December 5, 2020, at Westminster Presbyterian Church in Minneapolis. I feel so incredibly fortunate to have found the love of my life.

Ana amazes me with her dedication to rescuing dogs from overcrowded shelters. I've lost count of the number of dogs she has personally saved from euthanasia and found homes for. We have three of our own dogs: my sixth German shepherd, named Coconino, and two rescues, Luna and Chum.

Meanwhile, I have concentrated on developing my spirituality. I like the Sufi saying, "These things we speak of (God) cannot be found by seeking, but only seekers find it."

I am a seeker.

Ana and me

Wedding day, December 5, 2020

CONCLUSION

"May you leave an excellent legacy to
10,000 generations."

—*Zen Manual of Leadership*

I have lived my adult life defying conventional norms, like opposing the Vietnam War and running for offices without the DFL Party's endorsement. I've always faced naysayers, including family and friends, who contended that I was wrong; that I should instead bow to the conventional "wisdom"; that if I didn't, I would lead myself and others to failure.

My most important successes came when I defied conventions because I believed that what I was doing was right. I achieved what others thought was impossible because I believed in and trusted myself.

What have I learned from all those years, from all my successes and failures, trials and tribulations? So much and too little. But I must admit that, to my deep disappointment, I fear so much of what I stood for, fought for, and worked for throughout my career is now being damaged or destroyed.

The path I forged was very different from today's dominant politics. I have always said that there are no saints in politics, only shades of sinners. But there are shades, and they do matter.

I learned from my father and my uncles a commitment to social responsibility. My father's favorite quote was from the

Bible: "For unto whomsoever much is given, of him shall be much required" (Luke 12:48). He and his brothers felt an even greater responsibility to our society than to the retailing success that built our family name and my inheritance.

My uncle Don was instrumental in creating the Nicollet Mall and bringing the Twins baseball franchise from Washington, DC, to Minnesota. My father was a principal sponsor and lifetime trustee of the Minneapolis Institute of Art (MIA). My uncle Wally was at the forefront of many state and national environmental organizations. My uncle Ken championed the corporate "Five Percent Club," whereby corporations contributed five percent of their pretax profits to community improvement projects. My uncle Doug generously supported the YMCA.

Those principles of civic involvement and responsible stewardship forged Minnesota's greatness in the 1970s, '80s, and '90s. Business leaders throughout our state were also civic leaders. Our citizenry supported government services with their votes and their tax dollars.

Minnesota was not a low-tax state at any point in my lifetime. That philosophy predominated in southern states, which resulted in inferior public school systems, inadequate public services, substandard housing, and high crime and incarceration rates.

However, the commonly shared principles that had characterized Minnesota and created the state–local public financing system known nationally as "the Minnesota Miracle" crumbled into partisan divides in the new century. My Republican predecessor opposed any state tax increases to offset growing budget deficits, which led to greatly reduced funding for public education and other public services. Reduced state funding for K–12 education per student dropped Minnesota to the bottom half among the fifty states. State funding for higher education, in inflation-adjusted dollars, dropped to its lowest level since the early 1970s.

When I took office in January 2011, in the face of an enormous $6.2 billion deficit projected for the upcoming biennium, Republican legislators stridently rejected raising taxes on even the wealthiest Minnesotans. Their "solution," in addition to cutting human services, was to increase the state's borrowing from local school districts and siphon off proceeds from an earlier tobacco lawsuit settlement—a one-time "fix" that was no solution.

Finally, with DFL majorities in both the Minnesota House and Senate in 2013, I was able to fulfill my campaign pledge to increase state income taxes on only the top two percent of the state's wealthiest taxpayers. That increase and an improving economy turned chronic budget deficits into surpluses and funded statewide, all-day kindergarten for Minnesota's five-year-old children.

Minnesota is not an inherently wealthy state. Our beauty is majestic, but we lack the allure of mountains, oceans, and warm winters. Instead, we have earned our success by well-trained minds and hard work. We educated our children well and taught them to work diligently and care about their communities.

Now, there is evidence that this common bond is eroding. Racial divides, socioeconomic divides, and rural–urban divides are widening. Too many people are fixated on "me–them" instead of "us." Instant, often anonymous, misinformation messages on the internet fuel those divides, and politicians pander to them.

We are at a crossroads. Will we succumb to the siren's song that lower taxes and lesser services are tickets to a better quality of life? That we can only climb up by pushing other people down?

Or will we recommit to Senator Paul Wellstone's axiom that "We all do better when we all do better," show compassion for the plights of our fellow citizens, accept if not appreciate our differences, and recognize that we are indeed *all* in this together?

At the national level, the trends are even more ominous. Back when I was being investigated and harassed for opposing the Vietnam War, I was consoled by believing that my generation would outlast Richard Nixon and his warmongers and rise to political power. We would abolish nuclear weapons, end world hunger, establish social and economic justice, and achieve all of this in time to retire and reach Satori before our passing.

Sadly, my generation has fallen far short of my lofty ambitions. We have certainly made important progress, but our gains seem overshadowed by our failures. And the most prominent political figure right now is Donald Trump.

Susan Wise Bauer's fascinating four-volume telling of *The Story of the World* recounts endless wars, conquerors, and atrocities. The saga continues today. But now, the scale of destruction, both of nature and of human lives, is so much greater. The devastation caused by the madness of Vladimir Putin afflicts millions in Ukraine and threatens the entire planet.

There doesn't appear to be any way to tame humankind's violent nature. The best we can hope for is to contain it. There is reason for hope. Only two decades separated the First and Second World Wars; we have made it for more than three-quarters of a century without a third.

Ironically, the risk of total annihilation is the greatest deterrent to its occurrence. And extraordinary advances in so many arenas to improve the human condition give more people more reasons to get along, or at least tolerate their differences, than ever before.

It's a race, neck and neck, between global sanity and insanity. Meanwhile, it's incumbent on all of us to do everything we can to tilt the scales toward survival and prosperity.

Thus, it's truly frightening that at this critical time for the world's civilization we face our own crisis within this country.

My friend Lee Sheehy reminds me that four pillars of a successful democracy are civility, honesty, facts, and the rule of law.

Donald Trump ascended to the presidency twice while shattering all four of those principles. Yet despite his incivility, dishonesty, lies, and lawlessness, a plurality of voting Americans returned him to the most powerful office in the world. I cannot comprehend what they find tolerable, much less appealing, in him.

I pray our country can survive, as it has other cataclysmic episodes in the past. I'm consoled that we have, as a nation, survived a Revolutionary War, a Civil War, two World Wars, slavery, Jim Crow, genocide of Native Americans, and a Great Depression. To mention just a few.

But there are no guarantees. When Benjamin Franklin was asked at the conclusion of the Continental Convention in 1787 what kind of government the delegates had formed, he replied, "A republic, if you can keep it."

That is what we have enjoyed for the past 239 years. The question now is: Will we continue to keep it?

James Madison wrote in 1788 that "The accumulation of all powers, legislative, executive, and judiciary, in the same hands, whether of one, a few, or many, and whether hereditary, self-appointed, or elective, may justly be pronounced the very definition of tyranny."

In the same vein, Supreme Court Justice Louis Brandeis said 138 years later, "The doctrine of the separation of powers was adopted by the Convention of 1787, not to promote efficiency but to preclude the exercise of arbitrary power. The purpose was not to avoid friction, but by means of the inevitable friction incident to the distribution of the governmental powers among three departments, to save the people from autocracy."

Now that separation of powers has been seriously eroded. Republican majorities control both the United States Senate and the House of Representatives. Six staunch conservatives comprise a strong majority in the Supreme Court. The congressional majorities are wholly subservient to their "Supreme Ruler," President Donald Trump. The Supreme Court seems willing to grant him almost unlimited license to force his very extreme and divisive dictates upon our country. This is a prescription for tyranny. And it's deeply, *deeply* alarming.

As I write this chapter, thousands of U.S. Immigration and Customs Enforcement (ICE) agents have descended upon Minnesotans like a rampaging gestapo, terrorizing, maiming, and even murdering our law-abiding citizens. It is excruciatingly painful to watch them being afflicted by the worst horrors in my lifetime.

And these atrocities are being dictated by our own national leaders: President Donald Trump and his administration. It is unthinkable. Yet it is happening with an overwhelming assault by paramilitary commandos, who are stealing innocent people from their schools, businesses, and even churches. People are afraid to leave their homes and go to work, to school, or to pray.

The Trump administration does not seem to care about whether their victims are violent criminals who should be deported or innocent Americans. The people snatched away from their families are being sent to unknown places, without access to communication, legal representation, or sanitary conditions. Their hardships are god-awful, but the president and his people do not care.

One high-ranking White House official said that strength, force, and power rule the world. Not morality, legality, or human rights. And right now, the enormous power of our federal government is theirs to abuse.

Administration officials also lambast our friends and neighbors who are peacefully protesting these rampages, calling them "domestic terrorists" and accusing them of inciting the violence. But lawful protest against oppression is ingrained in the American tradition, and its right is enshrined in the First Amendment of our Constitution.

Over 250 years ago, Boston citizens dumped British tea into their harbor, saying "Taxation without representation is tyranny." (Arrest and deportation without due process is also tyranny.) Patrick Henry famously said, "I know not what course others may take; but as for me, give me liberty or give me death!"

Almost two hundred years later, many thousand Americans were lawfully protesting President Nixon's wars in Southeast Asia. In November 1969, an estimated 500,000 of us assembled in Washington to protest those atrocities. We were tear-gassed, and some were beaten and arrested. At least no one was shot and killed.

In May 1970, after Nixon spread the war into Cambodia and four Kent State students were murdered, another 150,000 of us descended upon Washington to express our outrage. Again, many protestors were tear-gassed, beaten, and arrested.

Throughout our protests, we were denounced by Nixon administration officials as being dangerously un-American and fomenting domestic unrest. The critical difference is that back then we were protesting our government's atrocities against people in other countries. Today, brave Minnesotans are protesting atrocities against our own citizens.

As I write this, President Trump and his forces have the power to overwhelm their opponents. The secretary of Homeland Security boasts that she can send even more ICE agents to further trample any opposition. Her actions remind me of Vladimir Putin unleashing ever-more Russian troops against the beleaguered people of Ukraine. Like the heroic Ukrainians, Minnesotans' resistance to ICE was phenomenal and won the John F. Kennedy Profile in Courage Award.

But there's an old saying that those who do not learn the lessons of history are doomed to repeat its mistakes. Slowly, some fifty years ago, most of our citizens came to understand that it was their leaders who were "un-American," not the people opposed to them.

I'm putting my faith again in the basic goodness of most Americans, who will say, with us, "STOP."

As the American patriot Thomas Paine said in 1776, at another turbulent moment in our country's history, "These are the times that try men's souls. The summer soldier and the sunshine patriot will, in this crisis, shrink from the service of their country; but he that stands by it now, deserves the love and thanks of man and woman. Tyranny, like hell, is not easily conquered; yet we have this consolation with us, that the harder the conflict, the more glorious the triumph."

I have five grandchildren whose futures depend upon our success. We cannot let them down.

HUMOR

"I don't make jokes. I just watch the government and report the facts."

—*Will Rogers*

You can't be effective in politics (or in life) without a sense of humor. You also can't survive without a sense of humor. As one of my mentors said, "The situation might be hopeless, but it's not serious!"

Early in my first campaign for public office, for the U.S. Senate in 1982, I stopped at a farm in Greater Minnesota. The farmer looked at my AMC four-wheel drive wagon and said, "You might be a city guy, but at least you drive a country car!" He went on to say, "Dayton, we're all born with original sin. You're just born with more of it than the rest of us!"

Years later, I added, "Well I might have been born with a lot of original sin, but after my campaigns, I have less of it than I used to!"

President George W. Bush was a year ahead of me at Yale University and was the president of my fraternity, Delta Kappa Epsilon. I told my Republican colleagues in the Senate that I had known the president longer than any of them. "Back in college, he and I were often in the same party. Why, I've seen him take positions that none of you have!" And he could say the same about me!

There's a saying that in the U.S. Senate, if you like and respect someone, you call him (or her) "my friend." If you don't like him, you call him "my good friend." If you detest him, you call him "my very good friend." There are a lot of very good friends in the Senate!

My friend Senator Tom Harkin said, "If you can keep your perspective while everyone around you is losing theirs, you obviously don't understand the situation!"

Tom also said that a friend told him, "Tom, you're such a 'Yellow Dog Democrat,' you'd vote for the devil himself if he were the Democratic candidate." Tom replied, "Yes, but I wouldn't vote for him in the primary!"

There are two kinds of people: Those with excuses, and those who don't need them.

I so much liked a joke my 2010 opponent, Tom Emmer, used against me that I used it on myself thereafter.

A man drives up to the governor's residence and says into the intercom, "I want to see Governor Mark Dayton." "Mark Dayton is not the governor," the trooper replied.

The next day, the same man returned. "I want to see Mark Dayton." "Mark Dayton's not the governor," was the same reply.

On the third day, the man drove up again. "I want to see Mark Dayton." The trooper, exasperated, exclaimed, "I keep telling you, Mark Dayton is *not* the governor. Why do you keep coming back?"

The man replied, "I just like to hear you say it!"

In the fall of 1981, California Senator Alan Cranston headlined my first big fundraiser, when I first ran for the U.S. Senate. He told the following joke:

In the Soviet Union, a man waited in line at the meat market for two hours. When it was finally his turn, he asked for some beef and was told they were out of beef. He asked for some pork and was told they were out of pork. Finally, he asked for some sausage and was told they were out of sausage. He stormed out of the store screaming, "This damn Communist regime. It can't take care of its people."

Outside, he was stopped by two men in trench coats. One said, "A short time ago, you would have been shot for saying that. But this time I'm just going to warn you: No more protests against the state."

The man walked home, and when his wife saw him empty-handed, she exclaimed, "Oh no! Are they out of meat again?"

"It's worse than that," he replied. "They're out of ammunition!"

After flying to Minnesota on four hours' sleep, Florida Congressman ("Senator"!) Claude Pepper told the following joke to some five thousand Minnesotans:

A minister and a politician died on the same day and arose together to the gates of heaven. There they were met by St. Peter, who led them down a long corridor to the rooms where they would spend their lives in eternal bliss. First, he stopped at the room reserved for the minister. It was a nice room but modestly furnished. Single bedroom, window overlooking the parking lot.

The minister was curious, so he followed St. Peter and the politician and watched with amazement as St. Peter opened double doors, leading into a beautifully furnished two-bedroom suite, with a well-stocked refrigerator and a beautiful view of the lake.

As St. Peter came out, the minister approached him and said, "I want you to know that I'm not complaining; I'm delighted to be here in heaven; but I just don't understand. I served the Lord all my life; this politician surely made many worldly compromises; yet he has this beautiful suite, while I have a small apartment. I just don't understand it."

St. Peter smiled, put his arm around the minister, and said, "Well, you see, it's like this. We've been having ministers coming up here for thousands of years, but this is the first time a politician has ever made it!"

I don't remember where I heard this next joke, but it falls into the category of that rare joke that's safe to tell a general audience.

Mr. Jones awoke one morning, lied to his wife and his boss that he was going to a conference, then headed across town to play a round of golf. The Lord saw this, summoned St. Peter, and said, "Mr. Jones has sinned. He's lied to his wife, and he's lied to his boss. I want you to devise a suitable punishment."

So the Lord watched as Mr. Jones teed up on the first hole, a par three, and hit a beautiful shot that landed on the green and rolled into the hole for a hole in one.

The Lord had great confidence in St. Peter, but he was

surprised, so he watched as Mr. Jones hit a perfect drive on the second, short par-four hole, which cut the dogleg and rolled on the green and into the hole for a second hole in one.

The Lord summoned St. Peter and said, "I don't understand. I told you to punish this man. Instead, he's played two holes, and he has two holes in one."

St. Peter smiled. "You're right, Lord. Two holes. Two holes in one. It's the most exciting thing that's happened to him in his entire life . . . and who's he going to tell?!"

Jim Hightower, the Texas columnist and progressive activist, has a great sense of humor. He said George W. Bush was "born on third base and thinks he hit a triple!"

He also said that the only things in the middle of the road are yellow stripes and dead armadillos.

Louisiana Senator John Breaux told this joke at the annual dinner of the Gridiron Club, a Washington journalism gathering. He said that before the 2000 presidential election, he thought a "dangling chad" was what Senator Bob Dole had before Viagra!

I can't swear this story is true, but supposedly when Louisiana Governor Edwin Edwards was indicted the second time for allegedly taking a $100,000 bribe to approve a gambling license, he replied, "Why, that's ridiculous. The people of Louisiana know me well enough to know that if I was going to take a bribe, it would be for a hell of a lot more than $100,000!" (He was acquitted of that charge but convicted on a third.)

Speaking of Louisiana politicians, I watched the following campaign ad on a consultant's "greatest hits" reel. In it, the powerful Louisiana Senator Russell Long was telling a group of constituents about what he had done for his state. I'm making up the name of the river, which I have forgotten, but the rest is almost verbatim.

Senator Long said, "Why I remember the day I got the Tuckabee River Dam for the people of Louisiana. President Kennedy called me to the White House and said, 'Senator, I called you here to talk with you about my Nuclear Test Ban Treaty.' I replied, 'Well, Mr. President, I'm here to talk with you about the Tuckabee River Dam for the people of Louisiana.'

"President Kennedy said to me, 'Why, Senator, what on earth does your dam have to do with my test ban treaty?' I replied, "Mr. President, the way I see it is like this. Seven members on my committee are for your treaty; seven members are opposed; and then there's me. So I'd say the Tuckabee River Dam has a lot to do with your test ban treaty.'"

The Tuckabee River Dam was built with federal funding!

Also, Senator Long supposedly asked his father, the legendary Huey "Kingfish" Long, if he should use ethics in his campaign. His father replied, "Hell, yes, son. Use anything you can get your hands on!"

This joke was not intended to have political connotations. However, it definitely applies to certain situations today.

A work crew was blazing a trail through a jungle. On the third day, they lost their compass. So the foreman sent a young apprentice climbing up the tallest tree to make a sighting.

"Stop! Stop!" the boy called out. "You're going in the wrong direction."

The foreman replied, "But we can't stop now. We're making so much progress!"

Governor Rudy Perpich lost his bid for election in his own right in 1978, after having become governor in 1976 via a Senate self-appointment scheme engineered by then-Governor Wendell Anderson. Perpich won in 1982 and regained his sense of humor. He said that before he lost in 1978, he had read that in third world countries they executed the losers. It wasn't until after he lost that he realized "that was an act of mercy."

It was about 9 P.M. in a Senate Armed Services Committee bill markup when Senator Ted Kennedy came in, accompanied by his Bernese Mountain dog, Splash. Splash immediately went seat by seat around the table, begging for leftover scraps of food. I turned to the senator sitting next to me, nineteen-year veteran Jeff Bingaman from New Mexico, and asked, "How much seniority do you need to bring your dog into an Armed Services Committee markup?" He smiled and replied, "More than I've got!"

At a DFL fundraiser, I was standing backstage with former President Bill Clinton. A Rolling Stones song came on. I said, "Next reincarnation, I want to be Mick Jagger." Bill glowered at me and said, "*I* want to be Mick Jagger."

I decided I was not going to argue with a former president!

Minnesota Senate Majority Leader Nick Coleman was a bona fide Irish Catholic Democrat. He joked that he was twenty-one before he knew that "Irish-Catholic-Democrat was three separate words"!

Minnesotan Walter Heller, who had served as President John F. Kennedy's chief economic adviser, said of the corporate executives seeking special tax favors from the Nixon administration, "Not only do they want a free lunch. They want a tax break for eating it!"

There are many funny stories from and about the great Winston Churchill. My favorite, verified by both Franklin Roosevelt's son and Churchill's valet, occurred when he was a guest at the White House during World War II. As was his wont, Churchill was lounging in the bathtub, dictating to his secretary, seated in the next room, when Roosevelt wheeled into the suite. "Where's Winston?" The secretary pointed to the bathroom. Roosevelt wheeled into that room, saw where Churchill was, and started to leave.

Churchill stood up in the tub, without a stitch on, and said, "Sir, the Prime Minister of England has nothing to hide from the President of the United States!"

Years ago, I was bemoaning the results of some election to Minneapolis Mayor Don Fraser. He gave me a wise, whimsical smile and said, "Well, Mark, I've always believed that in a democracy, if people want bad government, they're entitled to have it." (That certainly applies to today.)

My stepfather, Lee MacPhail, President of the American League of Professional Baseball Clubs, said that he learned in baseball, "You're never as smart as people think you are when you're winning; or as dumb as people think you are when you're losing"! The same applies to politics!

Senator Gene McCarthy once said that a football coach "has to be smart enough to understand the game and dumb enough to think it's important."

Gleason's Law of Paranoia: "No matter how paranoid you are, they're doing more than you think they are."

My corollary: "Gleason didn't know the half of it."

"You're not paranoid, if they really are out to get you!"

A friend asked U.S. Senate Chaplain Edward Everett Hale in 1903, "Do you pray for the senators, Dr. Hale?"

He replied, "No, I look at the senators and pray for the country."

Former Vice President Dick Cheney was reportedly asked not to return to Yale University after his freshman year. When President George W. Bush spoke at Yale's 300th commencement, he said, "All you C students, take heart: You, too, can become president of the United States. And if you only make it through one year, you can become vice president!"

WISDOM

Some of the following gems of wisdom have already appeared. They're worth reading again.

"For unto whomsoever much has been given, of him shall much be required."

—*Luke 12:48*

"Not shaken by adversity, not hankering after happiness. Free from fear, free from anger, free from the things of desire. I call him a seer, and illumined. The bonds of his flesh are broken. He is lucky and does not rejoice; he is unlucky and does not weep. I call him illumined."

—*The Bhagavad Gita*

"(God) cannot be found by seeking; yet only seekers find (Him)."

—*Sufi saying*

"May you leave an excellent legacy to 10,000 generations!"

—*Zen Manual of Leadership*

"If you realize that you have enough, you are truly rich."

—*Lao Tzu*

Its corollary: "More is never enough."

—*Mark Dayton*

"Let nothing disturb thee. Let nothing dismay thee. All things pass; God never changes. Patient endurance attains to all things. Who God possesses, in nothing is wanting. God alone suffices."

—*St. Teresa of Ávila*

"The credit belongs to the man who is actually in the arena, whose face is marred by dust and sweat and blood, who knows the great enthusiasms, the great devotions, and spends himself in a worthy cause; who at best, if he wins, knows the thrills of high achievement, and if he fails, at least fails daring greatly, so that his place shall never be with those cold and timid souls who know neither victory nor defeat."

—*John F. Kennedy, paraphrasing Theodore Roosevelt*

"I do the very best I know how—the very best I can; and I mean to keep doing so until the end. If the end brings me out all right, what is said about me won't amount to anything. If the end brings me out wrong, ten angels swearing I was right would make no difference."

—*Abraham Lincoln*

"Never give in, never give in, never, never, never, never . . . except to convictions of honor and good sense."

—*Winston Churchill*

"If not now, when?"

—*Paul Wellstone*

"Better the occasional faults of a government that acts in a spirit of charity, than the constant omissions of a government frozen in the ice of its own indifference."

—*Franklin D. Roosevelt*

"We hold these truths to be self-evident: That all men [and women] are created equal, that they are endowed by their Creator with certain unalienable rights, that among these are life, liberty, and the pursuit of happiness."
—*Thomas Jefferson*

"Democracy is the worst of all forms of government . . . except for all the rest."
—*paraphrasing Winston Churchill*

Winning does not tempt that man.
This is how he grows.
By being defeated decisively.
By ever greater foes.
—*Rainer Maria Rilke*

"Every step in personal growth needs isolation, needs inner conversation and deliberation and a reviewing with the self."
—*Joost A. M. Meerloo*

"One grows or dies. There is no third possibility."
—*Oswald Spengler*

"The path of spirituality is a knife-edge between abysses."
—*Aldous Huxley*

"Patient and regular practice is the whole secret of spiritual realization. Do not be in a hurry in spiritual life. Do your utmost and leave the rest to God."
—*Swami Shivananda*

"The heroes, saints, and sages—they are those who face the world alone."
—*Norman Douglas*

"Strength of numbers is the delight of the timid. The valiant in spirit glory in fighting alone."
—*Mohandas Gandhi*

"War is barbarism. . . . It is only those who have neither fired a shot nor heard the shrieks and groans of the wounded who cry aloud for blood, more vengeance, more desolation. War is hell."
—*William Tecumseh Sherman*

"Hatred can never put an end to hatred; love alone can. This is an unalterable law. People forget that their lives will end soon. For those who remember, quarrels come to an end."
—The Dhammapada, *translated by Eknath Easwaran*

"The political leaders with whom we are familiar generally aspire to be superstars rather than heroes. The distinction is crucial. Superstars strive for approbation; heroes walk alone. Superstars crave consensus; heroes define themselves by the judgment of a future they see it as their task to bring about. Superstars seek success in a technique for eliciting support; heroes pursue success as the outgrowth of inner values."
—*Henry Kissinger*

"If men were angels, no government would be necessary. If angels were to govern men, neither external nor internal controls on government would be necessary. In framing a government which is to be administered by men over men, the great difficulty lies in this: you must first enable the government to control the governed; and in the next place, oblige it to control itself."
—*James Madison*

"The moral test of government is how that government treats those who are in the dawn of life, the children; those who are in the twilight of life, the elderly; and those who are in the shadows of life—the sick, the needy, and the handicapped."

—*Hubert Humphrey*

"Are you a politician asking what your country can do for you or a zealous one asking what you can do for your country? If you are the first, then you are a parasite; if the second, then you are an oasis in the desert."

—*Kahlil Gibran*

"Things won are done. Joy's soul lies in the doing."

—*William Shakespeare*

"Aeschylus wrote: 'In our sleep, pain that cannot forget falls drop by drop upon the heart and in our own despair, against our will, comes wisdom through the awful grace of God.'"

—*Robert F. Kennedy*

SELECTED SPEECHES, 2011–2018

— INAUGURAL ADDRESS, 2011 —

"Let's Get Minnesota Working Again . . . By Working Together"

Thank you, Chief Justice Gildea.

Vice President Mondale; our excellent Lieutenant Governor Yvonne Prettner Solon and other distinguished guests; my wonderful sons, Eric and Andrew, and family; my friends; my fellow Minnesotans.

I am honored, humbled, and grateful to stand before you as Minnesota's Fortieth Governor. I especially want to thank my fellow citizens, who voted for me, and placed your trust in me. I will do my very best to serve you well.

To those who voted for my two worthy competitors, I will do my very best to also serve you well.

I believe we all share the same aspiration—for "a better Minnesota"—for ourselves, our children, and our grandchildren. We may disagree on the details. May we never forget, however, that our honest disagreements and our freedom to express them are the essential rights and great strengths of our democracy.

Yet what a difference a decade makes. Ten years ago today, I was sworn into office in the United States Senate. Back then our country was on top of the world and on course to stay there. Tragically, two massive federal tax cuts, two lengthy wars, and two devastating recessions have damaged our preeminence and our prosperity.

Here in Minnesota, two state tax cuts, two wars, and two recessions later, we stagger from one huge deficit to the next. 208,000 Minnesotans are out of work. And a state which used to lead most others in economic growth has fallen toward the bottom.

The past decade has left our country, our state, and many of our citizens worse off than before, with lower standards of living, larger debts and deficits, and less assured of future success. The stakes now are high. This coming decade will determine whether we suffer the historical declines of previous superpowers, or write a new chapter for future historians. If anyone can do it, we can. And we must.

Previous generations of Minnesotans and other Americans faced graver dangers, under worse conditions, with fewer resources, than we do today. They summoned their collective knowledge, courage, and resolve. They persevered. And they prevailed. By working together.

They won their independence. They preserved our nation. They overcame the Great Depression. They worked their way to the top. By working together.

Now it's our turn, our challenge, and our responsibility. Now is the time for us to summon our best, to be our best, to do our best.

To all Minnesotans, I say: Let's get Minnesota working again . . . by working together. That is what we are called upon to do—for ourselves, our children, and our grandchildren.

To the 201 Minnesota legislators, who will take office tomorrow, I say: Let's get Minnesota working again . . . by working together. That is what we were elected to do.

We were all elected by just a fraction of Minnesotans; but our responsibility now is to serve all Minnesotans. If we serve only the people who voted for us, we guarantee destructive division, and we risk paralyzing gridlock. We must do better than that. The people of Minnesota expect better from us than that. Their futures depend upon us being better than that.

I have three top priorities, and I ask all of you to work with me cooperatively and constructively to achieve them.

1. To bring more jobs to Minnesota.
2. To balance the state budget fairly.
3. To improve government services.

My top priority is to get Minnesotans working again. The 208,000 who are unemployed. The thousands more who are underemployed, stuck in low-paying, dead-end jobs. Whose economic security is shattered. Whose hope for a better future is threatened.

Their futures are also our futures. As our great United States Senator Paul Wellstone said, "We all do better when we all do better."

To all do better means we all must find common ground in our shared desire for a better Minnesota. In our shared love for our state. In our shared appreciation for all it has given to each of us. Now, the future of Minnesota depends on us—on all of us working together.

To Minnesota's business owners and executives, working men and women, farmers, and civic leaders, I say: Let's get Minnesota working . . . together. We can't succeed without you. You can't succeed without one another.

As we work together to put Minnesota back to work, we have many advantages: talented, hardworking, productive people; strong companies; innovative small businesses; good schools, colleges, and universities; valuable natural resources; and a priceless quality of life.

Let us recognize all that is good about Minnesota and make it better . . . by working together. My second, urgent priority is to clean up the state's financial mess, a responsibility I will share with the new legislature and, ultimately, with all of you. Some people think eliminating a $6.2 billion deficit, almost 20 percent of expected revenues, will be simple and easy. I don't. As my friend and former colleague Senator Tom Harkin of Iowa likes to say, "For every complex problem, there's almost always a simple solution. And it's almost always wrong."

My proposed budget solution will be reasonable, balanced—and painful—because I see no easy alternative. I will insist that any final solution make Minnesota's overall tax burden more progressive, not more regressive. I respect that no one likes paying taxes, and almost everyone would like to pay less. Which is why it's essential that everyone paying taxes knows everyone else is paying their fair share. And also knows that I will do everything possible to assure those hard-earned dollars are spent only to provide the best possible public services—for a better Minnesota.

To those who sincerely believe the state budget can be balanced with no tax increase—including no forced property tax increase—I say, if you can do so without destroying our schools, hospitals, and public safety, please send me your bill, so I can sign it immediately.

Otherwise, let's begin tomorrow, and in May conclude, this challenging, complicated, and essential process, by working together. And let's always remember that working together requires responsible cooperation and reasonable compromise, as well as sharing the best ideas we have.

Third, we must improve the services we provide our citizens, starting with education innovation, and including more affordable health care, better natural resource protection, streamlined business regulation, improved transportation, and greater cost efficiencies throughout government.

While everything is important, education is first and foremost. Nothing is more essential to our state's success than providing all our students with the world's best education. Yet nothing has divided educators, policymakers, and parents more in recent years than how best to provide it—and how adequately to fund it.

Meanwhile, we're failing our students—and thus failing our future. Overcrowded classrooms, like the thirty-six children in a fifth-grade classroom in Rochester. Four-day school weeks, as in Warroad, forcing children to stay at home alone while their parents are working. Unaffordable college tuitions, leaving the single mother in Marshall with a master's degree, $100,000 in debt, and no job.

Better education for everyone is essential to getting Minnesota working again . . . and to keep Minnesotans working in the future. To give everyone the skills necessary to succeed in an ever more competitive global economy. Doing so must be everyone's shared responsibility. That is why I am asking every business in Minnesota to adopt a school. And contribute to its improvement. To visit the school and see its realities. To meet with teachers, students, and administrators and find out what they need to improve their school—now your school. A little money, a lot of help, technical expertise, remedial reading volunteers, adult mentors, new books, used computers. Make that school's progress your shared responsibility.

Other areas of health and human services also need our help. To all Minnesotans, I ask you to remember the words of the Roman philosopher–leader Cicero that in a democracy, the most important office is that of citizen. I ask you to remember that our state's success is also your responsibility. I invite you to get involved in the betterment of your communities.

I ask every adult Minnesotan, who is physically able, to volunteer a part of one day, every month, at a school, hospital, or social service agency, as I did this morning at the Wellstone Elementary School and will continue to do as governor and thereafter. Whatever you can do to help, whomever you choose to help: whether the young, the old, the sick, or the disabled, you're helping to get Minnesota working again . . . by helping one another.

In conclusion, let me note that Saturday was the first day of the second decade of the third millennium A.D. What we do during the next four years will affect everyone who follows us, who will inherit their Minnesota from us. Their futures and ours are intertwined, and they are our responsibility.

All of us want—and need—a state that works better than today. One in which everyone has a good, well-paying job, with affordable health care and secure retirement benefits. Where the world's most innovative companies employ the world's best-educated people to produce life-enhancing goods and services. Where strong economic growth and sound environmental protection are both honored and assured.

Our children and grandchildren, and their children and grandchildren, will inherit a state where people from all over the world now live here . . . together. How well they can work together then will depend on how well we work together now. How well we accept, respect, and even come to appreciate our many differences. How soon we realize that those differences are among our greatest strengths, integrate them, and put them to work for all of us.

They will be born and raised in a state where their well-being will depend on how well we take care of our youngest citizens. Their values will depend on how well we take care of our oldest and sickest citizens. Their success will depend on how well we rebuild our infrastructure, protect our environment, and create new economic opportunities for them and their fellow Minnesotans.

Their better future begins with us. So does ours. A better Minnesota for all of us depends on all of us.

So, let us dedicate ourselves to rebuilding a successful state, one that again is the envy of the nation, a leader of the world. Let it be written that we were Minnesotans who led the way to something better than before, who created something greater than ourselves, who achieved together what none of us could have accomplished on our own.

By working together. Starting now.

— STATE OF THE STATE ADDRESS, 2011 —

"A Five-Point Plan for Minnesota's Future Prosperity"

On January 29, 2002, as a Minnesota senator, I attended President George W. Bush's first State of the Union address. It occurred just four months after the terrible events of September 11, 2001.

He began with these words: "As we gather tonight, our nation is at war, our economy is in recession, and the civilized world faces unprecedented dangers. Yet the state of our union has never been stronger."

The president's words rang true. On the night of 9/11, I had joined with other members of Congress on the steps of the United States Capitol, which had been spared destruction that day by the heroic actions of passengers aboard United Flight 93, led by Minnesota native Thomas Burnett Jr.

We gathered, not as Republicans or Democrats, but as Americans. We wanted to show our nation and the world that, despite the day's horrors, our country stood strong, our leaders were united, and our government was working . . . together.

A few days later, we went together to the Pentagon and to Ground Zero.

Then I traveled with a small bipartisan group of senators to Afghanistan, just after American forces had routed the Taliban and al Qaeda and reopened the American embassy, though still surrounded by razor wire and Marines.

So, when I heard the president's words—"The state of our union has never been stronger"—I agreed that 9/11's disaster had united our country, our citizens, and our leaders.

I would like to say the same about the state of Minnesota today. After the most terrible economic disaster since the Great

Depression; after its harsh lessons that we are all Minnesotans whose lives, fates, and fortunes are intertwined; I wish I could say that we are all united, as we gather here this afternoon.

Whether we unite or whether we divide is hanging in the balance. The challenges we face threaten to divide us, rather than bring us together. Partisan posturing and narrow agendas threaten to overwhelm bipartisan cooperation and compromise.

I do see promising signs of bipartisan accord. I appreciate the constructive relationships I have established with Speaker Zellers, Majority Leader Koch, and their leadership teams; as well as with Minority Leaders Bakk and Thissen and their teams.

On the other hand, in just the second week of the legislative session, there was a hearing held on the effects of a shutdown of state government next July. A shutdown which would occur ONLY if we fail to resolve our differences before adjournment 103 days from now.

On the night of 9/11, I stood with my fellow United States senators and representatives on the steps of our Capitol to assure our fellow citizens that our government had not shut down, would not shut down, could not be shut down.

It is absolutely unthinkable that we would even contemplate doing so here in Minnesota. So, I ask you, legislators; I invite you; I implore you—to join with me now, right here in our Capitol and pledge to the people of Minnesota that we will NOT shut down their government, our government—not next July 1, not any July 1, not any day ever.

It should not happen; it need not happen—not as long as we are willing to work together and to compromise our individual views for the common good.

Compromise doesn't mean we have to agree, thank goodness, because we won't. It doesn't mean we can't debate, because we will. It means we can disagree, debate, and then reach a shared solution to our state's problems.

If we do so, by working together, we can rightfully tell the people of Minnesota that we succeeded. We did the very best we could, given the very difficult circumstances we inherited.

And if we all succeed together, the people of Minnesota will win. If we fail, the people of Minnesota will lose. It's that simple. It's that inescapable.

Our shared success is essential to turn our state around and get us—all of us—working again. By all of us working together.

For many years, Minnesota was known as the state that worked.

Governor Wendell Anderson, who is with us here today, is the only Minnesota governor ever to ascend to the cover of *Time* magazine for his leadership in creating "the Minnesota Miracle." We were blessed with the largest number of Fortune 500 companies per capita of any state in the nation.

Most of them were started here by Minnesotans, like my great-grandfather, and were built by business pioneers, like my father, Bruce Dayton, who is here today, into successful national and international corporations.

They didn't succeed alone. Thousands of talented, well-educated, and productive Minnesotans worked hard together with them to achieve those tremendous successes.

Minnesota's economic ascendancy and social vitality were true public-private partnerships, and they occurred by the thousands throughout our state. In the fall of 1983, I traveled to Thief River Falls, as Commissioner of Economic Development, to award the first Enterprise Zone tax incentives, which Governor Rudy Perpich and the Minnesota Legislature had authorized that spring, to a seven-person business called Artco. Those business leaders and their hardworking employees built that small business into Arctic Cat, which employs well over a thousand people there.

It stands alongside DigiKey, another remarkable business success story, which its brilliant founder, Dr. Ronald Stordahl, started in his garage and which today employs some two thousand Minnesotans, who fulfill orders worldwide within twenty-four hours with 99.85 percent perfection.

Unfortunately, due to a combination of factors, Minnesota's economic success stalled during the past several years. During the last decade, Minnesota, which previously had been among the best states in the nation for economic growth and job creation, had one of the worst-performing economies.

According to a *Wall Street Journal* analysis, real median income in Minnesota fell by nine percent from 1999 to 2008, over double the national decline of four percent. Only two other states had a worse decline.

As a result, our per capita income fell from seventh highest among the states to fourteenth in 2009.

Our employment growth averaged in the bottom ten among the fifty states during the past decade.

Last December, there were over 77,000 more Minnesotans unemployed than in December 2002, just before Governor Pawlenty took office. There were 5,881 fewer people working in Minnesota than there were eight years ago, even though our state's population grew during that time by over 286,000 people.

And it is worth noting that this decade of poor economic performance followed two consecutive cuts in the state income tax rates by Governor Ventura and that Minnesota Legislature in 1999 and 2000.

Fewer people paying lower taxes has meant state per-pupil aid for our students from kindergarten through twelfth grade has been reduced by 14 percent in real, after-inflation dollars during the past eight years. Tuition in our state's two-year public colleges has risen to the third highest in the nation; tuitions in our four-year universities are among the top ten highest.

Ten Minnesota school districts have gone to four-day school weeks, not for educational reasons, but rather for lack of money.

Class sizes have grown, while thousands of talented teachers have been laid off. The average salary of those teachers who remain is two percent below the national average.

The number of road miles in poor and mediocre condition has more than doubled. Minnesota's rank among the fifty states in road condition has fallen from eighth to twenty-seventh.

Anyone who drives our state's deteriorating roads and highways, or is stuck in ever-longer metro traffic jams, or waits longer times for poorer bus service, wants a better Minnesota than this.

Any parent who has to find childcare for their children because of four-day school weeks, while they're working five, wants a better Minnesota.

Any fifth-grade teacher in a classroom with thirty-six students wants a better Minnesota.

Any college graduate, saddled with many thousands of dollars in student loans and unable to find a job, wants a better Minnesota.

Anyone unable to find a job wants a better Minnesota.

Minnesotans want a better future. Minnesotans deserve a better future.

I can envision a better future.

I know what we must do to create that better future for all of us.

To progress, we have to invest. We have to invest in jobs; in education; in transportation; in the health of our people, communities, and environment; and in the transformation of government.

That is my Five-Point Plan for Future Prosperity. Invest in more jobs. Invest in better education. Invest in improved transportation. Invest in the health of our citizens, our communities, and our environment. Invest in the transformation of government services.

Investments require faith and trust. People invest in the

future only if they believe in that future. They invest only if they trust their investing partners. They invest only if they believe that others will do what is necessary for those investments to succeed.

To create together a successful Minnesota, we need to believe once again in each other and in our collective talents, abilities, and wisdom. We need to believe that our fellow Minnesotans are acting in good faith, doing their best, and that they, like us, want the best for their children, their communities, and our state.

So let us believe again in Minnesota. Let us believe again in one another. Let us invest together in our better future.

It begins with education.

I want to recognize and thank two of our most distinguished citizens, the retiring leaders of our two largest higher education institutions: the president of the University of Minnesota, Robert Bruininks, and the chancellor of the Minnesota State College and University System, James McCormick.

President Bruininks has led the University of Minnesota with great distinction as its fifteenth president since 2002. He has served the university for thirty-nine years, as professor, dean, executive vice president, provost, and president. Fortunately for all of us, he will continue his outstanding service to the university in a faculty position.

Chancellor McCormick began his service to Minnesota in 2001, as the leader of the MnSCU system of thirty-two higher education institutions statewide. He has given us a decade of strong, visionary guidance to bring those vitally important institutions together as one system. We thank him for his outstanding service to Minnesota.

Three other very distinguished educators are with us today.

Dr. Efe Agbamu is Minnesota's Secondary Principal of the Year.

Dr. Agbamu is currently principal at Park High School in Cottage Grove, where she instituted an International Baccalaureate program. She is recognized for her "ability to achieve academic and community goals, for improving teaching and learning and encouraging a positive school environment for staff and students."

James Sonju, the principal at Rochester's Lincoln K–8 Choice School, is Minnesota's Elementary School "Science and Mathematics Principal of the Year." He was selected for his work integrating cutting-edge science throughout the curriculum and revolutionizing the way his school teaches science.

Ryan Vernosh is Minnesota's Teacher of the Year. He is a sixth-grade teacher at Maxfield Magnet School in St. Paul, where he has taught since 2006. He says the two biggest issues facing education are the achievement gap and social justice. "These gaps are unacceptable and are my driving force as I prepare to teach every day."

I salute these five great Minnesotans and all of our state's outstanding educators. They know, as I do, that better education is key to a better Minnesota. It is why I was so pleased to reaffirm last week my promise to increase state funding for public K–12 education every year I am governor, with no excuses and no exceptions.

Our children's futures are in our hands. Their futures are our responsibility.

I ask the legislature to follow my lead and increase state funding for K–12 education. That doesn't mean more money to maintain the status quo. To the contrary, every additional dollar we spend on education should be directed toward improving the quality of that education.

Starting with the experiences we provide our state's children in the very first months and years of their lives.

I have been greatly impressed with the careful thought

being devoted by many dedicated adults to the best use of our resources for early childhood education.

That is why I will reestablish the Governor's Council on Early Childhood Education and the Children's Cabinet, both to be led by Education Commissioner Brenda Cassellius.

This is a terrific opportunity for continued public–private partnerships, involving business leaders, foundation executives, parents, educators, and everyone else who cares about our children and their success.

Then we need to commit more state money to providing all parents with the option of affordable all-day kindergarten for their children. How can states like Alabama, Louisiana, and Mississippi fund all-day kindergarten, while we in Minnesota do not?

Despite our deficit, my budget will propose increased funding to expand the number of children who can receive all-day kindergarten. I ask the legislature to help me find the additional money as soon as possible to make all-day kindergarten an option for every child in Minnesota.

In our shared desire to improve our elementary and secondary schools, our colleges, and our universities, I urge all of us to work together—instead of against one another.

For too long, teachers and other educators have been battered by continuing criticisms of their commitment, their ability, and their effectiveness. For too long, words like accountability, responsibility, and acceptable progress have been used to imply that there is none.

To say that is untrue does not mean we are satisfied with every aspect of our educational services today. It means that we are going to take a different approach to making them better.

We are going to listen to one another's concerns; we are going to work cooperatively and constructively; and we are going to enlist the best ideas from the real experts: the parents, teachers, principals, and superintendents who are most in touch every day with our students and their needs.

As someone said, all the reform we could possibly use is available to us right now in those schools, colleges, and universities, which are educating students most successfully.

We need to identify those successes, share their strategies, and both encourage and require their use elsewhere.

I again ask every business in Minnesota to adopt a school, college, or university: to become actively involved in making them better. They will benefit from you, and you will learn from them.

Another crucial area of investment is in transportation. Minnesota suffers today from the failed legacy of twenty years of declining investments in our highways, roads, and bridges; in our public transit systems; and in other critical infrastructure. Our decline has been worse than most other states, which means we are falling further behind in what I consider one of the most important "business climate" measures: the quality and capacity of our transportation systems and other infrastructure.

It doesn't have to be that way. Look at our Metropolitan International Airport, where new investments have been made continuously during those same twenty years.

It's not perfect, but it's remarkable. Virtually an entire new airport has been constructed while continuing to operate the old one. It is rated one of the best-managed airports in the country and even the world.

Or consider the recently completed Highway 62 interchange, also built while remaining open for traffic.

It's not perfect; yet it's a big improvement, and it provides for better public transit as well.

The notion we don't know how to invest in critical infrastructure improvements, or to implement those projects efficiently, is foolish. What's even more foolish, however, is our failure to make necessary investments in them. The results are deteriorating highways throughout Greater Minnesota and worsening congestion in our metro system.

Roads, highways, and public transit are to our state's economy as are arteries to the human body.

If the arteries are healthy and efficiently transport blood, oxygen, and nutrients throughout the body, everything works at its best. If, however, the arteries become decrepit or clogged, the body's performance suffers.

Minnesota is at a critical juncture with its transportation systems. Our investments are inadequate to maintain their condition or expand them to serve our growing population.

Their further deterioration will seriously constrict our future economic growth and damage our social vitality.

That is why I have asked Transportation Commissioner Tom Sorel to present to the legislature his ideas for better roads, highways, and transit systems, and to begin the discussion of how best to finance them. I invite others with transportation and finance expertise in both the private and public sectors to join us in that discussion.

I ask the legislature to consider creating a Transportation Finance Authority, chaired by the MnDOT commissioner, to bring together the best minds and their ideas for financing the transportation improvements upon which our future social and economic vitality depend.

Third, we have to invest in the health, safety, and well-being of our citizens, our communities, and our environment.

Fortunately for all of us, there are so many Minnesotans who go to work every day to make our lives better.

I especially want to honor today the men and women who risk their lives to keep our lives safe.

Colonel Eric Kerska is the Commander of the Minnesota National Guard's 1st Brigade Combat Team, 34th Infantry Division. The Red Bulls!

He will lead the 2,400 citizen soldiers of the 1st Brigade when they deploy in May to support, for one year, Operation New Dawn, the drawdown phase of U.S. military operations in Iraq.

Colonel Kerska has been a National Guardsman for over twenty-one years and a soldier for over twenty-seven years. In his civilian career, he is a battalion chief for the Rochester Fire Department—a job he will put on hold while he serves his third tour of duty.

He is joined today by his wife, Tina, who is equally a Minnesota hero for her sacrifice in giving up her husband for the next year to protect our country.

With us also is a family of Minnesota heroes: 1st Sergeant Gary Wenzel, his wife, Cathy, and their eighteen-year-old son, Private First Class Todd Wenzel.

1st Sergeant Wenzel has been deployed twice. During his eighteen-month tour in Iraq in 2004–05, Cathy Wenzel founded "Project Backpack" for military sons and daughters; and another organization, "Minnesota Veteran Family Support," providing families with services before, during, and after military deployment.

Today, the Wenzel's oldest son, Andrew, is on his way to Afghanistan; and Todd will be deploying with the 1st Brigade Combat Team later this spring.

Colonel Kerska and Private Wenzel, please extend to all of the 2,400 men and women in your Red Bull unit our deepest gratitude for their heroic service to our state and nation, and our heartfelt prayers for all of your safe return.

Closer to home we are protected by the courageous women and men who wear the uniforms of law enforcement officers throughout our state. We are honored today by the presence of the Police Officer of the Year, Adam Bailey.

Officer Bailey has been with the St. Paul Police for six years; previously he served with the St. Louis Park Police.

He was named the Minnesota Police and Peace Officers Association's Police Officer of the Year for his outstanding service.

Officer Bailey has also been awarded the City of St. Paul's highest honor—the Medal of Valor—for his extraordinary heroism in the line of duty.

To Officer Bailey and all the Minnesotans in uniform who risk their lives every day and night to keep all of us safe, please accept our deepest gratitude for your dedicated and heroic service.

In addition to protecting the safety of our citizens, we must do everything possible to protect their health and well-being. The best possible and most affordable health care for all of our citizens is far too important to become a political football in the 2012 Presidential Superbowl.

Minnesota has long been a national leader in health care innovation, and our citizens everywhere have benefitted enormously from that leadership.

When my mother was hospitalized in New York City before her passing, I learned there is no private or public hospital there, at any price, which provides a quality of care that is routine throughout Minnesota.

Nor can one find the quality of doctors, nurses, and other health care providers.

Those professionals, clinics, and hospitals are absolutely priceless. All Minnesotans need and deserve access to them at the most affordable prices. We can have our honest disagreements about how best to achieve that goal.

Let us promise, however, that our disagreements will be based upon honest differences over policies, not politics.

Fourth, we need to transform how we provide our citizens with the best public services, most efficiently, at the lowest cost.

This is a clear but daunting challenge: How do we improve government services and performance while we also cut costs?

Minnesota is not alone. Republican and Democratic governors and legislators across the country are grappling with this crisis.

The best of them are realizing, as my son Eric's business school professor told him, a crisis is a terrible thing to waste, and they are getting down to business. That is what we need to do in Minnesota.

Improving government's efficiency and service quality while reducing its cost has bipartisan support—and leadership in both the public and private sectors. I want to thank General Mills for their support of our state's Enterprise LEAN business process improvement initiative. This initiative has improved service and cut costs; it will be expanded.

We need to do more, and we will. I want to combine the best private sector expertise with our public sector experience to make Minnesota government the best in the world.

Our administration will lead the way. I have asked Lieutenant Governor Yvonne Prettner Solon and our Chief of Staff Tina Smith to head this effort, along with MMB Commissioner Jim Schowalter, Administration Commissioner Spencer Cronk, and Office of Enterprise Technology Commissioner Carolyn Parnell.

I have asked them to immediately identify cost savings. For example, Minnesota has already spent $168 million in this biennium on office technology, like computers and desktop printers.

Local governments spent an additional $228 million. What if we pooled our purchasing power to get a better deal for Minnesota taxpayers?

We will examine every area of expenditure and contracting to find ways to cut costs, while improving services.

Longer term, we need transformational change to improve the productivity of government and bring it fully into the twenty-first century. The opportunities are huge, and the savings can be enormous.

This reform will succeed best if we work in partnership with our state employees.

The good ideas for improvements and efficiencies often come from the people who work in government every day. Treating them with the dignity and respect they deserve will be essential to our success.

Fifth, and most important, we need our business leaders to believe in Minnesota, to invest in our state, and to create more jobs for the thousands of our citizens who want to work.

We also need better working partnerships between our state's businesses, colleges and universities, other civic organizations, and state and local governments.

We all agree upon the need to create more jobs. Putting more people to work throughout Minnesota is essential to our economic recovery, to our social well-being, to a better future for all of us.

I am pleased to report to our fellow citizens that the legislature and I have found areas of cooperative agreement.

We agree that our state's permitting and approval processes for new and expanding businesses have been taking unreasonably long; and we are united in our determination to shorten them, while protecting our citizens and our environment.

Two weeks ago, I signed an executive order to begin that streamlining process immediately. DNR Commissioner Tom Landwehr and MPCA Commissioner Paul Aasen have been working with legislative leaders of both parties to put those and other improvements into legislation.

I thank Speaker Zellers, Majority Leader Koch, and the other legislators who are working with us to achieve this progress. May it characterize our cooperative spirit throughout the rest of the session.

I hope that we can find that same cooperative spirit to pass the statewide bonding bill, which I proposed last week.

Those investments will help build a better Minnesota for generations to come. National economists, commenting on continuing high unemployment, say a crucial factor holding back job growth is that construction has not yet revived.

That is my bonding bill's initial purpose: to put up to 28,000 unemployed Minnesotans in the private sector construction industry back to work.

And, through those long-term improvements, to benefit all Minnesotans for years to come. I want businesses everywhere in Minnesota to feel wanted, valued, and appreciated by everyone in our administration.

I have asked the heads of our Departments of Agriculture, Natural Resources, the IRRRB, and the Tourism Office to work closely with businesses in those important industries, which are so vital to our state's prosperity, especially in Greater Minnesota.

I want to thank Jason Thormodson, an eleven-year-old future farmer and mechanic from Madelia, for reminding me yesterday how very important agriculture is to our state.

DEED Commissioner Mark Phillips will have overall responsibility for our business outreach; and I have asked him to revitalize the former Star Cities for Economic Development program, which I inherited as DEED commissioner from the administration of Governor Al Quie.

Governor Quie is here today, and I want to honor him for his outstanding service to our state as our congressman, our governor, and our leading citizen.

His Star Cities program trained local officials, Chambers of Commerce members, college and university presidents, and other civic leaders to work in partnership and lead their cities' economic growth efforts.

Those local economic development teams need to be better supported by state officials, and I promise that their efforts will be given the highest priority by everyone in our administration.

I will be personally available to assist them in any way I can. I thank Representative Fabian for asking me to join him and Senator Stumpf at North Star Agri Industries' recent ground-breaking in Hallock.

I appreciate Representative Hamilton and Senator Magnus inviting me to Jackson for AgCo's exciting expansion, which will bring over one hundred new jobs to our state.

I stand ready to go anywhere in our state, nation, or world where there are jobs to be gained for Minnesota, and to assist the businesses that provide them.

And I am especially grateful to our super volunteer, Senior Adviser Kathy Tunheim, and my good friend Tom Borman, who will help me reach out to Minnesota's business leaders.

Some will criticize me for proposing next week to ask those successful businessmen and -women and other wealthy Minnesotans to pay higher taxes.

I ask them for their forbearance during this fiscal crisis, which I did not create but inherited, and now, with you in the legislature, must solve.

I ask Minnesota's business leaders and other most successful citizens to give us two years to turn this ship of state around. Not by savaging essential public services, upon which you and your employees also depend, but rather by transforming the ways in which government operates here in Minnesota.

And, with your help, to reduce the need for those services by putting people back to work throughout our state.

My father's favorite quote was from the Bible: "To whomsoever much has been given, of him shall much be required."

You have achieved so much. I ask you, please, to help your state, your children and grandchildren, your friends and neighbors, to regain what you and I have enjoyed so much and benefitted from so greatly during our lives here in Minnesota. Please—help us restore Minnesota to greatness.

I invite you to contribute your expertise to help us regain that greatness—at the state level, and at the county, city, township, and school district levels.

Adopt a school. Volunteer in one of them. Teach a social service agency how to become more cost efficient.

Help the legislature and me to balance the state's budget more wisely. Contribute your ideas, your talents, and your wisdom. We need you now more than ever.

In closing, I ask all Minnesotans for the same forbearance. I ask not to be finally judged by the budget I am required to submit next week.

I ask you to remember that I was not given a blank slate on which to write my best proposals for our state's future. Neither was the legislature. We were left a horrendous fiscal mess, a decade of economic decline, and state agencies poorly managed.

All of that must be turned around. All of it will be turned around, but not by tomorrow, and not entirely by the end of this legislative session.

We will, however, *turn it around*—and move Minnesota ahead once again—to reclaim our former greatness.

I approach this monumental assignment with the utmost dedication and determination. I know Lieutenant Governor Prettner Solon and our exceptional cabinet do as well.

I believe our 201 legislators feel that same awesome responsibility.

I urge them to approach their difficult decisions, as I do, with caution and care.

We will be properly judged by effects of our decisions and actions on the lives of our fellow Minnesotans—this year, next year, and for years to come. Whether we make their lives better or worse.

Together we must shape a strategy that will create a better Minnesota, for all of us and for all who will follow us.

We must reverse Minnesota's past decline. And return our state to a path of growth, success, and prosperity.

We can; we must; and we will.

By all of us working together . . . to get Minnesota working again.

— STATE OF THE STATE ADDRESS, 2013 —

"Building a Better Minnesota"

In a state of the state address, as in life, it's important to assess where we are, remember how we got here, decide where we want to go, and then determine how best to get there.

Comparing the state of our state today with conditions when I took office two years ago, we have made important progress. We have much more work still ahead of us; however, we are on the way to a better Minnesota.

According to our Department of Employment and Economic Development, there are over 72,000 more jobs available in Minnesota today than when I took office two years ago. Almost 52,000 of those jobs were added in the past year.

Minnesota's job growth in 2012 was the twelfth best among all fifty states; and we outperformed three of our four neighbors. Iowa ranked thirtieth best; South Dakota was forty-fourth.

Wisconsin, which by the way is open for business, helped bring up the rear at forty-second. And, help spread the word across the St. Croix, their unemployment rate last month was 20 percent higher than ours, while our per capita income was 12 percent higher than theirs.

Only North Dakota, in the Upper Midwest, topped us in job growth last year, and their percent increase led the nation.

Our exports of agricultural commodities increased by 13 percent in 2012, compared with 2011. Total exports of all Minnesota goods and services have achieved eight straight quarters of record growth.

Our students' educational attainments have improved. Math scores for all tested grades improved by 5.3 percent from 2011 to 2012, and reading scores improved overall by 1.3 percent. We have led and continue to lead the nation in important measures of health, including the lowest heart disease death rate and the lowest percentage of obese or overweight children. We have the second-longest life expectancy for all our citizens, and we're number one for males.

I'll let Health Commissioner Ehlinger explain that discrepancy, and I expect that Representative Kahn will soon have a bill to correct it.

Last year we eliminated premiums and expanded health care access for 16,000 more Minnesota children; and we were recognized for providing the Best Long Term Care Services in the nation by the AARP Commonwealth Fund.

No one should be satisfied or complacent. However, these and many other improvements are encouraging.

We have also made great progress in restoring fiscal responsibility and operational integrity to Minnesota government, which also tells us a lot about what got us to where we are today. I became governor after a decade of deficits in both our federal and state governments. They squandered their positions of financial stability amidst consistent economic growth, which they enjoyed at the beginning of the twenty-first century and which were then projected to continue for at least the next decade.

Few politicians can resist the opportunity to cut taxes. President Bush proposed two large tax cuts in 2001 and 2003, which I opposed as a senator and Congress passed. In Minnesota, Governor Ventura convinced the legislature to reduce income tax rates in both 1999 and 2000. Both leaders assumed that the strong economic growth during the last half of the 1990s would continue. Unfortunately, both were wrong.

Also wrong were the politicians and economists who promised that cutting taxes would lead to more economic growth, jobs, and revenues. Instead, the two federal tax cuts were soon followed by two recessions, the second the most severe since the Great Depression.

In the decade after Minnesota's income tax reductions, our economy fared worse than the nation and most other states. And at both the federal and state levels, big tax cuts followed by serious recessions produced large budget deficits, which threaten our current fiscal strength and future economic prosperity.

The solutions to those deficits were very clear. However, they were also very painful; so they were postponed, then postponed again, and again. Unfortunately, avoiding financial problems usually makes them worse. Fixing them then becomes even harder.

Thus, when I became governor in January 2011, the state budget forecast projected a $6 billion deficit for the next two fiscal years. It took six months of difficult negotiations with the Republican-controlled legislature to finally agree upon a balanced budget.

Those decisions were hard for all of us and far more painful for all the Minnesotans denied needed services and assistance. But we had to enact a balanced budget, and we did.

Since then, an improving state economy and savings from health care reforms have boosted our finances by $2.5 billion for this biennium, enabling us to restore our reserves and repay over 60 percent of the previous school shifts.

We have repaired much of the fiscal damage we inherited, but we're not done yet. We face another deficit, projected at $1.1 billion, for the next biennium; and we still owe our schools another $1.1 billion.

My budget for the next biennium would lift us out of this miserable deficit-to-deficit cycle. It would eliminate the $1.1 billion deficit, balance the biennial budget, and begin the following biennium with a projected surplus that would enable us to pay back the remainder of the school shift.

My proposals have already aroused considerable controversy. Such debate is healthy in our democracy.

The genius of our system of governance is that no one gets to have it all her or his way. Starting with the governor.

Some will characterize any legislative changes in my budget as my loss. I don't see it that way at all. The winners I care about are the people of Minnesota, whose collective best interests I was elected to represent. As were you in the legislature. Whatever outcome does the most to improve the lives of the most Minnesotans makes winners of us all.

However, before we refocus on that controversy, I think we should look farther ahead. Former Governor Arne Carlson liked to say, "If you don't know where you're going, any road will take you there." I appreciate that wisdom more every year.

Where do we want to go? Where do we want Minnesota to be in a year, in a decade, or more? We will not agree on every aspect. However, if we can discover our shared goals, perhaps we will find greater accord on how best to achieve them. We can also better assess whether the path we're now on will lead us to them.

This perspective also broadens the time horizon of our decision-making. We must consider not only what is right for Minnesota today but also what is best for Minnesota in the future. So, what do I believe offers the best hope for a better future to most Minnesotans? I want Minnesota to provide the best jobs for our citizens, the best lives for their families, and the best environment for our businesses to provide those jobs.

Those who measure "business climate" only by tax rankings will question my strategy, although many surveys rate Minnesota lower in overall taxes than most are led to believe. We're fifteenth among the states in taxes, according to the Minnesota Center for Fiscal Excellence. And we rank eleventh highest in per capita income.

However, Minnesota has not been considered a "low tax" state during my almost four decades of public service. And the facts show that states offering businesses and their top executives the lowest taxes usually offer the rest of their citizens the lowest incomes, the fewest public services, and the highest crime rates.

Furthermore, their job growth typically lags "high value and high performance" states like Minnesota.

So, yes, I absolutely meant what I said. I want Minnesota to provide the best jobs for our citizens, the best lives for their families, and the best support for our businesses to provide those jobs. I want Minnesota state government to provide the best value for everyone's hard-earned tax dollars and the most efficient, effective services anywhere.

I want Minnesota to offer the world's best educations for ALL of our citizens, children and grandchildren. Educations which begin early in life and continue throughout life; so that all of us can learn the skills, and relearn the new skills, necessary to succeed in a rapidly changing and ever-more-competitive global economy.

We know that our exceptional citizens, who are more inventive, harder working, and more productive than people anywhere, have been the most important contributors to our state's economic progress and social vitality. Most of us agree that our citizens' superior educations have been crucial to our previous successes.

And many of us agree that providing all Minnesotans with the best, most advanced, and yet affordable educational opportunities will be even more essential to their future success, and thus to ours.

I will return shortly to consider whether we are on a path toward that goal.

I want all of us, and especially Minnesota's future generations, to live in a healthy environment; in safe, inclusive communities; and with the same rights and protections as every other American citizen.

A healthy life starts with, and depends upon, clean air to breathe, clean water to drink, protected natural environments to enjoy, and a secure ecological future. No one can endure the severe droughts or floods of recent years; endure (or, some, enjoy) our milder, snow-scarce winters; lather on sunscreen to walk outdoors without being greatly alarmed.

If you're not, talk with my good friend and world-premier polar explorer Will Steger, who is here tonight, about the drastic climate changes he has witnessed.

Even more alarming is that our state and our nation are still not doing enough to reverse this path toward global catastrophe before it is too late.

In Minnesota, we have made real progress in areas like energy conservation, more efficient farming and manufacturing practices, and the development and use of clean, renewable energy, especially wind energy, instead of polluting fossil fuels.

The question is: Are we progressing fast enough? Are we doing all we can to utilize other renewables, such as solar, and also to make Minnesota the best place to locate these new industries and their jobs?

Many of you who served in previous legislatures deserve great credit for your pioneering work to expand our use of clean energy, including Lieutenant Governor Yvonne Prettner Solon and former Senator Ellen Anderson, who is also here tonight.

I challenge this legislature to work again with our state's visionary clean energy advocates, large energy providers, large energy users, other stakeholders, and my administration to use your past achievements as springboards for Minnesota's next big leap toward a sustainable energy future. Safe, inclusive communities benefit all Minnesotans. Doing everything possible to stop the terrible acts of violence, which end young lives and victimize innocent people, should be an urgent priority for all of us.

Those strategies deserve and require more time than I have available tonight. Let me focus on one initiative, however, and enlist everyone's support.

Studies show that the highest incidences of juvenile delinquency and teenage pregnancy occur during the weekday hours after school. Years ago, there were more organized, supervised after-school programs for young people. The ones remaining do exceptional work; but there are not enough of them, and they struggle to find the funding to continue.

Two years ago, I challenged businesses to "adopt a school." Some businesses, to their great credit, were already involved in improving our schools, and others accepted my challenge.

Some, however, especially smaller businesses, have told me it was just too big an assignment to adopt an entire school.

So, I invite you to "adopt an after-school program." It might involve a financial contribution, the donation of new or used equipment, or your employees as part-time volunteers. There are so many from which to choose, and so many young people who need better options than unoccupied time, streets, and gangs.

In the coming weeks, we will be releasing more information on how you can help. In the meantime, if you need help finding a worthy program, give me a call. I believe most of you have my home phone number by now. If not, it's 651-201-3468.

For the next two weeks, however, I'm taking calls at home only from "adopt an after-school program" volunteers. On anything else, please call my office, at 651-201-3499.

Let me mention one other cause which is controversial but consistent with my faith and my principles. And, more importantly, consistent with this country's founding principles and its

Constitution. I believe that every Minnesotan should have the freedom to marry legally the person she or he loves, whether of the same or other sex.

Last year, Minnesotans began a conversation about why marriage matters, and we found our common belief that it is about love, commitment, and responsibility. I want Minnesota to be a state which affirms that freedom for one means freedom for everyone and where no one is told it is illegal to marry the person you love.

I realize now that I could fill the rest of the evening, and most of tomorrow morning, with my goals for "a better Minnesota." I doubt that anyone wants to sit here for that long, and we're not set up to serve breakfast!

Many of my goals, however, are contained in my budget for the next biennium, along with new and continuing strategies to help us attain them. My budget addresses two overriding imperatives: First, to erase a $1.1 billion deficit and balance the rest of it, while continuing to improve the efficiency and quality of state services; and second, to make the investments necessary to move Minnesota ahead.

How does it meet the first requirement? The old-fashioned way: by decreasing spending, enacting cost-saving reforms, and raising revenues. My budget is balanced, fair, and honest—there are no gimmicks, no games.

I reduce projected state spending while increasing investments in more jobs and better education. I continue our significant progress in improving the quality and the efficiency of state services.

And I raise revenues responsibly for the first time in many years, while also making our tax structure fairer for hardworking, middle-income Minnesotans.

My budget would reduce overall state spending for the next biennium by $1.8 billion below what was projected when I took office in 2011. Back then, the state budget forecast predicted that laws enacted by the previous governor and legislature would result in expenditures of almost $39.7 billion during fiscal years 2014 and 2015. My current budget proposes spending $37.9 billion in that biennium, $1.8 billion less than originally forecasted.

That's worth repeating. My proposed budget for the next biennium would spend $1.8 billion less than was forecasted for those two years when I took office.

Those who criticize my supposed lack of spending reductions evidently do not understand that many of the $2 billion cuts we made two years ago for the current biennium were permanent; and lowered spending by $2.5 billion in the next biennium before I made my new proposals.

Take state funding for higher education, for example, which comprises the University of Minnesota, the MnSCU system, and student financial aid. Facing an overall $6 billion deficit, the 2011 legislature and I had to cut state support for higher education by 12 percent, to $2,568,000.

Last November's budget forecast assumed the next biennium's expenditures for higher education would be the same as in the current biennium. Take a look. There are no spending increases for higher education; so, the previous 12 percent cut would continue into the next one. However, that significant cut is only the latest reduction in state support for higher education. Last weekend, I searched the Department of Management and Budget's computerized archives, looking for a previous biennium when the State of Minnesota spent less money, in real dollars, to support higher education.

I couldn't find one in records, which go back to the 1996–97 biennium. I did learn that in real dollars, our state spends $569 million less on higher education in the current biennium than we did sixteen years ago.

I asked the MMB staff to look back even further, into the paper records. They found that the last time we actually spent less to support higher education, in real dollars, than we are in fiscal year 12–13 . . . was in fiscal year 80–81.

I'll say it again. In every biennium since fiscal year 80–81, real state spending for all of postsecondary education has been higher than it is today.

My budget would add $240 million in higher education funding for the next biennium. That counts as spending increase, which technically it is. However, it falls over $100 million short of restoring the funding cut from fiscal year 10–11; and it still leaves state support for higher education hundreds of million dollars below the real levels twenty and even thirty years ago.

No wonder the most recent comparison of the fifty states by their expenditures for higher education per $1,000 of personal income ranked Minnesota only thirty-second. And no wonder tuitions keep rising, making a Minnesota college education less and less affordable for students and their families.

How much lower will we reduce our spending for postsecondary education, either in real dollars or compared to other states? Experts everywhere say that the quality and affordability of higher education is key to our future economic success. Does anyone believe that continuing to reduce our commitment to higher education is the path to a better Minnesota?

Analyzing other areas of state government spending yields similar results. During the past decade, our state leaders reduced expenditures for many public services, both in real dollars and in comparison to other states. The latest survey places Minnesota thirty-third among the states in total expenditures for K–12 education per $1,000 of personal income; thirty-seventh for health and hospitals; nineteenth for police protection; and forty-eighth for fighting fires.

Are we better off today after all those reductions in public services? I say no. Trying to cut our way to a better Minnesota is a failed experiment.

That is why my budget takes a balanced approach. Real spending cuts are partly offset by responsible increases, mostly for better education from early childhood through postsecondary and for job creation incentives. Both are critical to assuring future economic opportunities and enhancing our quality of life.

Overall spending reductions and selective increases are one part of my balanced approach to eliminating the deficit, balancing the budget, and moving Minnesota ahead. Another important strategy is to expand the significant reforms which my administration has made during its first two years in reducing the costs of services and improving their efficiencies.

We have instituted more reforms and achieved greater progress during our first two years than in all of the previous eight years. I will briefly mention just a few.

Today, Minnesota has retaken its rightful place as a national leader in health care reform. The cost of providing health care for increasing numbers of our citizens has for years been the most rapidly growing part of our state budget, as is true for virtually every other state. Curbing those cost increases, while expanding quality and affordable health care to all of our citizens, is crucial. Our Department of Human Services contracts with managed care providers and insurance companies for most of its health care services. Thus our first target for reform was the way the state had previously contracted for those services; and we have already achieved significant cost savings.

Commissioner Lucinda Jesson's tremendous success in negotiating a one percent profit cap on existing contracts and putting the largest new contracts out for competitive bids have saved state and federal taxpayers over $1 billion.

Our reforms do not stop there. My new budget proposes a comprehensive redesign of the fastest growing part of our HHS budget, our long-term care system. By providing more choices to keep seniors and people with disabilities in their homes, with better care, we save $151 million in the short term. More importantly, we will have built a system that is financially sustainable when the age wave descends upon Minnesota starting in 2020.

Last week we announced yet another reform measure that will change how the state pays for public health insurance, providing better care for 100,000 Minnesotans and saving taxpayers an estimated $90 million.

Finally, Minnesota is one of the leading states in implementing this country's sweeping and far-reaching reform of providing and paying for health care.

Over the next two years, our public programs will provide health care to an additional 145,000 poor Minnesotans who do not have insurance today. These are people who otherwise access care through costly emergency room visits, harming their health and driving up the price of health care for all of us.

And through the creation of a Minnesota Insurance Exchange, we will enable individuals, families, and businesses to make more informed decisions about good, affordable health care coverage.

In education, we have worked with DFL and Republican legislators, business executives, and other civic leaders to establish state support for early childhood learning programs, a quality rating system, and scholarships for low-income children.

My new budget would expand significantly early learning opportunities for children statewide. My proposal to provide state funds for optional all-day kindergarten would provide a continuum of learning from early childhood into first grade and beyond.

Two years ago, we worked with the legislature to make administrative and legislative reforms that streamlined businesses' permit application processes. We shortened the time taken by the Pollution Control Agency to review permit applications to a maximum of 150 days for all but the largest projects.

We are now progressing toward the next goal of reducing those timelines to ninety days.

We're not done reforming. In fact, we're just getting started. Back in 1998, when I first ran for governor, a campaign that most people have forgotten and I would like to, there was a television commercial for the soft drink 7UP. Contrasting itself to Coke and Pepsi, it proudly called itself the "Un-Cola."

In my campaign, I proposed making an even-year legislative session "the Unsession." Except for responding to a fiscal or other emergency and passing a bonding bill, the session would be devoted to eliminating unnecessary or redundant laws, rules, and regulations; reducing the verbiage in those that remain; shortening the timelines for developing and implementing them; and undoing anything else which makes government nearly impossible to understand, operate, or support.

I suggest making next year's legislative session the first "Unsession." After this session is concluded . . . on time, in May . . . I will ask my agency heads and legislative staff to begin making lists, checking them twice, and working with any legislators, other public officials, and citizens who wish to spearhead these reforms.

The third component of my balanced budget approach raises state revenues, which will be necessary to eliminate the deficit and still prevent further reductions in the services and assistance that many Minnesotans need.

Raising revenues requires asking someone to pay more taxes. Making taxes fairer requires asking more of those citizens and corporations who now pay less than their proportionate share.

Few people like paying taxes, even when they're fair. No one likes paying more taxes, even when necessary to make them fair.

But when taxes are unfair . . . and remain unfair, not only do the people who are forced to pay more rightfully resent it; but they also lose faith in their elected officials who won't change it.

Today, more and more hardworking, middle-class Minnesotans believe that the state's tax structure is unfair to them.

And they're right. The facts compiled by the nonpartisan staff at the Minnesota Department of Revenue show that the richest Minnesotans pay less of their incomes in state and local taxes than most other Minnesotans. Large multinational corporations headquartered here admit their effective tax rates are well below the 9.8 percent paid by many smaller businesses.

Thanks to the excellent work of Minnesota 2020, I recently became aware of a new study by the Institute on Taxation and Economic Policy which confirms the Department of Revenue's analysis. It found that middle-class Minnesotans pay 26 percent more state and local taxes per dollar of income than do the top one percent of our state's income earners.

When people who have the most pay the least, this state and nation are in trouble. When lobbyists protect tax favors for special interests at the cost of everyone else's best interests, this state and nation are in trouble. My goal is to get us out of trouble.

As I see it, we have three basic budget options.

Plan A is the one I have proposed, or something close to it.

Plan B is to stick with our current tax structure, or something close to it.

Plan C is something better. No one would be happier than me to see a good Plan C. I'm still looking and I'm sure listening. But without one, our choices are between Plans A and B. Let me briefly address some of my concerns with Plan B, sticking with the status quo. Most of us want stability and certainty in our lives. When confronted with the need for change and its resulting uncertainties, it's human nature to hunker down, hang on, and hope that the established order will return.

Today's reality, however, is that the old order doesn't show any signs of coming back. Our state and our nation are engulfed by the new, global economy. We either act now to move ahead or let ourselves fall behind.

Retaining the current tax structure doesn't even solve our current budget problems; much less advance our state to a better future. It still leaves a $1.1 billion deficit, which I insist must be resolved through honest, responsible measures. It leaves important services severely cut. And it leaves us unable to make the new investments, especially in jobs, economic growth, and education that I believe are essential to a better Minnesota.

I have a respectful but strong disagreement with some of the other elected officials here tonight about the value of public investments in, and incentives for, economic growth. My father and uncles taught me the paramount importance of continuous private and public investments in improving the communities in which people work and live. In my job, I apply that principle to the "community" of Minnesota.

For two years, my proposals to make capital investments in the downtowns of major cities, like St. Paul, Duluth, Rochester, Mankato, and St. Cloud, and investments in smaller but equally essential projects throughout Minnesota were rejected by Republican legislative leaders. Despite a lagging construction industry and good Minnesotans in the building trades unable to find work, they just said no.

Well, just saying no just won't work . . . not in Rochester, where the renowned Mayo Clinic wants us to help them continue to outclass their competitors in other states and other countries . . . and to continue doing so from Rochester. I thank Mayo, whose CEO Dr. John Noseworthy is with us tonight as a guest of Speaker Thissen, for giving Minnesota this chance to partner with them and help assure their world medical preeminence for decades to come . . . in Rochester, Minnesota.

Our vitally important agriculture economy is crucial to our state's future. We cannot afford NOT to keep making new investments to support innovation, new production efficiencies, and even greater prosperity. That is why state funding for the Agricultural Growth, Research, and Innovation Program must remain a high priority. I have shared with University of Minnesota President Eric Kaler, who is here this evening, my high priority to return the university's medical school to the national prominence it has previously achieved; and he has told me that he shares that goal. That turnaround, however, will require public investments.

I have talked with MnSCU Chancellor Rosenstone about the critical importance of his campuses retooling their programs to prepare their students for the jobs of the future. I know that the chancellor is addressing this imperative. However, revising curricula, modernizing equipment, and upgrading technology all will require public investments.

And I have not even mentioned tonight . . . nor does my budget address . . . the critical need to invest in improving our highways, roads, and bridges statewide; our public transit systems; our aging infrastructure; and the list goes on.

We can choose, as others in our positions have before us, to ignore these growing problems, avoid fixing them, and hope they don't crash down upon us while we're in office.

Or, we can lead. That is what the people of Minnesota elected us to do. That is what they need us to do.

They need us to lead our state forward. Not back to failed ideologies of the past, now masquerading in new jargon. Not remaining locked into what might have worked in the past but is faltering now, and will likely fail in the future.

It is an awesome responsibility—to know that Minnesota's future will depend, in part, on the choices that we are called upon to make.

Those choices will not be easy; and some of them will not be popular. But it is time to prove that Minnesota's leaders are capable of more than ideological skirmishes and political stalemates, which offend our state's citizens and jeopardize our state's future.

This is our time and our responsibility . . . to work together and build a state that works. So, if you're coming to this State Capitol during the next four months, bring your best ideas and your sincere convictions. Bring your work boots and your hard hats. If you're interested in nothing more than throwing rocks and casting blame, send the rest of us a letter . . . or a postcard. But if you really want to pitch in, all the way in, even sacrifice a little of your self-interest for everyone's better interests . . . welcome. We need you. Your state needs you.

And please remember always. You're here to serve the best interests of all the people of Minnesota. Not just your clients. Not just your constituents. Not just the people who agree with you. Or who agree with me.

You are here. I am here. We are all here . . . to serve *all* of Minnesota. To serve the cause of a better Minnesota.

So, let us begin.

— SECOND INAUGURAL ADDRESS, 2015 —

Thank you, Chief Justice Gildea. It has been an honor to work with you during the past four years.

Justice Page, thank you for your extraordinary service to the people of Minnesota. Justice Lillehaug, it is great to have you up here.

On a personal note, I'd like to welcome the members of my immediate family who are with me today. My father, Bruce Dayton, who is now ninety-six years old, is here with his wife, Ruth. My brother, Brandt, and my sisters, Lucy and Anne, have traveled from New York City and Helena, Montana.

You just saw my wonderful son Eric and daughter-in-law Cory—along with my grandson, Hugo, who makes four generations of Daytons here today.

I give special thanks to my father, Bruce Dayton. Dad, you have been a guiding light throughout my life. I would not be standing here today without your love and support. Thank you.

Vice President Mondale; Senator Klobuchar; our constitutional officers; other distinguished guests; and my fellow Minnesotans.

Thank you for the opportunity to serve as your governor for four more years. I especially want to thank you who voted for me and placed your trust in me. I will do my very best to serve you well.

I will do my very best to serve all Minnesotans well.

We gather today at a much better time than when I took this oath of office four years ago. Back then, both our state and nation were struggling to recover from "the Great Recession." Minnesota's unemployment rate was 6.8 percent; nationally it was 9.1 percent.

Since then, our country's economy has improved; and our

state has helped lead the way. Minnesota's unemployment rate has dropped to a remarkable 3.7 percent.

We have added over 191,000 jobs during the past four years—and we're not done yet. Recently, it was reported that our nation's economy grew at a five percent annual rate during the third quarter, the fastest pace in over eleven years. The Dow Jones Industrial Average topped 18,000.

Many economists are now optimistic that our country is entering a period of more robust growth. Yet, recent reports also show that inequities in Americans' wealth and income are at record highs.

Perhaps that explains the large divide between the new optimism on Wall Street and the persistent pessimism on Main Street, where real wages and median family incomes have continued to fall, even during this recovery.

Two-thirds of Americans currently believe our country is "on the wrong track." Only one-fourth say it's now going "in the right direction."

But what is the "right direction"? Many Americans would like to go back in time—to regain what they had before. The world, however, has moved into a new era—marked by globalization—where companies and countries engage in fierce competition to create the lowest-cost production sites in the world and reap the profits from doing so.

This dispersion of economic activity has cost millions of Americans their jobs, their economic security, and their confidence in the future.

The world today offers many good opportunities. Yet, while there are many roads to successful, fulfilling lives, there is, essentially, just one path. It is through education, training, and the development of marketable skills.

Surrounded by low-cost competition, the United States retains one enormous advantage—the inventive and entrepreneurial abilities of our people. Most of our challengers, be they companies or countries, have not mastered the complexities of conceiving and designing new products and services; then organizing and financing them; then managing a group of people to produce or provide them.

In Minnesota, we have a further advantage—one that has been our greatest asset for generations. Our citizens have long known that a good education is the key to our success. Now, we need to realize that a good education is the key to our survival.

And that an excellent education unlocks the door to unprecedented opportunities. Our future success—the health of our families, the vitality of our communities, and the prosperity of our state—will depend upon our making those excellent educations available to all Minnesotans.

We're partway there.

We have ample evidence that most of our students are now receiving good educations. Many are getting great educations, from talented teachers, professors, and other educators throughout our state.

But are all of our students learning what they will need—to find good jobs and achieve success in the world that awaits them? If we're going to improve people's lives in our state, we have to improve their educations. We have to create a state of educational excellence.

How? By investing in it.

There's a big difference between spending and investing. Spending is for now. People spend money to buy what they need or want right away.

Investing is for the future. People invest money now to produce future benefits and rewards. Wise financial management requires understanding this difference. And striking a proper balance between them.

In the coming months, we will make important decisions about spending or investing a projected state budget surplus of

$1 billion. We could spend it to provide goods and services for more people. We could spend it to provide tax cuts for some people.

I recommend that our top priority be to invest it in a better future—first and foremost, by investing it in excellent education. This means elevating our citizens' educations from good to excellent.

And making that educational excellence available to everyone.

To begin, we need to make quality educational experiences available to all our children, even before they reach school age. In one of the best initiatives of my first term, we now offer free, all-day kindergarten throughout Minnesota. We have created better opportunities for five-year-olds everywhere to develop the intellectual and social skills they will need—not just to survive, but to thrive.

This new effort has also shown us the number of children who are not ready for kindergarten. If our response is to do nothing—or too little—to remedy the disparities, we know that they will later cause worse crises for those kids—and for us.

So, we must expand and improve our early education and childcare programs. Additionally, some children's needs go beyond early education. They must be better protected from neglect and abuse.

We must do more to prevent the mistreatment of Minnesota's children and to intervene quickly and effectively when necessary. We must also develop the mental health resources to help them overcome those traumas.

I don't have the expertise to design those initiatives. However, we have many legislators, educators, doctors, social workers, judges, and others who do. During the next five months, let us decide what more we must do to save our children. Then, do it.

After we get healthier, better-prepared children into our schools, we need to elevate their academic experiences—from better elementary and secondary school academics, to better emotional support and career guidance, to postsecondary educations that will better lead to success. I don't want to spend more education dollars on what is being done now. And I won't spend more on doing less.

I'll oppose four-day school weeks, less time in classrooms, or shorter school years. The era of shortchanging our students' educations is over.

Instead, I want investments for more time in studies and other developmental activities. For year-round school options. For after-school and special help services. For advanced high school and college courses in skills needed for the jobs of the future.

In the face of such intense global competition, for the sake of our children and the continued growth of our economy, we cannot do anything less.

Some critics will say: Invest more money in education? But we spend so much already! Unfortunately, no—we don't. According to the most recent U.S. Census report, Minnesota presently ranks twenty-fourth among the fifty states in per-pupil elementary and secondary school spending.

Our state's support for higher education in real dollars recently fell to its lowest level in thirty years.

During the past four years, we started to reverse the previous decade's disinvestment—with all-day kindergarten, early childhood scholarships, per-pupil aid increases, and more postsecondary assistance. But those new investments have only returned Minnesota's education expenditures to the national average—and that's not good enough.

Now, with $1 billion surplus, the question is not: "Can we afford to provide Minnesotans with the best educations?" It is: "Can we afford to continue providing less?"

The answer, obviously, is "No!"

For that reason, and for the sake of our state's future, I will dedicate the next four years to regaining our state's position as a national and global leader in education excellence.

I want all Minnesotans to have access to the best possible educations, to the skills and training they will need to achieve their highest aspirations.

In the days ahead, I will talk about other essential investments—including transportation. I also recognize that there are other important, unmet needs in the lives of many Minnesotans. I know that many advocates sincerely believe their needs—or their clients' needs—should be our state's top priority—and funded accordingly.

I look forward to working with the outstanding legislative leaders who are here today, and with their colleagues who will begin tomorrow, to better address those needs.

In closing, I note that much attention has been given recently to the divisions within our state. Most of them are familiar. During my forty years in and around Minnesota governance, those resentments have simmered and, occasionally, erupted.

There's Greater Minnesota against the Metro Area. Central cities versus suburbs. Urban schools against rural districts. East Metro versus West Metro. Cities, counties, and townships compared to other cities, counties, and townships.

Someone always believes that someone else is getting a better deal.

Those rivalries are not going to disappear. However, they cannot be permitted to blind us to the larger truth that we are all ONE MINNESOTA.

What binds us together is much more important than what pulls us apart. What helps one region usually benefits our entire state. Not always, but usually.

Economic growth in one area pays for property tax relief in another. Good farm prices in southern Minnesota boost sales and revenues in metro stores. Shops in Duluth do better when the Range is at full production.

Better transit in the West Metro adds to the vitality of the East Metro, and vice versa. Counties benefit when cities within their borders are thriving—and when other cities in other counties are thriving.

What helps some Minnesotans usually helps all of us. So let's cheer each other's successes, not resent them.

And finally, let's remember that not only are we all one, we are also number one. When it comes to promoting Minnesota's virtues, we're too modest. Besides, we're often so focused on what we think is wrong, we forget everything that is right. And—if we do remember—we're careful not to talk about it.

But we do need to talk about it. Not as an exercise in collective self-esteem, but because we're competing with forty-nine other states and many countries to attract the best and the brightest—students, scientists, nurses, doctors, mechanics, machinists, entrepreneurs, executives—the talent upon which our future success depends.

When it's all added up and all sorted out, most of us live in Minnesota because we want to. We know we're not perfect; but we're very good—and getting even better. Let's not forget that our state is often recognized by national and international experts as among the best or even the very best.

Casting all Minnesota modesty aside—we should be proud. Because we so often are the best. And because when we are, we have earned it. Through smart minds, good ideas, and hard work. Through all of us pulling together and making our state—despite lacking the advantages of ocean beaches, or rocky mountains, or fossil fuel riches—into a place unique and extraordinary.

A state upon which we proudly emblazon our motto: "L'Etoile du Nord," "The Star of the North," and bequeath it even brighter to future generations.

— STATE OF THE STATE ADDRESS, 2018 —

Madam President, the Majority and Minority Leaders, and Members of the Minnesota Senate; Mr. Speaker, the Majority and Minority Leaders, and Members of the Minnesota House of Representatives.

Madam Chief Justice and the Distinguished Members of the Minnesota Supreme Court and the Court of Appeals.

My fellow constitutional officers.

And my fellow Minnesotans.

Especially my about to be five-year-old grandson Hugo, sitting up there.

Some people have suggested I conclude my speech now, to make certain I can walk out by myself.

However, this is my final state of the state address, and there is more I want to say. So, cross your fingers, Hugo, 'cause here we go!

As I prepare to leave office, I want to thank the people of Minnesota, who twice voted for me to serve as their governor. And thank the legislators, supporters, and allies who helped us succeed.

To my fabulous staff, fantastic commissioners, and other key appointees, you have my eternal gratitude.

You deserve so much of the credit for our administration's successes.

Your dedication has been extraordinary; your wisdom exceptional; and your resilience remarkable.

I want to thank my family, who have counseled me wisely, supported me steadfastly, and endured me patiently: my sensational sons, Eric and Andrew; daughter-in-law Cory; grandsons Hugo and George; my former wife and dear friend, Alida Messinger; my father, siblings and spouses, uncles, aunts, and cousins. Without you, I would not be here today.

My father used to say, "Time flies when you're having fun; and even when you're not." Being governor was not fun when I took office in January 2011. State government was in terrible financial condition, with a $6.2 billion deficit forecasted for the next two fiscal years. The state had "borrowed" almost $2 billion from our public schools, and had used millions of dollars more in shifts and gimmicks to mask the full extent of the deficit.

You might remember that I campaigned for governor in 2010 on a pledge to raise state income taxes on only the wealthiest two percent of Minnesotans, and not on the other 98 percent.

In 2013, with DFL majorities in both the House and Senate, we passed that two percent increase on the top two percent of our taxpayers.

The change has made Minnesota's tax system more progressive and has been crucial in turning chronic budget deficits into steady surpluses; paying off the state's debt to our schools; eliminating other fiscal shenanigans; and building a $1.9 billion budget and cash reserve.

We have restored fiscal stability and integrity to state government. I thank those Minnesotans who did pay higher personal income taxes, and the great many others who expanded their businesses and created over 280,000 new jobs since I took office. The hardworking people and businesses of Minnesota are the sources of our renewed economic prosperity and the foundations of our future success.

What must we do to continue that success? Tax cuts are some people's answers. Tax cuts are always some people's answers.

In 1997, what is now the Minnesota Center for Fiscal Excellence published its first "How Does Minnesota Compare?" with the other states. In fiscal year 1996, Minnesota's individual income tax collections per $1,000 of personal income ranked us third highest among the states.

A Republican governor. Third-highest income tax state. In

fiscal year 2002, the last year of an Independence Party governor's term, Minnesota still had the third-highest personal income tax collections among all the states. In fiscal year 2010, the last year of my Republican predecessor's term, Minnesota's personal income tax collections per $1,000 of income were the sixth highest among the states.

In the center's latest report, published last September, Minnesota's personal income tax ranking for fiscal year 2015 was again sixth highest, the same as it was in fiscal year 2010.

Minnesota has not been a low tax state during my career. And it's fortunate, because states with the lowest taxes generally rank among the lowest in per capita income, household income, educational attainment, home ownership, and public health.

By contrast, Minnesota's total job creation, average household income, and state economic output have improved steadily—both in real terms and relative to other states.

It's not that raising taxes is, by itself, a good thing; it's that investing those revenues in education and infrastructure produce far better returns in improving our economy's vitality and our residents' well-being.

They produce more jobs and better jobs.

If we, and our successors, preserve our state's fiscal integrity and invest our present tax system's revenues in even better education, infrastructure, and transportation, we will continue to offer better jobs, with higher incomes and other benefits to our residents.

If we don't, we won't.

During my two terms, we have made substantial increases in our state investments in education—in our people—starting from early childhood; to universal, all-day kindergarten; all the way through elementary, secondary, and postsecondary education.

This school year, nearly 80,000 children are attending all-day kindergarten and early learning programs thanks to those wise investments; and those 80,000 children are getting better starts in school and life because of them.

Business after business tells me the number one reason they are locating or expanding in Minnesota is because of the superb quality of our workers.

One major industrial operation in northern Minnesota told me just last week that his company has fourteen plants throughout North America. When he is recruiting new customers, he brings them to his plant here in Minnesota—to show off his workers' exceptional productivity, the quality of their products, and their skill in making them.

Those qualities are ingrained in our state's people, which they pass on from one generation to the next.

But they must be nurtured, trained, and employed to achieve their full potentials.

Minnesotans understand the importance of education, but what most don't realize is how badly the state's financial support had slackened in the years before I became governor. When I started, the state's funding for elementary and secondary education per $1,000 of personal income was in the bottom half of the fifty states.

Most recently, we ranked eighteenth, according to the Minnesota Center for Fiscal Excellence.

That's better, but it's not good enough.

And it explains why our public schools are constantly having to hold special property tax referendums to ask for what should be funded by the much more progressive state income tax.

With us tonight is Mr. Corey Bulman, a high school teacher in the Mound Westonka school district, who was Minnesota's Teacher of the Year.

It is thanks to you, Mr. Bulman, and Minnesota's thousands of other dedicated teachers that last year, our students once again topped the nation on ACT college entrance exam scores. Our teachers and our students deserve our strong support.

State government's funding for higher education has also declined. In 2012, state support for the University of Minnesota, Minnesota State, and financial aid was, in real dollars, the lowest it had been since 1981. Once again, we have restored some of that loss, but we have still shifted too much of the costs of attending our state colleges and universities onto students and their parents.

Both Minnesota State and the University of Minnesota were funded well below the systems' requests last year. The university just announced that with $10 million of additional state funding in this session, it will not need to raise tuition this next school year. I will include that $10 million in my supplemental budget request, along with an additional $10 million for Minnesota State, and I urge the legislature's bipartisan support.

Our two outstanding postsecondary leaders, University of Minnesota President Kaler and Minnesota State's Chancellor Malholtra, are with us tonight. Recognize them please. I salute you both, and thank you for your service.

Further damaging the future success of our colleges and universities is the chronic inadequacy of our state's capital investments in their campuses. It's almost impossible to provide world-class educations in antiquated buildings with leaky ceilings, dilapidated bathrooms, worn-out exteriors, and in classrooms without advanced technologies and other learning aids.

That is why my bonding bill provides more money for capital improvements on Minnesota State and University of Minnesota campuses than either system requested. I know they asked for less than what they need, because they thought that was all the legislature would support. Well . . . surprise them!

If we invest more in education, future generations of Minnesotans will be more successful. If we don't, they won't. Another priority of my bonding bill is infrastructure. Since I could not meet all local needs, I made, as my priority, water infrastructure, especially projects to make our residents' water cleaner and safer. In addition to the $105.7 million in last year's bonding bill, I would provide the Public Facilities Authority with an additional $167 million to ensure that more Minnesotans have the clean water they need.

Over 170 local water infrastructure projects across our state cannot move forward without this funding.

Please provide that safety in your bonding bill.

Another crucial area for infrastructure investments is in transportation, which also was poorly financed for years. Everyone driving in our state knows that traffic congestion and highway conditions keep getting worse, wasting their time and straining their sanity.

After years of my urging, the legislature has started to increase state expenditures for road and bridge repairs and improvements. Unfortunately, most of that additional money has been taken from the general fund, $588 million last session.

That's a convenient solution—for as long as state budget surpluses continue. However, some people are now proposing to transfer ALL revenue collected from sales taxes on motor vehicle repairs and maintenance from the general fund to the highway fund, and even dedicate it constitutionally.

Such a transfer would cost the general fund $1,354,000 over just four years. It would further undermine the structural surpluses in future bienniums.

While I support additional investments in our transportation infrastructure, I strongly urge legislators to consider carefully the fiscal impacts of this deceptive solution, and instead look to sustainable, long-term financing for the roads, bridges, and modern transit systems that Minnesotans need.

The people of Minnesota want to see an evenly divided legislature . . .

Restoring fiscal stability to our state budget is one of the most important legacies I can leave Minnesota.

During my final year in office, I will not support any budget, tax, or policy proposals which would threaten that stability. I urge legislators to do the same.

We face other major challenges. After several years of lowering the state's uninsured rate under the Affordable Care Act, 116,000 Minnesotans have lost or dropped their health insurance during the past two years. Our state's uninsured rate jumped from 4.3 percent in 2015, the nation's second lowest, to 6.3 percent last year.

The number one reason was that people could no longer afford it. Or they were fed up with being charged higher premiums and deductibles for lesser coverage.

Therese and Brian Romsdahl, who grow corn and soybeans and raise beef cattle in Butterfield, have joined us here tonight. Therese and Brian, thank you for being here. You feed our nation, you feed our world. We thank you.

Like most Minnesota farmers, Therese and Brian are being hurt by exceedingly low commodity prices.

Now they are being charged $33,000 this year for their health care premiums. $33,000. That's outrageous and it's wrong.

Meanwhile, some insurance companies have stopped offering individual coverage because of lower returns and Washington's uncertainties. This exodus has caused many Minnesotans, especially those living in rural areas, to lose their previous insurance carriers and often their established networks of doctors and providers.

"Pay more for less" has never been popular. People quickly ask, "What are my other options?" Right now, for affordable health insurance, they have none.

However, this legislature has the opportunity, and the responsibility, to offer Minnesotans another option.

For twenty-six years, MinnesotaCare has given lower-income working families quality, affordable choices when purchasing their health insurance. I believe we should give all Minnesotans that option.

After its start-up, the operating costs of this new "MinnesotaCare Buy-In" would be paid entirely by its members' premiums, so there's no ongoing expense to other taxpayers.

For some families, the MinnesotaCare Buy-In may offer better health care coverage at lower costs. That is exactly what competition is supposed to do for consumers.

Legislators have a very clear choice. They can side with big insurance companies, who don't want this competition; or they can side with Minnesotans, who do.

Our Minnesota lawmakers face another clear choice this session. They can side with the NRA, who strongly opposes commonsense solutions to reduce gun violence in our schools and communities, or they can side with the schoolchildren of Minnesota who are begging us for it. And I salute all of the Minnesota students who took a stand today to march to tell us adults that they need safe schools.

On Monday, four state senators courageously stood together on the side of our students. I thank them for their legislation to extend criminal background checks to all gun purchases and require all lost or stolen firearms be promptly reported to law enforcement.

Will you stand and be willing to be recognized? Thank you. Please? We should take attendance at these things, no way to find out who's [here] . . .

Those changes will help keep guns out of the hands of people who shouldn't have them.

They will save lives.

I want to thank the many legislators in this chamber—from both parties—who are fighting for these and other lifesaving measures to reduce gun violence in our state. I will sign any of that legislation the minute it reaches my desk.

Helpful when you clap, gives me a chance to hydrate.

The recently passed federal tax bill is extremely complex and defies a simple solution. If we conform state personal and business taxes completely to the federal changes, some Minnesotans would owe more state taxes, while others with the same incomes would owe less. If we do nothing, the federal changes would cause significant increases in other people's state taxes.

Either way, thousands of Minnesotans would be hit with state personal income tax increases. That is not fair; and it's not right. Minnesotans deserve better.

Last year, the legislature reduced business property taxes for each of the next ten years.

The federal bill just cut the corporate tax rate by a whopping 40 percent. Combined, they provide huge tax cuts to Minnesota businesses.

So, our number one priority—which will be reflected in my budget on Friday—should be tax fairness for individual Minnesotans and their families.

I am very proud of our state, proud of what Minnesotans have accomplished here. *U.S. News and World Report* recently rated Minnesota the second-best state in the country, up from third best the previous year.

USA Today said we're the nation's Best-Run State; AARP ranked us the very best state in which to retire.

And CNBC says we're the third-best state for business.

We're not perfect; but compared to everyone else, we're very good.

I say again that the credit belongs to the people of Minnesota. We ARE our people, but we're only as good as all of us are.

That means ALL of us, in a state with rapidly changing demographics, in which 19 percent of our residents are now women, men, and children of color.

That is a very different complexion from years ago, and some folks still resist that change.

If we can educate them to move beyond racism, religious bigotry, and other hatreds, they will see that this new diversity is crucial to our state's future success.

There are simply not enough native Minnesotans to drive our future economic growth. There are already too few unemployed workers to fill our state's current job vacancies. And that labor shortage is expected to become even more acute. The additional workers we need to expand our economy must come from newcomers to our state.

Adjusting to this new reality is hard for some Minnesotans. Trying to push Minnesota back fifty years is neither a realistic option nor a good idea.

I want to be VERY clear. Minnesota is an inclusive and welcoming place for all and we all stand together in making that statement for everyone in Minnesota.

During the past few years, our state government has led by example. Since 2015, the percent of state employees with disabilities has grown by 40 percent; the percent who are men and women of color has increased by 50 percent. That's important progress, but we have much more to do to ensure our state government better includes and serves the rich diversity of our state.

As I conclude, I want to acknowledge all the important issues I did not address tonight. But my time is running out, so I must leave them to all of you.

I again want to thank the people of Minnesota who have supported my career in public service. It has given me so much—and so much more than I could ever return.

Best of all are the extraordinary people I have encountered throughout our state. People I could never meet any other way. Shouldering their hardships and celebrating their achievements have cemented the bonds of our common humanity.

We are each so uniquely different; yet we are all so much the same.

From my experiences in places like Iraq, Afghanistan, and the poorest parts of New York City, I have come to realize how much our lives are proscribed by where we land at birth on this planet.

And then by the economic and social environments in which we live.

I believe most of us are incredibly fortunate to live in Minnesota. Despite our challenges, there is nowhere else that compares.

Previous generations worked hard to build and then leave us what we have here. Now it's our responsibility to make it still better for generations to come.

Our model should be this magnificent State Capitol building, which just a few short years ago was in dangerous disrepair. But all of us here set partisanship aside. We came together, worked together, and even kicked ourselves out of this building until its restoration was completed.

Look at what we accomplished by working together. Just imagine what more we can do if we continue.

Thank you very much.

IMAGE CREDITS

Page 6
Painting by Nicholas R. Brewer from a photograph from the Lee Brothers Studio, MNHS Collections

Page 7
Photo by Norton and Peel, MNHS Collections

Pages 8, 10, 11 *(left and right)*, 13, 38 *(top and bottom)*, 40 *(top and bottom)*, 45, 48, 50, 56 *(top and bottom)*, 63, 64, 78, 79, 85, 87, 88, 90, 92, 93, 100, 108, 111, 112, 117, 124, 125, 131, 133, 137 *(top)*, 139, 141, 149, 156, 159, 162, 164, 169, 183, 199, 203, 206 *(top and bottom)*
Courtesy of Mark Dayton

Page 15
U.S. News and World Report Collection, Library of Congress, Public Domain

Page 19
Drbogdan, CC BY-SA 4.0, https://creativecommons.org/licenses/by-sa/4.0, via Wikimedia Commons

Page 20
Schomburg Center for Research in Black Culture, Art and Artifacts Division, New York Public Library, public domain

Page 21
Photo by Sterling Doughty, public domain, via Wikimedia Commons

Page 28
Warren K. Leffler, public domain, via Wikimedia Commons

Pages 33, 57
MNHS Collections

Page 49
United States Congress, public domain

Pages 137 *(bottom)*, 143, 161
Office of Governor Mark Dayton and Lieutenant Governor Tina Smith

INDEX

Page numbers in *italics* indicate a photograph
MD stands for Mark Dayton

Perseverance is set in Hoefler Text, a typeface designed by Jonathan Hoefler, one of the architects of the modern type industry. Steeped in the virtues of classical typography, Hoefler Text is a comprehensive family of typefaces from the dawn of the digital age.

Interior text design by Wendy Holdman